Some Observation

Civilization of the western

Barbarians

Particularly of the English, made during the residence of some years in those parts.

John B. Swazey

Alpha Editions

This edition published in 2023

ISBN : 9789357967235

Design and Setting By
Alpha Editions
www.alphaedis.com
Email - info@alphaedis.com

Contents

TRANSLATOR'S PREFACE.

THIS Translation of the Work of Ah-Chin-le is trustworthy as to the meaning of the Text—though the literal translation has not been, in many cases, attempted.

Preserving the Spirit of the Author, the Translator has desired to be intelligible in good, readable English. Where it is impossible to give the precise thought of a mind so differently cultured, the *nearest* English is given. It is hoped that the inherent difficulty of the task may excuse errors of grammar and style.

The Translator has been so absorbed in his Author, that he fears he may have often slipped in his Syntax, and been rude in his manner. However, with whatever faults, he hands the volume to his Countrymen—thinking that they may be as much interested in it as he has been; and may derive as much amusement. If it do not commend itself for its Wisdom, it may, at least, for its novelty—that is, as a genuine expression of intelligent *Chinese* opinion, concerning the "*Civilization of the Western Barbarians, and particularly of the English.*"

The Author's own Preface explains the Origin of the Work, and its claims to consideration.

THE RETREAT,
Shanghai, China, 1875.

J.Y.S.

AUTHOR'S PREFACE.

AH-CHIN-LE, Mandarin, and member of the exalted *Calao*, to the Illustrious *Wo-sung*, Mandarin, First class, President of the most Serene, the grand Council, *Calao*; virtue, health, and the highest place in the Hall of your Sublime Ancestors! Trained from my youth for many years in the school of the Foreigners [Fo-kien], so as to be versed in the languages of the chief Barbarians of the West, and particularly of the English, afterwards perfected in the latter at our port of Shanghai, and sent by your Illustrious command upon a private mission with the Imperial Embassy to the outside Barbarians of the far West to curiously seek into the state of those Peoples, and report upon the same to your Illustrious mind—that being so informed exactly, your Wisdom might, in those matters appertaining to the Western Barbarians, enlighten the Son of Heaven (our Celestial and Imperial Majesty [Bang-ztse] most renowned and exalted) when, in Council, things touching those outer Barbarians should be considered: these, my poor words, in so far as to your Illustrious Wisdom it has been thought proper to make general, are now produced: that the happy subjects of our Central, Flowery Kingdom, may understand more perfectly the condition of those outside Barbarians, respecting whom so very little is known, and may the more cautiously guard the Sacred Institutions [Kam-phfe] of our Celestial Land—wise, peaceful, powerful, and teeming with an industrious and contented people, before the Western Barbarians had so much as the rudiments of learning.

Ah-chin prostrates his poor body before your Illustrious Benevolence, and craves forbearance that these, his unworthy *Observations*, are not better ordered:—the circumstances of travel, fatigue, agitation of mind, hurry and confusion, have been unfavourable for that due ordering of the same which a respect for your Illustrious Wisdom required—in this particular the precise Report, submitted to the Exalted, the *Calao*, through the hands of your Illustrious Greatness, is more perfect. These are minutes, rather, jotted down and fastened for better reordering, if, at another time, it should be judged fit. May the Sovereign Lord of Heaven [Chang-ti] keep your Illustrious mind and body!

AH-CHIN-LE.

NOTE.—These *Observations* now following were made in England, and refer chiefly to the *English* Barbarians, who pride themselves upon being the most powerful and most enlightened of all the outer Barbarians, and, in fact, of any People in the whole, immense World.

AH-CHIN.

CHAPTER I.
OF THE RELIGION AND SUPERSTITIONS OF THE ENGLISH.

THE worship of the supreme Lord of Heaven [Chang-ti], is not unknown to these Barbarians, though degraded by many Superstitions.

The purity of the divine and original Worship (as with the vulgar in our Celestial Kingdom) is too simple. About 500 or 600 years after our Confutze, in the time of the Romans, there appeared in an obscure province of their Empire a new Sect of devotees, who asserted that they had among them a Son of Heaven. This Son they called *Christ*; and those who adopted this new deity were called *Christians*. This was nearly 2000 years [met-li-ze] ago. The Sect increased and spread. One of the Emperors of the West adopted the new god, and enforced the worship of him upon the subjects of the Empire.

All the Western Barbarians derive their knowledge from the Romans; whose power, indeed, they over-turned, but whose civilization they imitated. Particularly, the Bonzes (Priests) of the new *Superstition*, joined to the Chiefs of new powers (which arose upon the ruins of the Roman Empire), preserved some remains of the ancient Learning, and enforced the new Superstition. What little of letters remained was almost entirely with the Bonzes. This event was much the same as the introduction from the Hindoos into our Central Kingdom of the worship of the Hindoo god, *Fo*; and, curiously, these events happened at about the same time.

It is to be observed that in our Illustrious Kingdom there is a tendency to superstitious observances. We have several *Sects* [pho-ti]; but our *Literati* merely tolerate and do not worship. A simple and pure homage to the Sovereign Lord of Heaven [Hoang-chan-ti] is an act of the Wise: and even the *Sects* make their *Spirits* subordinate to Him. The Western Barbarians, however, dishonour the true worship by strange "rites"—even by incredible superstitions, when the intellectual culture is considered. It is not long since, in the monstrous credulity of the people, directed by the Bonzes, it was believed that the *Devil* (Chief of the *Evil Demons*) would enter into an individual—generally some old, ugly, and friendless woman—and, *by her*, turn the milk sour, drive the cattle mad, torture children, shrivel up the limbs, blast with the *Evil Eye*; and even plague with disease and with horrible death! And these wretched women, and sometimes men, themselves often fancying that the Devil was really in them, were seized upon, dragged through mud and mire, fearfully maltreated, and put to death by the horrible torments of fire, upon this wild accusation: and this terrible scene was not caused by a maddened rabble of the common sort, but under the lead of the Bonzes, and according to the Laws of the Land.

The great, central figure of idolatry is the Pope, who sits enthroned in Rome; and is, generally, a very old man, not always remarkable for wisdom nor virtue. He claims to be the sole vicegerent of the Christ-god, and only visible divine Head—all who do not worship him are really not true worshippers. Yet, there are many *Sects* of this *Superstition*; and in England, the Sovereign is held to be the true Pope and Head! The English Pope now worshipped is therefore a woman—the Queen! Such a thing seemed to me to be too wild—a phantasy—I could not comprehend. I knew that this Sect—the Roman—had long ago followers in our Flowery Kingdom; and our annals show was tolerated: not, however, for the *Superstition*, but for the Bonzes, who were masters of some useful knowledge. Personally, I never knew any native devotees of the Superstition—in fact it has steadily diminished in repute, and its few and scattered adherents are very obscure. So I was, and am still, puzzled by this extraordinary *Sect*. I have read the *Creed*; a sort of verbal incantation, made by devotees in the temples.

One day, I begged of a good-natured, large-bellied, Priest to explain to me; and ventured to ask him if the *Creed* was really an Article of Belief, or only a formal and meaningless Invocation—like some of the mummeries [phin-zi] of our Superstitious Sects. He looked surprised; but when he saw that he was thus accosted by a "*Heathen Chinee*" (as these Barbarians always contemptuously call the inhabitants of our Central Land), he merely said: "Why, you have in China our Missionaries to enlighten your darkness; have you never met them?" "No; I have heard of them at Shanghai; but they do not speak our tongue, nor do we understand them; and their teachings, even if understood, would attract no attention from the *Literati*, who would consider them as unworthy of notice as any other Superstition." "How so? our Religion is no Superstition; it is the true and *only* true Religion, revealed by God himself to his chosen people, and miraculously preserved for all believers." "I bow before your Illustrious mind and body; but we have, and have had from time immemorial, just such pretensions; they are as old as history." "I will not argue; but look at the excellency of our divine religion!" "Where shall I look? If you mean the excellency of certain moral principles, there is nothing peculiar to your *Sect* in them. They have been taught in our schools for thousands of years—they *are* excellent; they show the divine in man—man is of the divine; morality comes of that." "But look at your frightful vices; at your Pagan worship—see the effects of idolatry!" "I bow to your Illustrious mind." I saw my effort to obtain any reasonable explanation was fruitless; I made my obeisance and left. What an illustration of ignorant and superstitious conceit! Vice, thousands of miles beyond sea, so dreadful; the vice at hand, defiling every corner, unseen! The only true Religion of this Priest will not see, or, seeing, he will not believe that it is Vice—or, at any rate, idolatrous—pagan Vice! I could not believe, at first, that the *Superstition* was more than a Form, kept up merely for the advantage of the Priests. The sharp intellects of the Barbarians, applied so fruitfully to useful arts, seemed stultified, if I held to their actual belief. I doubted the honesty of the Priests; I knew the bad character of many of the Bonzes of our Superstitious Sects. Now, better acquainted with the imperfect civilization of the people, I am not moved by these ignorant and bigoted displays. Poverty, vice, and drunkenness; crimes of violence and fraud, are rife among the Barbarians. The Temples, ordered and maintained by the *Queen-Pope*, are, for the most part—especially in great cities—empty. The Sects of the Low-Caste people, despised by the High-Caste, are far more zealous worshippers, though not better *Christians*. The funds raised to support the great Temples and the Priests, are nearly all absorbed by them, and the Temples left ruinous. The lowest Castes do not worship, but curse the Sovereign Lord. Yet, our Illustrious Kingdom is called *Pagan*— *Heathen*—words implying every degradation; and our people fit only to be turned over to the endless torments of Evil Spirits!

Like our Confutze, the principles of morality and general benevolence are taught in the sayings ascribed to Christ. Yet fighting in the most brutal manner is allowed in the Schools, although the teachings of Christ, commanding Charity and Peace, are conned over in the daily lessons; and horrible Wars for the subjugation of other Peoples, incessantly waged! Still, if we may believe these Barbarians, all true religion and virtue are possessed only by them! The education of the people has been disregarded; and now, when the wisest of their great men has, with great difficulty, caused a decree to issue for the teaching of the neglected masses, at least, in some rudimental learning, the purpose is likely to fail. The Priests demand that the *Superstition* shall be taught, and those of one *Sect* insist that they shall lead; denouncing a differing *Sect*. Each *Sect* denounces every other: and, so far is the contention carried, that the teaching of the people is lost sight of; the special *Superstition* of a Sect being held by its adherents far more important than merely "Secular" teaching! It must be understood, that though, commonly, there is but little real reverence for the Supreme Lord, and less benevolence, yet, such is the hold which the Bonzes have got of the imagination (by means of the *devil and hell*, which are greatly feared), that they are a *power*. Their demands, therefore, as to the education of the people, will be respected; and the matter be left, largely, in their hands. This, owing to the bitterness existing among the Bonzes of the Sects, will cause the whole attempt to fail—to fail, as a general measure. The Lowest orders, for whom the design was chiefly devised, do not hold the Bonzes in esteem, and will not be so readily led by them, even were the Priests themselves in accord. The Sects and the Priests not only fight upon this subject; they are usually at strife upon any matter wherein their coöperation is desired. One leading rule of the *Sacred Writings* commands, *Peace*. In respect of all who differ from them, these Sects say that the true meaning is, *War*! Each Sect dislikes and denounces every other; and the members of all damn to everlasting torments the whole human race but themselves! This place of eternal torture in "fire and brimstone" [Zan-tan-li] is called Hell [Tha-dee]!

In the ceaseless conflicts of the *Sects*, the most dreadful crimes have been committed. The chief events recorded in the annals of the Western Barbarians for many ages, and even to this time, have been only bloody wars, massacres, and vile intrigues, springing out of these conflicts: horrible crimes, again and again repeated, and under circumstances too dreadful for belief. And when I have looked into the causes of these shocking events, there seemed to be no more involved than the manner of interpreting some obscure word or phrase in the *Sacred Writings*; which to a wise man would be unimportant, however interpreted, or if never interpreted at all!

At this moment, the best intellects among the English (who boast that they are superior to all other Barbarians), are hotly disputing as to the proper mode of wearing vestments, of holding or of not holding candles, of standing and posturing, and other matters equally important, when the Priests officiate in the Temples. The most trivial thing in the *Superstition* is esteemed of such consequence, that an error respecting it may be fatal to the "soul" [pan-tzi] in the future life! Some of the most learned fear the words and "missives" of the poor old man, who sits in Rome (already referred to), and is worshipped by most Christians out of England (and by very many in it) as the only delegate of the *Christ-god*. They fear this Pope— fear that by his connection with the *Evil One* he will "*play the devil*" among them. And though of precisely the same Christ-god *Superstition*, merely because of a difference of opinion as to the visible "Head" of that Superstition, really believe that this poor old man (called by the larger portion of Christians, with profound worship, Pope, *Holy Father*) may, by his wicked devices, allure into his worship, and bring under his power, the English Barbarians; to the everlasting destruction of their souls!

This notion of an *Evil-one*, universal among all the Barbarians, I never well comprehended. We have in our Flowery Kingdom Sects which believe in good and bad *Spirits*; although our *Literati* smile at such things; that is, in the vulgar forms. But the Christians assert that the Devil is too strong with men for the Supreme Lord—and the English *Sect* say that the Pope is a very child of the Devil! To be sure, their Sect is the feeblest of all, and merely separated from the great Pope-sect upon points not touching the superstition itself, and really on selfish and personal grounds. They know that the Pope justly claims a direct and regular succession from the *Christ-God*; that he and his adherents, forming the vast majority of *Christians* (as all the sects call themselves) are believers with themselves in all the main "*dogmas*" [ka-nti] of the Superstition; yet, none the less, they are the children of the Evil-one, and fit for Hell. And not the vulgar only, but the learned actually have a horror that the Pope may be again worshipped in England. A calamity too terrible for contemplation!

The Pope-worshipping Sect repay this hate with an equal abhorrence, and send the English *heretics* to the awful Hell, with the same satisfaction.

All the Western Barbarians worship this new *Christ-God*, but, like our devoters of *Fo*, divided into many Sects, as I have already intimated. The benignant *Fo*, teaches his idolatrous devotees how to differ without hate. But, these *Christians* are always at strife, bitter and irreconcilable; not as to essentials, even within the Superstition itself, (to say nothing of genuine morality), but as to things trivial and absurd. One will say, "Be baptised or be damned to the eternal Hell!" But another says, "Baptism is only a symbol, one may be saved without it." Then, "What is baptism?" Some say "The Priest must immerse in water;" but another, "No, the Priest must sprinkle the face only." Yet another, "Water is itself nothing, Priest nothing, unless before either, the baptism of the 'Holy Spirit' have occurred." To perfect the "rite," all say that the Priest must offer proper "Incantations," and generally in the Temples before the Idol. The contestants damn each other to everlasting torments for not being *truly* baptised.

All the Sects say, "You must believe in Christ or be damned;" but do not agree as to what this *Belief* is, and go on damning each the other for not having truly believed.

It is impossible, however, to make intelligible the countless vagaries of the Sects. They all fight under the same *Christ-God*, whom they all address, among other titles, as the "Prince of Peace" [Tchu-pe]. They all profess to follow His precepts, one of which is to love all men, even enemies (not *friends*, one of these angry disputants once said). These revered Precepts are written in the *Sacred Books*, and all the Sects swear their oaths upon these, and resort to them for the unchangeable rules of belief and practice. They all declare that the *Sacred Writings* are so plain that a man, "though a fool, may understand," and so clear, "that he who runs may read." Yet, they curse each other to the eternal torments for interpreting erroneously. The truth is, that *the Books* are most obscure, and differences of interpretation are inseperable from their use; the terrible thing is, that Superstition has made these differences so important. The *Sacred Writings* are contradictory, and teeming with things indifferent, meaningless, or trivial. Written at widely different periods, by many hands, long ages ago, in an obscure and barbarous dialect, for different objects, their true meanings cannot always be rendered. But few, even of the Priest-class, can read them at all in the original. They are mainly Records of the Laws, customs and wars of an obscure and terrible race, here and there interspersed with Invocations to the Gods of that race, and with their Proverbs, or words of wisdom. This tribe, called *Jews*, revolted from their masters, the Egyptians, and fled into a desert region lying west from the Hindoos. The man who led them in this revolt was learned in the laws and customs of Egypt, and upon these he founded his own system. He declared himself to be directly called by Jah (Jehovah) to be their High Priest and Judge—that they were to obey him who received from Jah immediate instructions—that, in fact, to disobey him was to disobey Jah. That he was to lead them forth to found a new State, and that the power to announce the will of Jah alone resided with him and his successors, in this High Priesthood, and that they could only be successful over their enemies and prosper, by an implicit obedience to Jah, by the mouth of the High Priest.

This event took place in our dynasty, *Shang*; and our annals, referring to the Western Barbarians of the ancient times, make mention of some things— obscure movements of tribes, and of the great works performed by the Egyptians; and of a servile race, condemned to toil on these structures: and, possibly, this revolt of the Jews may have been contained in these references. However, the whole matter would have been lost ages ago, nor have left a trace, but for the singular circumstance that the ancient records of these Jews have in a good measure escaped destruction. This happened not by any chance; but from the fact that the High Priest, pretending to be the very mouth of Jah, made all his utterances *Sacred*; and the Priesthood, inscribing and preserving the Jewish "Rites," worship and institutes of all kinds, guarded these writings with extreme care; which the reverence of the Superstitious people enhanced. Thus these *Institutes* of the Jews, declared to be by the Priests the very will of Jah, came to be "*Holy*" [Kan-ti]— inviolable! Now, the Barbarians regard this preservation of the Jewish Records as an evidence of their divinity, and a clear warning to man not to disregard them; and when they assert (as, by the High Priest, they constantly do), "Thus saith the Lord-God-Jah," they accept the declaration, and bow before it, as the very word of Jehovah! But we know that similar "*Sacred Writings*" are common in the East, and that these pretensions of the Priests are as universal as *Superstition* itself; in fact, form the chief features in it.

The new Christ-God was a Jew; and, though, singularly enough, in the words ascribed to him, in those parts of the *Sacred Writings* assigned to him and his immediate followers, there are bitter denunciations of the spirit and of the letter of much in the old, Priest-made part; and he distinctly says that his office is to give new and reformed rules; none the less, his immediate followers, being Jews, naturally looked upon him as Great High-Priest, speaking as did their ancient High-Priest (High-Priest and Christ-God)— the very "mouth-piece" [Mu-te-pi] of Jehovah! Adding to the High-Priest a *Messiahship*; for they believed him to be the mysterious *Messiah* of their Sacred Writings, foretold by their wise *Seers* long ages before! The great High-Priest who should deliver them from all their enemies, and lead them to a universal dominion! Very few of the Jews themselves, however, adhered to this opinion: in fact, Christ was put to a shameful death by them as an *Imposter* [Kon-ti-fe]. And by the Jews, in general, he was and is still considered to be a misguided fanatic. The Romans at this time held the Jewish province, and continued to do so. Meantime, the followers of the Christ-God, as I have said, spread by degrees, after his death, into other Roman provinces. New Superstitions were often greedily received; the Western Barbarians had always readily adopted new gods, and new Superstitions. This idolatry was, however, held in contempt by the learned; but it slowly spread among the lower orders, and penetrated to Rome itself.

The Roman soldiery, in some instances, made it conspicuous; and, after some generations, a Roman Emperor, thinking he saw some miraculous evidence of its divine force (in the workings of his own dark imagination), forced this new Superstition upon his Empire. That Empire embraced the Western world. The Barbarians who succeeded to them adopted, largely, their laws; their worship, and their religious rites. Thus, these Western Barbarians are *Christians*; and, though they detest the Jews none the less, hold to their "Sacred Writings" as the very words of Jah—whom they also worship! This they do because they follow the few Jews who accepted Christ as Jehovah, rather than the *whole people* who rejected him!—follow the few who accepted Christ as the Messiah-God promised in the "Sacred Writings;" and hold with them that these are the only *Revelation* of the will of Jehovah to man! By *Jehovah* meaning the only Supreme Lord of Heaven!

The remarkable thing is that this enormous pretension is not ascribed to *Christ*, but is obscurely announced in certain writings of the early Christian Jews. Thus these Western Barbarians, scoffing the name of Jew, accept of his ancient and ferocious god, and adopt the barbarous *rites* of a blood-thirsty and obscure tribe of the desert, make the records kept by the Priests of the tribe *Sacred*, and curse to *Hell* the whole Jewish race for not accepting the interpretation of *a few of their number*—the few, and only a few, worshipping Christ as the true *Christ-God*. That is, these Barbarians better understand the subject than the people into whose hands the matter was entrusted by Divine wisdom.

When one considers, then, the foundation of the great worship of the West, one wonders not at the Sects and strife. Founded in dark and cruel *institutes* of ignorant antiquity, the attempt to engraft a better system failed, because in this attempt the Priests were still *Jews*, who, adoring Christ, adored him as Jehovah and a Jewish High-Priest. What follows becomes more intelligible, but not less astonishing. The new worship has its divine *Revelation* from Jah, interpreted by its Priests, who introduce Christ as their great High-Priest, and the *Christ-Jehovah* of the new worship. All are *damned* to the everlasting Hell who do not believe these Priests, worship this new god, and accept as the very Divine *Word* these *Jewish writings*. This superstition suited the dark imaginations of the Barbarians, and was, in truth, not unlike their own, and may have had a common origin.

The intellectual activity of succeeding ages has been mainly devoted to these *Sacred Writings*; and the disputes, as to the meaning, never-ending. Every word has been criticised. *Sects* have been formed upon a syllable— appearing and disappearing. Now one would madly starve, another feast. Some fanatics would live in caves, some on inaccessible mountains; some tortured themselves, and held women to be unclean unless they married *Christ*. Some would only shout their invocations, others would only commune with the god *inside*. Some *would* kneel, others *would* stand. Sometimes a sect more wild than usual would organise vast bands of warriors, all wearing a symbol to show that they were Christians—usually a *cross* (because the Jews put Christ to death by hanging him upon a cross); and, placing Priests at the head, would rush to distant parts to root out *pagans*. These dreadful slaughters of distant tribes were called *Crossades* (from the symbol referred to). Some Sects destroyed society by another fanaticism; they forced men to live in caves or in dark stone chambers, shut off from all cheerful life, and from all intercourse with women; where they should constantly make invocations, lash themselves with thongs, and half-starve themselves; having skulls to hold before them, and awful paintings of Hell and devils to horrify them,—if perchance they may propitiate the *Christ-God*, Jah. Women also being driven into similar, horrid imprisonment in stone vaults, where the whole life is spent in invocations and sufferings, without so much as seeing any man.

These and numberless other things grow out of the interpretations, ever-changing, of the *Sacred Writings*; which, to the dark imaginings of Priests and devotees, seem ever to give such utterances as fit to their feelings. To the Priests they are an unfailing arsenal of power.

For many ages nearly all the Books written—mainly by Priests—were in respect of the *Sacred Writings*; called commentaries, homilies, disputations, doctrines, invocations, sermons; endless in name, and nameless.

This *Literature* is less in repute than formerly, and immense collections of huge writings are now rotting away in the dismal alcoves of *Libraries* [Buksti], as great stone buildings for keeping Books are called. This *Literature* is rarely looked at now, excepting by the Priests and antiquaries [ol-olphoo]; much of it is obsolete in form, or in the Roman—not now so much in vogue as formerly. A large portion of the writings, and a larger portion of the "speeches" [phi-lu-tin], however, are devoted to the same subject; but the style is modern, and less obscure, though not less deformed by a dark and irrational superstition.

To my poor mind, were all these innumerable productions of gloomy and bewildered intellects—misled and crazed by a monstrous Idolatry—swept for ever away, nothing would be lost—nothing, unless the most astonishing monument ever builded by man. However, it is doubtful whether to lose even this is not better than to have *anything* left of so monstrous a Pretension.

Whilst thus the Barbarian *brain* wasted itself in this wretched work, and piled up its ponderous tomes of useless, and worse than useless, Literature—holding knowledge in general as vain, and *Science*, when, in Priestly interpretation, not according to the barbarous *Sacred Writings*, as a thing to be accursed—activity of body, during the same ages, did *its* dreadful work. Directed by the Priests, one *Sect* denounced another as *damnable*, and the stronger attempted to destroy the weaker by "fire and sword." New contentions would arise, to be crushed out by bloody execution; only to spring up again, to be again extirpated. Every *Sect* as it appeared would fight for supremacy. All worshipped the Christ-God, and sought the same Sacred Writings; and all invoked His aid, and pointed to those Writings for their authority—to exterminate a weaker *Sect*; to deliver over whole provinces to rapine, slaughter, burning, destruction; cities in conflagration; women, children, as well as men, not merely slain, but put to death with tortures unspeakable; massacres, by treachery and surprise, of thousands and tens of thousands! To such work was the activity of body largely directed by Priests and the savage chiefs. For ages these atrocities were perpetrated. History has no parallel of horror; human nature seemed to have become possessed by the *Devil* of the Superstition, and exceeded its *diabolism* [pau-di-ki]. In the name of Christ, fire, slaughter, and rapine, spread over the whole immense world. Wherever the Priests of this dark superstition became powerful, everything which opposed them perished. It was a cardinal principle that men could be saved from the dreadful Hell only by the aid of the Priests, and by accepting of their interpretation of the *Sacred Writings*. The system erected by the Priests was called the *Church*, and none could be saved unless they were in the pale of *Holy Church*—unless they, in the manner directed by the Priests, performed all the rites of worship. These not merely were directed to the worship of the Sacred Writings, the Christ-God and Jah, but to the mother of God and to the

Pope. In England, by and by, the Priests threw off the Roman Pope, and set up the English Sovereign, for the time being, as Pope, and put men and women to death by fire and torture for still preferring the older Idol.

Nor is this madness, this fanatical fury, wholly expended. Education has not yet raised these Western tribes into the enjoyment of a rational worship—of a rational morality—of a life, calm, tolerant, and beneficent. They have never attained the civilisation of our Central Kingdom, and to the wisdom of our illuminated Confutse.

There is morality to be found among them, and a few worship, purely and simply, the God of Heaven, and look with untroubled hearts upon the senseless superstitions. The masses are, however, still held in them; and the High Castes either hold to the prevailing idolatries, or pretend to do so. This old Jewish Worship, with its *rites* and pretensions, fastened upon tribes by Priests and the Roman power, is still dominant in the West. In England to-day it is the same superstition, only the Queen is Pope, instead of the Man at Rome. For this the English are *damned*, as worthy of Hell-fire, by Roman Pope worshippers; and the English return the curse. A constant *Bugbear* [Do-nki] to the English mind is, that the more powerful Roman Pope may get into England again; then, what horrors! Nor does this frightful *chimera* alone alarm the lower people; the most learned Englishmen, and their wisest, exert their minds in writing and in preaching against this terrible thing.

To me this seemed strange—incredible. The English Barbarians are, in general, sharp enough; they are learned in many things; they can see the absurdity of Eastern superstitions; they denounce the Roman-Pope worship as worthy of *hell*; but they worship a Queen-pope at home, and the same Christ-Jah-god and "sacred writings" which the Romans worship. They believe, as do the Roman-pope worshippers, that all who do not worship the *sacred writings* and the *Christ-Jah-god*, and accept of the Priest-*Church*, will inevitably burn for ever in fires of Hell; yet, because of the separation as to Pope worship, each regards the other *sect* with a hatred only appeased by sending each the other to the dreadful Hell! How incredible that the human mind—the active and skilled human mind—should alarm itself and others for fear of the worship of a Pope—a man: and really think the condition of the human soul would be hopelessly wretched—if it mistook the right object of worship—the idol of Rome, or the idol of England! The intellect truly employed would be directed to the overthrow of *the superstition* and its objects of idolatry altogether. The Roman or the English Pope—the Roman or the English *sect*—what matter? Both alike indifferent and worthless to an intelligent worshipper of the SUPREME LORD OF HEAVEN (Hoang-chan-ti). His worship is elevating, supporting a clean morality, tolerant, benevolent—a morality found wherever man is found; debased, more or less, as man be debased, or as he may be sunken in vicious or cruel superstitions.

To restore a pure worship is to help on a better civilisation among the Barbarians. Nor would a respect for the morality ascribed to Christ do other than help in the same way. The misfortune is, that that morality has been overlaid with Jewish and Priestly additions and inventions. There are some of the English *literati* who dare to teach a purer worship, discarding the *superstition* in its grosser pretensions; but they are not listened to.

It is difficult to understand what is accepted as *true* by the differing *Sects*— but their differences may be disregarded—and I will refer to what all the Sects of the *Great Superstition* subscribe to, aside from the matter of *Pope*.

One, only God: in three parts—each part a very God!

> 1. *The Judge and destroyer* of mankind; for all are damned to Hell! This is the Jewish Jah.
>
> 2. *The Son*, begotten of Jah upon an immaculate virgin. Sent to mediate with Jah and appease His fierce anger, so that some may escape Hell—that is, those few who have "*believed in*" *and worshipped the Son*, the Father, and other things. For as to what is to be believed, form the points of endless contention, as I have hinted.
>
> 3. *The Holy Ghost*, or Comforter, whose function I have never comprehended. It appears to be a divine *Effluence*, entering into the devotee, to warm, exalt, and enlighten him; especially to comfort him and to support him in his dire conflicts with "*the flesh, hell, and the devil*" (as the Superstition reads). It is an "awful mystery" in the *rites*, and has crazed many a worshipper; for those who fancy themselves to be in the possession of this *Effluence* feel like gods, and conduct themselves as scarcely accountable to mortal control; though others feel an absorption, as they say, into the divine nature—a notion like that of some of the fanatics of the Hindoos and of the East.

As powerful, indeed more powerful over men, is the terrible Satan—*Devil, Evil One*. There are many names and shapes. This monster was once (according to the superstition) chained down in hell-fire, for having raised a rebellion against Jah, who, however, let him loose again, and gave him wings to fly from his fiery prison to the world, where he should wage war with Jah, in a covert way, by his craft drawing away mankind from Jah to his worship and to his designs; that, however, he should never prevail to overthrow Jah, and the only result would be to increase the number of the countless devils of low degree already in Hell, by adding to them nearly the whole human race!—for to that torment all go who do not worship in spirit and in truth, according to the superstition. This awful strife between Satan and Jah always proceeds. The Priests say that, for "some wise purpose," Jah suffers Satan to succeed in his snares; and his victims continually fall into the everlasting place of Fire, prepared for the devil and his victims. The Priests say that this wholesale destruction of mankind was a thing predetermined by Jah, and that he created the Devil to accomplish the work; but they do not explain why the torments should be everlasting; as men are themselves short-lived, one would think a reasonable superstition might have limited the fire-torture to, say, twice the length of mortal life!

Our *Literati* will readily recognise some parts of this horrible superstition—perhaps the main features, as Oriental—going back to the dimmest dawn of tradition, and to the early and grotesque forms of the human imagination, dark and uninstructed. The *Hell*, however, is a terrific expansion of the horrible, suited to these Strange Barbarians.

Besides these great deities, there are Arch-angels, Angels, Saints male and female, Spirits good and bad—the latter *Imps* of Satan (whatever the word may mean), who enter into human beings, and take on the human form: in this disguise, called Ghosts, Wizards, Bogies, Witches. However, good people can tell these devilish *Imps*, and avoid them (so they be *good*, that is, true worshippers of the Idols of the Superstition); for the smell of brimstone sticks to them, and the tail and cleft-hoof—inseparable from devil-imps—will always show somewhere to *the good*. But, if unawares the Imps catch them, they are only to say *Christ*, or *Jehovah*, or call on some Saint, and the Imp will at once vanish like a vapor!

It will be seen that this Superstition is as populous with gods and spirits as are any in the East, and some of the forms more frightful and ridiculous.

There are dissentients—some, who, not dissenting to the chief gods, yet conjecture that the good and bad *spirits* merely symbolize good and bad propensities in human nature. But real objectors are few and timid, afraid of punishment—if not here, then after death. For the Superstition so long rooted has engrafted its terrors in the very blood, and men are born with the *Horror* in them; they can never free themselves from it. A few, however, do dissent; but, like our *Literati*, they do not care to oppose vulgar ignorance openly, nor is it safe; they feel a contempt, but repress its too-marked expression. "Why render themselves uselessly odious?" they say. The Priests, very likely, often disbelieve much of what they say; but not unlikely their emoluments (*livings*) have some effect upon their conduct, though not upon their private convictions. In our Flowery Land there is a maxim: "A common man's brain is in his belly."

I have had a High Bonze say to me, when I have suggested some objections, "Oh, we do not know anything about such things; the morality is good, and we need a devil for women, children, and the common people: it is safer to let things alone."

"But," I have rejoined, "*Is* it quite well, in the long run, to teach falsely?"

"I do not say it is well to teach *falsely*. I said, I do not know—who does? Men more learned than I believe strongly, men wiser than I have "gone to the stake and perished by slow torture of fire," made *martyrs* (we have no such word) of themselves, rather than deny these things. They were probably right. I simply take things as they are."

"But," I replied, "surely misguided fanaticism, of which the world is full, is proof of nothing whatever, unless of the sincerity of the madman—not always of that."

"My dear Ah-Chin, you are very quick, and no fool (I beg pardon), but you do not understand it. The Superstitious parts are mere forms; and as to the *horrors*, as you call them, I think them indispensable; they are better than the Police." (The Police are the officers who arrest offenders in the streets and public places.)

The Bonzes who talk in this way are, usually, what are derisively termed "hunting and fishing" Bonzes, not remarkable for strictness of conduct, though quite as likely to stick to the Temples, like our Bonzes; they are not likely to pull down the roof which shelters them. The Superstition is less revered than formerly, and its wilder parts are less obtrusive. Its pretensions are not moderated in terms, but the practice is more moderate. Sects do not put each other to death, at present, though so much of the old bitterness remains that no one can say what horrors might follow upon unexpected changes. Gradually wise men endeavour to drop out of sight the Jewish and Priestly creations, and, inculcating morality, take the *Christ-God* as symbol of Charity, and his moral precepts as the basis of a moral Philosophy; or (to be less offensive to the Superstition) *Christian Philosophy*. In this way they seize hold of what is true in the Great Idolatry, and endeavour to ignore the grosser parts altogether. They hope to bring about a rational worship without violence, by a gradual disuse and forgetfulness of the irrational, and are willing to yield something to ignorance, if they can by that means, in the end, enlighten it. They allow to Christ an exalted character, large in the divine faculty, and divine as man is divine in possessing that faculty—to say, *the moral*. In this, much as we see in our exalted *Confutze*, who lived and taught long before the period ascribed to Christ, and from whom the Western tribes, doubtless, received their moral notions.

The religion of Wise men is the same at all times and everywhere. Wherever some intellectual culture exists, men will be found who understand and practise the rules of morality; and wherever this is general, there is the higher civilisation. This higher civilisation, resting upon a general morality among a people, has for its base a rational recognition of the Sovereign Lord and man's dependency and accountability to Him; *Father of men*; and Himself the source of this morality. He, *in this faculty, reveals Himself*, and shows to man *his* sole claim to a divine relationship.

This higher civilisation does not mistake intellectual achievement as its title to enlightenment. The sharp and active brain is quite consistent with the base and low; and may be indifferent to superstitions and degrading idolatries. But the moral faculty, active and large, at once refines and exalts the intellect; then men are truly *wise*, and degrading superstitions die.

The object, then, to which the true worshipper aims, everywhere, is to bring man out of a debased into an enlightened recognition of the Supreme Lord and of this simple relationship; to teach that the human race form one family, united indissolubly to each other, and to the Supreme Lord, by the divine moral faculty, to which the intellect is subordinate; that by this they may be all truly enlightened, and worship simply and truly, with grateful and serene trust, the Supreme Lord and Father of all. This worship can never be other than beneficent. It is only the expression of gratitude; the desire for better wisdom, for still larger charity, a well-doing and serene life, at peace with itself and all beside.

To a civilisation resting upon this simple and direct worship and morality, few barbarians have any perception; their pride and gross superstitions have made it impossible.

The temples are often very grand and beautiful, built of hewn stone, with lofty domes, towers, bells, and spires. The priests are very numerous, and divided into many ranks. The lowest are the curates, who do the "*dirty*" work, as the English phrase it. They are but little better than beggars, though mentally often superior to those who half-starve them, whilst the higher ranks (by whom they are hired) live luxuriously.

The *Sacred Writings* say that Christ was Himself a mendicant, and that his first followers were but little better; that he denounced, in bitter terms, all pride and luxury; that the true object of life was not to think of oneself, but of others; to give to the poor, help the distressed, and the like. In truth, this benevolence and the moral precepts of Christ (as I have already said) are its *salt* [pho-zi].

I have, in the temples, heard a High-Caste Priest eloquently exalt this benevolence, and pointing out the divine charity of the *Master* (as Christ is often called),—heard him say, "My brethren, give to the poor, help the suffering, do good whenever you can, give your all to Christ."

I have said, "This is excellent; I will talk with this benevolent Bonze." On one occasion I did so. The High-Caste had dined; I was ushered into his presence; the fruits and the wine were still before him. I approached and bowed low before him, and dared to ask, "Is your illustrious body well?" He slightly nodded, and waved me to a seat. I expressed my admiration of his benevolent morality, as shown in his exalted *invocation* in the Temple. "Oh, that was of course; we do not rely upon morality." I begged pardon, but did not understand. He added: "Morals are well, in their way. Charity is a good thing, if the purpose be sanctified; but nobody is saved by his goodness." He saw my bewilderment. "Oh, I deplore your darkness; I grieve over the errors, too fatal, even in our Christian land." I could only bow. He continued: "When will the darkness of superstition give way, in the East, to our glorious religion? When will the worship of Christ spread over the whole benighted world?" I ventured to hint that I had called to speak my thought of his noble benevolence. "Oh, yes, we must give. But the true worship—knowledge of, and belief in, the *Redeemer*—ah! that is the only means of salvation; those are the vital things." I said, "The poor are everywhere, and need help." He looked at me suspiciously for a moment, and then brightened; he saw I had not come to ask for anything. "Yes; the Scriptures say, 'The poor ye will always have with ye,' and we cannot alter it." "I am told that your Low-Caste Priests are good men, and do nearly all the work. I know one of these who is very kind. Your benevolence is like our *Confutze*, who had a tender regard for the poor and distressed."

"Ah, our divine *Master* taught charity; but one must go higher than that." "Pardon my poor mind, but do you *not* really give to the poor, in your temples, as your exalted Wisdom taught?" "Ah-Chin, you mistake; but one must overlook your darkness of mind—no offence—*Society* takes all I can spare, and I give to Curates from my revenue." "Society? I do not comprehend." "Well, no; you know nothing of the incessant calls. We must visit and receive visits; keep up equipages, servants; then there are always poor relations, and the poor Curates (these are the 'poor relations' of our order)." "But the Curates are poorly paid, I am told, and deserving." "The Curates are well enough; but more fuss is made than need be. I was a Curate, Ah-Chin, myself." "Your illustrious did not need aid, perhaps?" "Well, yes; I got Curate-fare—cold shoulders of mutton, and other colder shoulders." I saw that there was something which I was not to understand. "Pardon, but the *Society* is not to be put before the Christ-God?" "I beg, sir, you speak not in that way. I pardon much to your darkness. Do not again profane our blessed and holy religion."

This alarmed me; I did not know what portended. I bowed very low, and humbly craved permission to take my leave. I really feared punishment—perhaps of the *Cangue*, or pan-tsee. I afterwards knew, no more than the reproof of the High-Bonze was imminent; though, had the common people caught a *pagan Chinee* who had dared to speak, in their notion, disrespectfully of their Idols, he would be fortunate to have no worse treatment than a *ducking in a horse-pond* [phu-it-mu-dsi-wo].

What but slow progress is to be expected when a people—even the *Literati*—are so superstitious? for the errors there, make obstacles everywhere. It is but just now that nearly the whole population of the province of Ireland (one-third of the kingdom) have been relieved from maintaining the English Idolatry, though they detested it.

The intolerance of the devotees prevents better men from reforming abuses, even in the Temples. If a Priest dare to moderate the excessive absurdities of the Superstition, he at once endangers his *Living*, and is likely to be degraded and driven forth to neglect and poverty.

I, myself, knew a Wise Priest of rank, who very innocently published some comments upon the *Sacred Writings*, wherein he showed that the statements as they stood were simply impossible. Now, as I have said, the *Sacred Writings* are worshipped; and to doubt that they are the words of Jah is horrible—formerly punished by death, now by degradation, *excommunication*, and loss of revenue. This poor man did not express any doubt; he merely pointed out an error, which might be there *somehow*, and which he thought, in his simplicity, should be removed or explained. But the *Canon* [ban-gwo] of the Superstition allowed of no comment of that sort as to the Word of Jehovah! and cursed out of the Temples, with his Priest-robe torn off, and his money stript from him, the daring *blasphemer* [zw-an] must go!

This is an astonishing *Canon*; for if one allows that four thousand years ago Jehovah spoke words which were *then* inscribed—if one allows that the Jewish Priests kept annals and chronicles, and down through different ages preserved and added to their histories—if one allows that the followers of Christ after his death recorded some things concerning his life and his teachings, and that other followers wrote letters upon these matters—yet, one must also allow that all these writings were written at different periods, for different purposes, and in different and scattered records; all in obscure and unknown tongues; that they have been copied, re-copied, translated—that there are various versions—that, in respect of their meaning, and even of their right to be called a part of the Word, the highest and best cannot agree! Yet, through all the changes of great periods of time—through darkness, and wars, and every sort of ignorant credulity—through everything! *every word* of this huge collection of Obscure and Ancient Literature, and of an Obscure and Barbarous People, remains exactly as originally delivered by Jah! "Oh, certainly," says his devotee, "because *He has preserved them*." "Yes; but when a statement is absolutely impossible—as where 'the water covered the whole earth.'" "Oh, the *Word* does not deal with Science." I think not; Jah was not a god of science—he was, in fact, just as ignorant as the Jew-Priests who pretended to speak his *Word*!

Yet this inconceivable *Canon* goes further, and declares that this *Word* is the absolute, and only, and perfect *Revelation* of the Deity to man; that it contains the only TRUTH, and is the only way by which man, *under damnation already*, can have *any* hope, however small, of escaping the everlasting fire of hell! Upon this *Canon* all the Sects of the Western Barbarians erect their *Idolatries*—they call them Churches; but, as we have seen, they are for ever fighting as to the meaning of these very Sacred Writings!

Another *Canon* is, that Christ is the very God (Jah), and that the Holy Ghost is also the very God. And to deny this *Canon* is to go to Hell! Nor does it at all matter that one has never heard of this, nor that he could have never heard. The whole race of man before Christ was born, to this very hour, are either burning, and will surely burn, in everlasting fires of Hell, unless they have *believed* in this Canon! And Jah contrived that all this should be exactly so; though he did also plan from all time that his Son, Christ, should go down to the world and get himself put *to death*; and thus the great Jah, appeased by the sight of his Son *dying on a cross*, should be so far softened that some would escape Hell! Only a very few; because no one could escape unless he knew, and believed, and accepted, and *was born* into the very blood of this son! A mystery so incomprehensible, that Christians do not pretend to solve it, and are always trembling for fear that they may not have been *born again*!

How, under these circumstances, as Jah cruelly neglected to let the *Heathen* know that they could be saved—(indeed, they suspect no danger)—the good-hearted devotees of the Barbarians employ Bonzes to go over the great Seas to the *Heathen*, to carry them the *glad tidings*! These delegates from the Barbarians are called *Missionaries*, and the Temples and devotees are full of prayers and invocations for the Salvation of the Heathen! by which is meant the worship of the Barbarians duly adopted in our Central Kingdom, and in other regions of the wide world not under the sway of these Idolaters!

But our Flowery Kingdom, from so long ago as dynasty *Whey-Song*, has known of these missionaries; and we know of some now amongst us. They are harmless enough, and quite fully understand how to adapt themselves to circumstances, and draw the money necessary to their support. The Bonzes of the Roman Sect are the wisest, and care for nothing very idolatrous; if a *convert* will go so far as to be baptised [Wa-shti] they are quite content. They seek to be useful, and keep the obnoxious features of the Superstition out of sight.

There are also some Jews in our Central Kingdom. They have been known in some provinces from a time long before the supposed birth of Christ.

Another *Sect* of the region of the Western Barbarians (in the Eastern parts), who worship a god named *Mohammed*—a *Sect* merely an offshoot of the Jews, from whom they adopted the most part of their superstition, and equally fierce and intolerant—penetrated into our Flowery Land soon after its rise. It was about six hundred years ago that they established a slight hold amongst us, and are still to be found—never here in their weakness exhibiting any of the savagery of strength. In a large portion of the Western regions they were for ages as cruel and destructive as the Christians, and, in fact, waged wars with them for absolute mastery, during which all the horrors usual to those dreadful Barbarians terrified and maddened mankind. Finally, these two Sects, *Christian and Mohammedan* (so styled), divided the whole region of the Western Barbarians among themselves! and from that time have been less quarrelsome with each other, than have the *Sects* of the two great divisions in their intestine conflicts.

Thus, it will be acknowledged that the Barbarians are well disposed sometimes towards us,—or at any rate the devotees of their Superstition are,—and we must gratefully thank them for their sincere anxiety for the salvation of our *souls*; for our *bodies* that is another matter. They think us ignorant, even of the ordinary rules of morality. They do not know that before Greece or Rome had appeared in history, our worship of the Sovereign Lord and our moral precepts were established, purely, simply, and that our annals show that the Grecian and Roman culture largely borrowed from ours, though not the *Superstitions*. These were derived, probably, from some source common to the Western Barbarians, likely Egyptian, and though modified by habits of tribes, retained more or less of those original traits which appear in all

The Temples are numerous, though often quite deserted except by the Bonzes and their servants. The same revenues are taken by the Bonze whether there be any worshippers or not, and sometimes the prayers are said or sung to empty forms (seats)—not more empty than the prayers.

Next in rank to Curates come Rectors, who enjoy good *Livings* [mo-tsi], and have fine houses and gardens. The other higher ranks, are Arch-Bishops, Bishops, called Lords [tchou], who live in stone *palaces*, and have great revenues; but Society robs them of the larger portion of this revenue,—a barbarous injustice,—leaving the poor Lords quite destitute. I was told this; but I never happened to meet with a starved Bishop.

These *Tchou*-Bonzes intermarry with the High-Castes, perform the marriage ceremony for them, wait upon the Queen with invocations to the gods— baptize royal infants; that is, sprinkle them when eight days old, in the Temples with invocations, with many ceremonies, after which they are safe from the devil and the dreadful Hell; these are the chief duties of their exalted office. As great *lay-lords* (that is Lords not of the soul but of the clay—lay), they sit in the great Law-making *Council*; where their function is, to see to it that no law be made which in any way can injure the temples, or their own revenues and powers. One does not see that they are remarkable for the practice of the virtues which they teach; nor that they are meek and lowly followers of the Lamb (Christ-god); or that they very often "wash the feet of the disciples"—although they are commanded in the *Sacred Writings* to do these things; and also to succour the distressed, give to the poor, and other like acts of charity. I should have been pleased to see a Bishop kneeling and washing the feet of some devotee! but I never did. They discharge those duties which they owe to Society with honourable punctuality: keeping up neat equipages, sleek horses, and pious servants; and wearing the garb of their order with a scrupulous exactness, even to the shoe-buckles.

They quote the example of the Christ-god, who, when on the world, made from common water *good wine*; and are very choice respecting this article. As to charity, they are so robbed by Society, that, what with gifts for the *Heathen*, and poor relations (for whom they are also expected to get good *Livings* in the Temples), they have but little to spare. Then, too, "Charity begins at home" (the *Sacred Writings* declare), and he who does not take care of himself, and those who are dependent upon him, "is worse than a Heathen" (This is again from the *Sacred* words). For those poor and benighted creatures, sunk in dreadful idolatries, indeed, something must be put into the Missionary box!

The different *Sects* quarrel as to particular modes of Worship in the Temples. Some will have candles lighted, to please the idols; others say, they do not need candles, and are offended by the smell. Some say, You should make Invocations kneeling; others say, standing. Some say, one should face to the East, others say, to the North. Some say, you should pray aloud; others say, silent prayers are more acceptable. And very sharp quarrels and *new Sects* arise upon these matters. None are allowed to worship in Temples but devotees of the High-Caste Sect. All others must worship in Temples not dignified by a loftier name than *Conventicle, Chapel,* or the like.

I will state, briefly, what is the ceremony of Idolatry in the great *Queen-pope* Sect. She is worshipped in the Invocations, and receives, with her children, a place in the prayers.

When the great bells sound from the high, stone towers, the High-Castes go, richly dressed, into the Temples, uncover and bow the heads to the Idol, in silence—making Invocations, silently. By the command of the Jewish *Sacred Writings* the Seventh day (so, continuously, for ever) is devoted to the grand Worship in the Temples. This is a marked thing among the Western Barbarians—this devotion of one day in every seven to the Worship of Jah—as ordered in the Sacred Word. It is declared to be Jah's day—*Holy*-day. And it is so sacred, that there is danger of Hell to him who

"Does any work or play
Upon the sacred day,"

as the mongrel verse-makers of the *Superstition* have it! And the Priests vehemently denounce all who do not worship upon that day.

Some object to so great strictness; and the quarrel, as usual, is bitter between the strict and the not-so-strict Holy-day worshippers.

Those not-so-strict think that the poor, who work six days, should be allowed to go to the places of amusement on the seventh, and enjoy harmless recreations. The strict say they should be punished for desecrating the day by their neglect of worship; yet the poor cannot go in dirt and rags to the Temples. The High-Castes go there in rich attire, and would be incommoded by the poor—indeed, the High and Low Castes never mingle, not even in their worship. In truth, not many of any rank attend upon the Priests in worship. The devotees are mostly old women and older men, a few young people attracted by opposite attraction of sex, children and servants; a few pauper children may be huddled into a dark corner for fear of offending the idols.

The Priests face the Idol, and make Incantations, which are repeated, age after age, without any alteration; no Priest dare to make any the least change; the wrath of the gods would follow.

One peculiarity is, that the most abject *confessions* are made, by Priests and devotees, of heinous offences—making eternal punishment fitly their due. They beg for pardon and that *salvation* (meaning deliverance from the awful Hell) may be granted, not for any good in them, but wholly for the sake of the Son—the *Christ*. On my first attendance in a Temple, when I heard these fearful confessions and looked upon the fine women; the carefully dressed worshippers, I thought, "How dreadful, these High-Castes such wretches—incredible!"

I afterwards discovered that the *sins* [ly-ie], the offences confessed, were merely *ecclesiastical* (we have no term like it); nobody ever really confesses any wrong which he may have committed.

The grand act of worship is, however, the *Creed* (here again in our Flowery Land we have no term)—an Invocation and Declaration wherein all swear, under the awful penalty of eternal burnings in Hell and torments of Satan for ever, that they believe and worship all points of the *Superstition* with thankful hearts and undoubting minds. Repeating after the Priest, all standing, facing the Idol, uncovered, with eyes downcast and deep abasement.

The Incantations do not differ from the Invocations, only they are droned out in songs, more dismally, perhaps. The burden of both is to deliver the *true* worshippers from "the wiles of the flesh and the devil"; to overthrow, if possible, this awful demon, and to save sinners, of whom the worshippers declare themselves, in a hundred different ways, to be chief, "*miserable offenders*" [ka-nt-lm-mbi]. These, and lofty exaltation of the *Christ-God* and of the Father Jah, who, when He had given his word that nothing could save man from Hell, graciously allowed the Jews to crucify the Son, that in the Son's sufferings He, Jah, might let off some of the sufferings of mankind. Possibly some of the present worshippers might be among the lucky *saved*. For this *salvation* endless praises are to be Sung in the Temples below; and for ever and for ever in the great Heavens, through the infinite eternal worlds without end.

A Hymn of Praise in which all join ends the act of worship. The Priest *blesses* the people and invokes the mercy of the gods; and they, making due obeisance to the idols, retire in silence or to the music of the great organs.

A special act of worship, or Incantation, is always made to the *Triune-god*, that is, the *Three-in-one*, called HOLY TRINITY (*Threenity*). To omit this would, in the opinion of devotees, be so terrible a thing that no one would dare to stay a moment, fearing that, like Korah in the *Sacred Writings*, the very world would open itself and swallow them up. This *three-in-one* seems like a *Hindoo* god.

The Bonzes attend upon the sick and the dying, moderating their fears of damnation by insisting upon the most abject devotion to the Superstition, and intimating that, if they heartily grieve over their offences, and with undoubting minds believe in all the points of the *Creed*, then they may receive the *Sacraments*—that is, *Sacred Meats*; which having received, the devil and Hell may be set at defiance. These Sacred Meats are symbols of the very *body and blood* of Christ—a shocking *rite*, borrowed wholly from the old, savage Jews, who held that a *Sacrifice* must be offered up to appease the wrathful Jah on almost any occasion, and who sometimes even devoted human victims.

The Bonzes, in general, perform the Marriage Ceremonies, which they will have to be a Sacred *rite* in their Superstition, though some *Sects* think otherwise. However, the High-Castes do not consider a Marriage without a Bonze safe; some evil to the children, or other calamity, might ensue. Thus the Bonzes, for their services in this matter, obtain consideration and good fees [tin-tin].

After all, however, with the lowest Caste the Superstition is not much more than a *Fright*; its morality does not touch them, nor those things which refine. They have only a dim and low idea of the Sovereign Lord—debased, in so much notion as they do have, by the Jewish debasement. The devil-and-Hell part is familiar to them, and, in truth, fits well to the origin of the Barbarous tribes, and to their rude and savage character. As I have said, the Upper Castes consider this portion of their Superstition the really valuable part, in practical use. All evidence in the Courts, and every sanction, touching important interests or statements, rest upon this hold upon the fears of the common people. "Oh" (as an Englishman once said to me), "we must keep the devil and his *hot place* in our service, I tell you, Ah-Chin; or we should have 'the devil to pay' in good earnest!"

It is very difficult to change the Superstitions of a people, because rooted in their fears; and, in a matter wherein the imagination has chief power, and nothing can be *known*, even honest men of wisdom fear radical changes; they prefer to bear inconveniences, and dread the effect of *new doctrines* upon ignorant masses.

Priests, and the varied interests, and large establishments and revenues—in fact, a great portion of the whole community—are concerned in maintaining the Superstition, on selfish grounds, or think that their own interests are involved. The higher orders regard the *Established* condition of things in Worship and in the State as too *Sacred* to be touched. They denounce all who endeavour, in any faint degree, to suggest reforms, as "*infidel*" [un-ti-dsi]—a term of deepest reproach—agitators, who covertly would overthrow "our Temples, our Idols, and the Queen-Pope herself."

But they cannot wholly suppress the Thinkers; [kog-ti-te] (as the *reformers* are called); and these honestly think that some revision may be made with safety and advantage. They are sneered at by the larger part of the *literati*, and by all the priests, as *Tinkers*. A tinker is one who mends and patches, not a real artisan; and the majority will have it that nothing in England requires mending or patching. They are also stigmatised, sarcastically, as members of a *Mutual Admiration* Society. A society where the members laud everything written or said by any other member; and where, as the members think, all true wisdom alone illuminates the surrounding darkness. I suspect this society is a *mith* [pho-gti]; that the true sense of the sarcasm is, that the Thinkers overrate the value of their published thoughts, and that wisdom will not die with them. Certainly, some of the thoughts which I have seen in books, though not so gross and hateful as the Idolatry, are quite as useless. Only one thing I do respect them for—they do not subscribe to the pretensions of the priest; and are really influencing the people by giving them hints of value. They do act upon the upper classes, at least, with a reforming effect.

I have not referred to obscure *sects*, of which there are many. Some of these shout and howl; some keep absolute silence; some lash themselves into a sort of phrensy, and fall down in fits, fancying that they are possessed by the *Holy Spirit*. Some will only be *baptised* by going into a river, and there, under the Incantations of the Priest, be violently plunged all over in the water, both women and men. Still, all of these, and many others, hold to the *Sacred Writings* and the other Idolatries: the main points are alike in all.

The Roman Pope has many devotees among the English Barbarians; and was, not long ago, the Great and only Head. But a vile and cruel king, who wished to enjoy a woman and divorce his wife, with whom he had lived for many years, and by whom he had children, quarreled with the Roman Pope, because he would not suffer this bad thing to be done; and the English Barbarians, who disliked a foreign Pope, and the fierce chiefs about this king, even some of the priests of English birth, urged him to proclaim himself to be Pope in England, and to seize upon the revenues which the Pope had received from the English, and all the lands and properties of great value, which before-time had been given to the Temples and to the Priests. This was done; this king seized upon the wealth, and threw down the worship of the Roman Pope in England, and declared himself to be the new god in England—the Pope! And the English Barbarians worshipped, and have continued to worship, this new Pope accordingly. And some who could not honestly worship the new idol, and dared to adhere to the Roman, were burnt to death! Indeed this new idolatry was not introduced into England without terrible consequences. Massacres, burnings, imprisonments, wars, horrible crimes—persecutions, destruction of families, robbing, plundering—not even to this day have all the evil consequences ceased; though this bad ruler made this change in this particular of the great Superstition more than 300 years ago.

Thus, our Central Kingdom may see how powerfully Idolatry and Superstition are entrenched among the English Barbarians. A System interwoven with the very texture of their civilization; supporting, and, in turn, supported by the State; mixed up with customs and traditions, and endeared by its connection with family interests; rich in its possessions; powerful in all the Halls of Learning, and in its influence upon the fortunes and dignities of men; boasted of for its learning, for its history, and for its refining and reforming teachings; the *English Church* (as those Barbarians call their grand Idolatry) seems likely to stand for many generations. Yet agencies are, slowly, at work, which will remove the dark and horrible, and leave the simple and true. The Benevolence of the Sovereign Lord of Heaven never tires; and the pure worship and less corrupted morality will make way.

I hope I may be pardoned for the time which I have given to this subject; it is one worthy of deep attention. Besides, a little study of the literature and manners of the Western tribes, fastened upon my mind the impression that their History was mainly an account of the rise and progress of the Christ-god Superstition; and that, hereafter, whoever shall have the pleasing task of writing of their better civilization, will find it to be his main purpose to show the decline and extinction of that Superstition.

To wise men who worship the Supreme Lord only, and accept of His simple and direct Morality, there is, in all the broad and immense world, but a *single family*, ruled by Him. When this family recognises and worships Him, in direct and true sincerity, and practises the few and perfectly simple rules of His benevolent Morality, then it is an *enlightened*, civilized family.

The Western Barbarians do not understand nor practise this Benevolent Morality; until they do, their civilization will not be really better than a Barbarism.

We are not to suppose that a perfect morality will ever obtain, because man, being two-fold in his nature—divine and bestial—will now be ruled by the one, and now by the other part. The object of all education (discipline) is, therefore, to teach man how he may order these two parts. There is no antagonism [ha-tsi] between them, only it is indispensable that the *divine* part should rule.

That this may be, the *intellect* must be cultivated, not in difficulties, but in habits of thinking, of looking, or seeking out; of seeing the beauty, the order, the grandeur of the whole divine world. Thus employed it delights in itself; it feels the Mind like a bright thing, flying out to the great seas, and upwards to the everlasting stars. It loves to hear, to see, to look at and into everything. It can never cease to employ this delightful mind, thus stimulated in early youth, to exert itself; but it must be exerted innocently, benevolently.

That the subordination of mind and the animal may be secured, the Supreme, the Moral Faculty must, from the earliest years, be touched by wise fingers. Ah, how it responds, this divine part; how it, in the pure and warm glow of unselfish youth, recognises and worships with filial love its Father, the Sovereign Lord!—perceives the moral order and harmony, and loves to be orderly and obedient—early perceives that the true business of life is to preserve this order, and enjoy this peace.

Thus Man, a *moral-minded* animal, is first of all to be taught to understand his own nature, and to develop his distinguishing faculty. This done, the bestial part rises not above its office. It, too, performs its proper and useful end; and man is not a divided, but a whole and happy being.

All education, therefore, rightly considered, aims to this *Integrity* [Kom-fu] of a man—this secured, there are no limits to the mere objects of study or of examination.

Our *Literati*, directed many thousands of moons ago, by our exalted Confutze and Menzie, who, themselves were imbued with the ancient Wisdom, are familiar with these simple things. The Western Barbarians, mainly devoted first of all to the bestial part; to the enjoyment of the appetites and the passions; sunk in gross Superstitions, only by a few minds begin dimly to see.

CHAPTER II.
OF THE HISTORY AND GEOGRAPHY OF THE ENGLISH.

BEFORE commenting upon the Government, it is useful to speak of the geography and history of the English Barbarians.

The Kingdom consists of the following: England with Wales and Scotland, forming one large island; Ireland, separated by a channel of the seas, lying West; and several small groups of islets, scattered about the Coasts. It lies Westerly from the great, main Land of the Barbarians, from which it is separated by a narrow course of the seas. England and the Main Land form the region designated Europe. The whole Kingdom surpasses not in area or population some of our Celestial provinces: the extent being in the English square miles some 110 thousand [Si-re], and in people some 32 millions [Ken-ty]. In such narrow limits there are no rivers—only small streams, which, near the sea, owing to the flux and reflux of the great waters, become broad and deep.

In our Science and in our Annals the whole region and people are known as one only—but the different petty tribes are distinguished in our waters by the forms and colours of the *flags*, shown upon the masts of the Barbarian vessels. The English are less in people and in lands than many others; but by their fierceness in war, and the multitude of their big ships, they esteem themselves to be the most powerful of all.

The first account of them is recorded by one of the Romans, who, in our dynasty, *Han*, crossed the narrow sea from a Roman province, and entered into the island. It was then a Wilderness, and among the forests lived a few savages, clothed in skins. Sometime after, the Romans conquered the country, and established a Roman province—their dominion lasting four hundred [qua-cet] years—contemporaneous with our dynasty, *Hewhan*.

During the dynasties, *Han* and *Hewhan*, the various tribes surrounding the Roman provinces, grown more populous and better acquainted with the Military art, crowded, more and more, upon the Romans; and, gradually, destroyed their power. They were forced to leave England.

On their departure, and for several ages after, down to our dynasty, *Song*, the history of the Country is merely a tale of ceaseless struggles among the different savage tribes from the Main Land, to plunder and subdue it. The civilization disappeared. Nearly all signs of the Roman occupancy became obliterated; and the knowledge of letters would have been lost, but that the

Priests who accompanied some of the savage chiefs had among them some of the Roman learning. These Priests and chiefs had adopted the worship of the new Christ-god.

At length, one of these invading tribes having fairly mastered the country, and established a show of regular authority, the germs of knowledge began to grow. The victorious tribe had lands also on the main parts; fierce and warlike, it endeavoured to extend its power; and repeatedly made assaults upon others of the Barbarians of those chief parts. In these, the remains of the Roman civilization were considerable, and the knowledge of letters more common.

The position of the English, and their need of communication, made vessels indispensable; and they learned to build and to sail many ships. However, but little progress in civilization was made till our dynasty, *Ming*; when the Sovereign, then a Woman, called by the Barbarians, *Queen*, sent the first Embassy to our Central Kingdom—bearing gifts, and humbly approaching our Illustrious, begging permission to trade at one of our ports on the sea.

From that time to the present, the annals of these Barbarians are but little more than records of plundering expeditions into distant regions; of their fierce slaughters; their cunning or bold stratagems to extend trade, and establish dominion for the sake of trade and plunder. To obtain trade, by means fair or foul; to get strongholds abroad and subjugate others—these have been the great objects of the rulers and the people.

By their ships, manned with the most ignorant and debased, taught only in the work of sailing and fighting; stimulated by love of plunder, in which the meanest have a share; the very name of these Barbarians has become terrible in all the distant seas.

They first appeared within the waters of our Central Kingdom, in the dynasty *Tsing*, but did not venture then to assault our unoffending people; and only, by cunning and with low prostrations and humility, sought to traffic, in such way as should be acceptable to our Illustrious. Further time was looked to and greater force before showing their fierceness!

They have since seized nearly all the maritime parts of the Hindoos, and, penetrating the country with savage bands, have slaughtered the inoffensive people, and robbed the treasuries of Princes and the Temples of immense riches. They have, finally, subjugated the chief provinces of the Hindoos, and yearly bear away from them the ancient revenues.

Throwing off disguise, in our celestial seas, these Barbarians at length discovered their true character. To save our people from the effects of a dreadful poison, to which the lower orders had become habituated, our

Illustrious prohibited the importation of this thing, called by the English, Opium (Zle-psi). But these disregarded the just request; wished to pour upon us enormous amounts for the sake of the gains which the bad traffic yielded, and which was monopolised by them; and, when nothing else would serve, assaulted our unoffending people, fell with fire and sword upon our province of Quang-tun, and, rushing upon other maritime parts with their great ships, armed with prodigious cannon, threatened to burn and destroy. In our peaceful Kingdom we had no need of such things; we had no means to meet these destructive engines, contrived by *Christ-god* worshippers; and our Illustrious, to save further dreadful mischiefs to our unprotected people, granted trade to these selfish and cruel Barbarians! Yet this benevolence of our Illustrious only served to encourage additional demands; and we all remember how, coming with more ships, swifter with *steam*, and greater guns and men, these impious defiers of the Sovereign and Heavenly Justice have more recently fallen upon the Northern provinces, and slaughtered and robbed our people, our palaces, and even the precincts of our Illustrious himself! Who, awaiting and appealing to the Sovereign Lord of Heaven, doubts not the due chastisement of crime, which, in due time, shall heavily fall!

Meantime, in all other parts of the great Outer Seas, these English visited the coasts with their fire-ships, and compelled the natives to trade, either by fraud or by open war. In the great Sea towards the sunset, they, in this way, settled upon many Lands; and, in the course of some generations, their settlements in those regions, wishing to trade with others beside the English (which these would not allow) revolted; drove away the armed bands which were sent to subdue them, and formed a new power.

In this way, about 100 years ago, the Barbarians, called American [Mel-i-kan], arose. Their ships are known in our Central Kingdom by a flag, named "Starry," because of the *Stars* [Zen-ti] which are painted upon it. These people are ardent for trade, but not so mad and reckless; and not aggressive in their intercourse with others. They are not so domineering and haughty—humbly submitting themselves, in general, to the Son of Heaven, making tribute, and seeking his Illustrious protection to their trade and to their ships in our Central Waters.

During these events, the English Barbarians also sent their poor people and criminals into the Lands of the far South Seas, to make new places for their poor to toil in, to get rid of them, and to make safe, distant places, to keep their criminals in; subduing the tribes in those parts—thus making more trade. And in this way, and with their many big ships and cannons, they boast that they will bring the whole immense world, either to be tributaries, or to be completely subjective. And they please their devotees, because they say that this subjugation will "*Convert*" all the Pagans to the worship of the gods of their Superstition—and this great boon will abundantly compensate for all the wrongs and atrocities committed! In fact, they impiously pretend that they are commanded to subjugate the Heathen World, that it may be saved from the dreadful Hell!

The domestic events have not been important; though the Barbarians themselves think everything to be important which happens amongst them. They fancy that "Civilization and Progress" (famous words with them) depend upon the petty disputes arising—sometimes as to their Superstition, and sometimes as to some trifling thing in their Customs. One of the main events, is the story of a son of one of their Sovereigns, who drove his father out of the Kingdom, and rëestablished the Government in such manner, that, ever after, when the matter is referred to, one shall say *Glorious* [Twang-ba]. As well as I can understand, the things done were, that whereas, before, the Sovereign had been allowed to worship the Pope, if he wished (but in secret), afterwards he should not, but *be* the English Pope, solely. And, instead of a native dynasty, a foreign, and very base and stupid one, hateful to the English, was fastened upon them. These events, an outside observer sees, were followed by long-continued discontents, and civil war—wherein innocent persons suffered in their persons and their property; and very many were exiled, and very many were brutally massacred and put to death—not because of any other offence than adhering to the ancient Laws, and to the Sovereign whom this base son had dethroned! Yet, of this event, when one speaks of it, one shall say, *Glorious!*

The form of government has not changed; but the power has, during these periods, past into the hands of the Aristocracy [Fo-hi]. In the time of the Queen, who sent the humble petition to our Illustrious, the English Sovereign was Master—being Pope and Ruler; that is, High Priest and Sovereign. But the people, increasing and growing richer in ships and merchandize, began to feel the intermeddling of the Ruler. Previously, the people had been too poor and too few to be accounted anything; and grew up into an improved condition without notice. They now disliked to be taxed, and began a struggle with the Sovereign to limit his power in this thing—for they said, "If he can take a *penny* (a small coin), at his own goodwill and pleasure, he can take all." Now this is an absurdity—yet, it looked sound; and, at any rate, became the ground of the fight between the well-to-do people (the Middle-Caste), and the Ruler. *This* would make his will absolute; the *other* would make its will absolute! The Sovereign who first had this opposition seems to have been a fool, and the next, a knave—but neither had sufficient sense to arm soldiers enough to compel obedience, as was done on the Main Land—consequently, after a good deal of wretched fighting between the Sovereign helped by nearly all the High-Caste, and the *next* Caste in the Aristocracy and well-to-do people, these last succeeded, and put the Sovereign to death. As is always the case, during a civil war, *fanaticism* arose. It based itself upon two points—the right of the people to rule, and the right of the gods of the Superstition, *without any Pope*, to be worshipped. This was a departure from the original dispute only in part; because some had vehemently denied the whole notion of Pope-worshipping; and as the Sovereign was English Pope, this pretension embittered the strife. Now, the Aristocracy (High-Caste) upheld the Pope; but the Second-Caste and the people, opposed; and these, at length, for the time, carried all before them; destroyed the King, overthrew his worship as Pope; and established the gods of the Superstition, with such severity of worship (especially as to the *rites* and as to the *Seventh-day*), that, *Society* completely changed. Even the name of the State was changed! The point, of the *Rule of the people*, was in this vindicated; for the name of the State was—*Commonwealth*; and of the Ruler—*Protector*. Now, this so *radical* change was not real. It was the expression of that extreme agony into which Civil War hurries. The strong passions sway—the strongest rule. And the very able military man who organized the troops into the ways of an invincible army, though of the Aristocratic, High-Caste connection, happened to have adopted the most severe notions of the great Superstition; looked upon Christ-god merely as the *Jah* of the Jews; wished to make the *Sacred Writings* the law of the Land; and to get himself proclaimed to be the *High Priest* and ruler of this new Jewish State! This remarkable man, with his invincible troops, could not absolutely do this—but he did completely overawe and rule the State, causing himself to be declared *Protector of the Commonwealth*!

With the death of this strong man, there being no successor to his ability, repression soon relaxed; the Aristocracy came out of their seclusion; the gloom of fanatical worship brightened in the natural love of rational life. *Society* rebounded from the low depression; ancient feelings, habits, sports, reasserted themselves. Communities do not radically change, at once—such a thing to be beneficial, must be cautious. A tree, though misshapen, may not be plucked up by the roots violently, and forced into uncongenial soil; to improve its beauty and use, a different method must be sought: only, if the tree be actually dying, possibly, a complete and radical change may save it—at any rate it is the sole chance!

The troops, wholly devoted to their late great General, found no one on whom they could rely; and another portion of the Army in the far North, was induced actively to assist the Aristocracy. These, joined by the middle classes, who had wearied of the too gloomy worship and severe *rites*, hastened to recall a Son of him whom they had not long before put to death, and place him upon the *Throne*. They declared him to be Sovereign-pope: they restored the old form and name of government; and rescinded nearly everything done by the Commonwealth. In this *Restoration* (as the

English call it) is another event, considered by them, of great importance. In this Restoration (a natural effect of the *fanaticism* largely charged to the greater ignorance of the lower castes) the High-Castes again became predominant. They again took influence and power everywhere, and retained the fruits of the civil struggle in their hands. *They* had aided the resistance to the arbitrary will of the Sovereign; and they now grasped and enjoyed the power wrested from him. They, alone, could impose taxes. No Sovereign would again dare to tax the people (that is, the High-Castes) without their consent. But *they* would levy and raise taxes when they pleased. Thus holding the *Purse* of the State they had become supreme.

On the death of this Restored one (who turned out to be so base that the common people often deplored the loss of the late great General), a brother reigned. This man, as I have said (wishing to worship the Rome-pope) was driven out by his son, forming the epoch, *Glorious*. The present Queen is of the dynasty then established; and during this period the absorption of power by the High-Caste has gone on. Taught by the Slaughter of the late King, his successor feared; and the new dynasty was compelled by the Aristocracy to submit to those limitations of power, which effectually placed authority in their hands. To secure this authority, the Sovereign was not allowed any money to keep troops; and, if, on any pretence, troops were raised, they were immediately refused pay, and forced to be disbanded upon the least suspicion that they would be used to strengthen the Sovereign. The aristocracy had continued to strip him also of all private revenue; and had, in fact, reduced him to a dependency upon them for his daily subsistence [Bran-te].

Thus, the High-Caste, acting by the forms of the *Grand Council*, seized power.

It is proper to explain the substance and form of this Council.

It is divided into two parts—*Upper House, and Lower House.*

The *Upper* are the Lords [Cheang] of Lands and Lords of the Temples—(High-State Sect.)

The *Lower* are lords, brothers, sons, nephews, relations, and devoted servants of the Upper; and are far more numerous.

No rule can be made, nor law, without both these bodies consent to it. This they do by asking each one his opinion, and a majority decides. Everything of importance must originate in the Lower House, and first be settled there. Then, the will of the Lower House is communicated to the Upper House, and it is ordered to ratify it. The members do so, and the Sovereign (or somebody requested thereto by him) approves (as the English politely phrase it); and the thing, so approved, is a new Law. Now, no Sovereign dares not *approve*—it might cost him his head. The last one, many years ago, who thought he might risk it, soon gave up the attempt, and died in a madhouse.

It will be seen, that the power in the Lower House will necessarily fall into the hands of any one who can obtain adherents enough to his opinions to secure a majority of members. The most ready debater [Qu-iztsi], the coolest and self-possessed, who has made himself master of the wishes of the majority; or, who, to these things, or with only a part of them, has great wealth and influence—one, in fine, who knows and divines what is wanted, and has the ability to lead;—directs and orders the measures which are to be adopted. This man, who controls the Lower House, governs the State. He nominates those who shall assist him in the government, being the same who aid him in managing the House. Thus, the Lower House governs by its delegates.

All these men, who are really a COMMITTEE [ty-gi-te] of the House for the ruling of the Kingdom, act in the name of the Sovereign, and receive the ancient titles of office from him. The ancient forms are preserved; and these men, obeying the House, profess to obey the Sovereign—in fact, the Sovereign is pretended to be the source of honour and of authority; and the very Laws which have been made against his wish are declared to be his Laws!

Thus, both the Sovereign and the people are amused. The one, by the respect shown to him, the emoluments and influence of his high office, and of his Pope-ship; the others, by some semblance of political [in-tri-gsi] power. This consists in calling together a few of the people of second and lower caste, to choose a new member for the Lower House—but this is quite a comedy, [sham-li] for the most part. It gives the ignorant Barbarians a notion of self-importance, and tickles them with the fancy that they really have a part in the government of the State.

Whilst these changes in the ordering of things at home were in progress, the usual fierce and bloody expeditions of these Barbarians had not been suspended.

The Americans had succeeded in establishing their independent power, but not till they had waged a second war with their late masters, scarcely less important to them than the first. For the English, still looking upon them with disdain, insisted upon the right to stop any of the vessels of the Americans upon the high seas, and to seize and carry away to their own ships any one whom they pleased. They would do this, and force the victims of their insolent cruelty to fight for them in their horrible war-ships.

The American Barbarians resisted this outrage; and, forced to fight a bloody war, vindicated their just cause; so that never since have the English, or any other Barbarians, dared to board or outrage the ships or the sailors [mer-tsi] of the Americans.

This stubborn and brutal barbarity, love of plunder and traffic, have involved the English during the present dynasty in numberless wars beyond seas. They have internally avoided great commotion, although the low castes have occasionally perished in surprising numbers by famine and disease. In Ireland the depopulation has exceeded anything recorded. The poor people of the Northern parts also, driven away from their homes, have nearly disappeared, unless in the armed bands sent over the sea. With these, the poor and despised Irish are in great numbers also; and, indeed, the strength and ferocity of the armed bands depend upon these, the most degraded and lowest caste of the Barbarians. In this way, the most turbulent and ignorant have been drawn off, trained to use of arms, and used to spread and maintain the terror and power of the English. Many of the low-castes have been shipped away in great ships to distant parts to form new settlements, and to add to those already begun. By these means, and from the increase of riches from trade, and from plunder of remote regions giving employment to the low orders, great disorders have been avoided. The plunder of the vast treasures of the Princes of the Hindoos, and the trade which has been forced upon them, and upon others, have contributed to this end. The result of increased wealth has been, however, mostly to the gain of the High-Castes; who, holding the Lands, have found in the enormous increase of value in these an additional strength. The numbers of the rich have increased; and these always look to the Castes above, and draw away as far as possible from those below. The poor remained uneducated, and fell more completely under control. If one of their order benefited himself, he had no ambition higher than a desire to stand well with those above him. Thus Wealth, always joining itself to the Higher Castes, made the power of the Aristocracy [Fo-hi] quite complete, and the obedience of the common people assured. Of this High-Caste the Sovereign is merely the ornamental top.

The learning of the Romans made but little advance, until very lately. The great Schools had some of the High-Caste within their walls; the mass of the people remained ignorant, fierce, and brutal. The laws continued to be in a most dreadful state; the prisons, foul dens of disease, cruelty and crime; the administration of Law, and disposal of offenders, savage and barbarous in the extreme.

The learning took mostly a fantastic [pa-ntsi] form—pedantic, busied with the mere shells of words, and names of things. It busied itself chiefly with the old languages of the Romans and the Greeks. A man who could repeat aloud from memory the *modes* of a Greek word was a man of profound learning. Of our Central Kingdom, of the wisdom and knowledge of the great East, they knew nothing; but nursed an intolerable conceit in admiration of the trivialities of their own ignorance, and by disdaining to understand a civilization of which they knew nothing—branding it as idolatrous, dark, Pagan!

Still, gradually, intercourse and larger acquaintance with the main parts, revived the love of Roman art; and the Roman civilization once more revived. Roman architecture, sculpture, learning, laws appeared. The style of public buildings, houses of the High-Castes, Bridges, took on the Roman forms. The *Literati* became more numerous; and, with the increasing riches, larger numbers became instructed. A long, bloody and disastrous War, which ended only a few years ago, moderated the intolerant selfishness of the Barbarians. It left them so crushed down under the weight of innumerable taxes, that it began to be seen that these interminable Wars beyond Seas, were not paid for by the gains of trade, nor by acquisitions of territory. This moderation was strengthened by the better and increasing knowledge: and Wars are not, in general, so eagerly waged.

The oldest child of a Ruler succeeds—male first, and failing him, a female. The direct descent from the *eldest* always succeeds, to the exclusion of the younger.

It is justly claimed that this is an element of stability; though it contains a foolish omission. For there is no recognized authority which can set aside an heir in the direct Line for however good cause. Thus the danger of a violent succession is always imminent—and of this the English history has many examples. In our Flowery Land, this danger is averted by the wise customs of the great *Calao*.

In my Report, I have explained at length the rules which govern in transactions with foreign tribes; and shown the maxims needful for our Illustrious, in all negotiations and dealings with the Western Barbarians. As trade (particularly by the English) is the grand object, I have pointed out how to deal in this matter, in such way as to yield no more than is convenient, nor sooner than is expedient.

The *Committee* who govern, preserving ancient forms, administer through them, in the name of the Sovereign. These forms assume *three great divisions*, one of them being two-fold: *spiritual*, referring to the great Superstition; and the other *temporal*; this is quite nominal, for the "temporalities" always touch matters *spiritual* in some way.

The *First* is the Executive.

The *Second* is the Parliament.

The *Third* is the Judicial.

The Executive—that is that which executes—has two parts. Spiritual, (the ghostly, the unknown,) performing all things concerning the Sovereign-Pope, the Temples, the worship, the Bonzes. Temporal, ordering the military forces by land and by sea, seeing that the laws are obeyed, and ruling the Hindoos and other distant peoples and settlements. Also arranging all matters with other Christ-god Barbarians, and with all foreign peoples.

The Law-making, called Parliament, or place of talking [Ba-ble]. This is the Grand Council already referred to, divided into the Upper and the Lower House, together really forming one, where all Rules and Laws are made. Here rests the Supreme Authority; and this body is controlled by the *Committee*, as before explained.

The Upper House is composed of Lords, who sit there in right of birth, except the *Spiritual* Lords, who are the great Bonzes (called Bishops) of the Superstition. Formerly, this Upper was, next after the Sovereign, most powerful, and often over-ruled, and even dethroned him. But the greater intelligence has reduced its influence, and made innoxious its mischievousness. Even its aristocraticalness could not blind the Lower House to an *Imbecility* inherent in its very constitution. Born Law-makers! The proportion of idiots, worn-out and selfish *roués* (we have no similar word), narrow caste-bound egotists, at last, wearied even its congeners, and they left to the Lords [Tchou] the ancient Forms, but deprived them of all real power. This might not have happened, but that from the very nature of things the number of Peers (as a Lord is called, who has the hereditary law-making right) who are active and young is inconsiderable; and, for the most part, these prefer out-door sports, pleasures of wealth and travel, to sitting among the elders to be *snubbed* for youthful inexperience. The result is that all warmth, life, and interest, all generous disinterestedness, are unknown by these venerable egotists. They are sufficiently amused with hereditary titles, with the respect shown to their rank, and with the *playing* at Law-making. They are too conceited to see that they are "puppets," and too small to despise the *honours* which conceal their insignificance. Are they not exalted above and separated from the "common-herd"? [kou-tong].

They are completely engrossed with the trivialities of their rank (High-Caste). They wait upon the Sovereign like menials, tricked out in furs, feathers, and robes, and jewelled chains, stars and garters, sparkling in gems, silk hose, and the very shoes resplendent with precious stones! On great occasions they are allowed (and this permission must come from the Sovereign) to place upon the head a golden and jewelled "circlet," named *coronet*. With this head-gear glittering about their brows, they receive the respectful reverence of the people, and feel a greater exaltation than the gods. "Ah," as the Barbarians say, "who would not be a Lord!"

A special Superstition attaches itself to this head-ornament. That worn by the Ruler is called a *Crown*. When he places it on in public, the trumpets give a mighty sound, all the people bow in humble homage, and Nature is supposed to arrest the wheels of her majestic course to join in the rapturous shouts of delight! The act is rooted in the Superstition, and one of its most cherished things.

The highest ambition of a subject is to be permitted to take *Rank* and wear this *bauble*. There is no mean service to the Ruler, no intrigue, no sacrifice which may not be done or suffered to get this privilege—the right to shine in this coronet. And such an ambition is so honourable, that success condones every contemptible thing by which it is secured. Men are blinded by the glare, and overlook the mean being below: in his Coronet he is unimpeached and unimpeachable!

Nor is this ambition confined to the Lords temporal; the High-Caste Bonzes will not be remiss in those *duties* to the Sovereign and to his family, in those to "Society" and to the exalted Lords, upon whom they have to attend on all occasions of baptising and marrying and feasting, to give the *blessings* [fihu-lsi] of the gods of the Superstition—in nothing remiss which shall help them to secure the peculiar *head-gear* given to those of their order whom the Sovereign raises to the lordly rank called *Bishops*. It is called a *mitre*. Ages ago, in the obscure days of the Superstition, poor and miserable, the chief Bonzes were distinguished by a head-covering like two bits of board, united or *mitred* together, typical of the two-fold nature of their office. Thus arose the Mitre, now a resplendent and costly bauble, more lofty than the coronets, and showing the superiority of spiritual (priestly) dignity!

In these coveted distinctions, the Sovereign finds the source of nearly all the power really enjoyed; and by an artful use and distribution of coronets and mitres, often covertly manages the machinery of government to his own wishes. An unscrupulous and able man may make himself respected! I forgot to say that another jewelled symbol of priestcraft is bestowed with the mitre, so comical that one might suspect it originated in the love of coarse humour common to the Barbarians—but its true origin was in the same early and poor days of the Superstition, when the highest Bonze was only a "Keeper of the Sheep;" that is, his duty was to keep the poor devotees together and save them from the idolatrous *pagans*. The Christ was said to have called his despised followers "Sheep without a shepherd," and to have requested the chief of his followers "to feed his sheep." Thus it came about that these chief men took a staff, crooked at one end (similar to that used by a veritable shepherd), as typical of their duty.

With the mitre is, therefore, handed a costly *Crosier*—crooked and crossed staff—to enable the Lord Bishop to *pull in* the wandering sheep, or to catch hold of any which may have slipt down into deep holes, or other rough places! "Fancy a Lord Bishop catching sheep!"—said a jocose Barbarian to me once.

The crowning of a new Ruler is a grand *ceremony*, in which all the wearers of the little crowns (*coronets* and *mitres*) attend; and no Ruler is a RULER unless he be CROWNED, with all the superstitious *rites*. To this I may refer elsewhere. At present, I may mention that the history of all the Barbarians, and notably that of the English, is a story very often of the wars, assassinations, plots, and cruel deeds done to seize the *Crown*: for whoever could contrive to clap this thing upon his head was at once King! In the eyes of the superstitious invested with a sort of divinity! This feeling is well expressed by their greatest poet: "What a divinity doth *hedge* a King!" This is, doth encompass and protect a King.

When the Law-making Houses meet, the custom is for the Sovereign to attend in all his State, and *open* the Houses. That is, to swing open the grand doors of the Upper House for the Lords, and especially for the Lower members; who, on this occasion, are admitted to enter in and listen to the GRACIOUS SPEECH. The rush of the Low-members is frightful, for the *Doors* are only opened for a very short time. The speech itself is nothing— merely some polite phrases as to the health and happiness of "our beloved *Lords and gentlemen*" (as the form is), and some Incantation to the gods of the Superstition, "on the prosperity and successful trade of our subjects." The great Lords sit like gods, effulgent, exalted; whilst the Low-members crowd like school-boys, and as rudely as school-boys, below. This is another thing by which the childish Lords are amused with a notion of power.

The present Sovereign rarely opens the Houses, but delegates some great Lords to do it for her. And the ceremony is far less. The Crown and the Crown Jewels are, therefore, so rarely seen, that the divinity of the Ruler is in danger; for the Superstitious reverence and pope-worship attaches to the *Crown*. These Crown Baubles are, by the present Ruler, kept imprisoned and guarded in a huge stone castle, so strong that no force but of nature can throw it down, and are cautiously shown to the admiring and dazzled few who are allowed by the guards to see them, at "a penny a-peep" (as an American Barbarian said in my ear, on the day of my seeing them). In this he referred to the fee [tin] which is exacted before admission, and which (I was told) went to the privy-purse of the Queen to buy pins. The Barbarians boast that these glittering *gewgaws* cost more than all the Halls of Learning!

The *Judicial* is the remaining great division of administration. In this the Laws are explained and applied. No law is, by this department, ever made. It has no such function. None the less, it really makes new laws, and unmakes the Statute Law (that is, the Law enacted by the great Council of Law-makers) just as it pleases. In fact the chief business of this department is to *unmake* the Laws, and the chief business of the Council is to make *them over* again. And between the two, of the making of Law there is no end, nor any possible understanding. Were not the Barbarian body and mind very tough, they would infallibly perish beneath the weight of this inscrutable and ponderous contrivance. No one is benefited by it, but the innumerable officers who manage it, and the Lawyers, who fatten upon the fees [tin-tin] which it wrings from all the unfortunates who have to attend upon it. These Lawyers form a special and very exclusive Caste; often at dispute among themselves upon points of personal concern, and as to the emoluments and offices which appertain to the Caste, but always united (and so-called *Brothers*) as to everything outside, by which they can more effectually conceal and mystify the nature of their order, and the more adroitly plunder the uninitiated. This is the Caste which opposes every inquiry into abuses and every attempt to reform the administration; which shouts the loudest praises to the Superstition, puts in force all the terrors of the Caste and of the Law (as by them expounded) to destroy any one who does not adore the *glorious* event, and declare the Constitution and the Laws, the Crown and the Altar (meaning the Superstition), the most perfect of all human wisdom—indeed, *Divine*. I have explained the Glorious event. To the Lawyer-Caste glorious in fees and means of plunder; in abuses which, had the reforms introduced before that event been perfected, would have been swept away; reforms which that event postponed, and the subsequent wars and civil dissensions made not only impossible, but still more difficult in the future. In another place I propose to refer to this department—the *Judicial*—when speaking of *the Courts of* JUSTICE wherein the Laws are expounded and applied: because, as in these the daily course of the life of a people may be studied, I wish to look curiously into them. It will be readily seen, however, that for a stranger to find, beneath the thick and manifold wrappings and ponderous obscurities of the Lawyer-Caste, where *Justice lies smothered*, is no easy task.

The present Ruler is of the so-called *glorious* dynasty, and is more wise and virtuous than her ancestors, who were remarkable for obstinacy, meanness, stupidity, and debauchery. If one had a virtue, it was so misdirected by narrowness of mind as to be worse than vice. The best man of them was the most mischievous Sovereign, and the wisest thing done by any of the dynasty was to keep away from England. When they did nothing they did well; their activity was disastrous.

The Queen now reigning is esteemed by the Aristocracy because she leaves them to do as they please, and gratifies them by bestowing upon them and their devoted supporters *coronets*. She only demands for herself and her numerous children *ample provisions*; if in these she be gratified, she cares not to vex herself or her Lords by any disputes. She is very benevolent, filling the great palaces with *poor relations*, where they are supported—not by her. On the marriage of one of her royal children her munificence is unequalled; but she asks her devoted Lords to tax her subjects to pay for it!

Her allowances are, with wise *policy*, made very ample, that a *splendid Court* may be kept up, to give places to the aristocracy, and to gratify the love of display. In this the Lords are generous; it costs *them* nothing, the taxes upon the people cover the expenses. There are murmurs that the crown is never shown; that Royalty is hidden from view, and that the reverence of the people wanes; that the allowances designed and heretofore used to maintain a grand *Court of respect and honour* are misdirected, and get into the private pocket of Royalty for merely personal objects. But he who should dare openly to say this, unless of a very High Caste, would assuredly have his ears *cropped* [ku-tof.]

The reign has not been without bloody wars; one of which was to uphold a sick *Turk* (an outside Barbarian, who hates the very name of *Christians*, and calls them *dogs*), and whom the English Barbarians themselves despise. Yet, they rushed with great ships and armed bands to attack another *Christ-god* tribe, who threatened the sick Turkish chief; because, as they thought, their trade was best secured by helping the Turk! This foolish war cost thousands of the lives of the English sailors and armed bands, but what is far more consequential to the Barbarians, many millions [li-re] of gold. It ended in nothing at all; for the great tribe which lost in the war some ships and some forts, taken by the English, have now rebuilt them more strongly than before, and again threaten the sick Turk more than ever!

When the American Barbarians had a domestic contention—some of them wishing to deliver a poor people held in slavery, by a custom in some of their provinces, from the cruel wrong—the English Barbarians sided with those who wished to keep the slaves. They did this notwithstanding that always before they had almost quarrelled with the American tribes for allowing this very thing! Now, however, because they did not like to have that people great in ships, and because they thought it would be safer for them and better for their trade, to have the American tribes broken to pieces, insidiously aided those who fought to hold the slaves, in every way they could without open war. But the slave-holding tribes were overpowered, and the slaves set free. Presently, the American Barbarians demanded that they should be repaid some of the *monies* which this treacherous conduct had cost them—the lives could not be repaid. The English Barbarians, fearing the American tribes—very valiant, and having many ships—finally submitted to pay a heavy penalty for their wrong doing!

Lately, also, the English Barbarians have stood silent and seen another tribe on the Main Land (which aided them just before in the War for the Turk, and, in fact, saved them from being shamefully beaten) completely overthrown and mercilessly sacked by another tribe—when a kindly word would have saved great suffering. But it does not displease the English Barbarians to see another tribe weakened—and their trade was not touched in this war—in fact, perhaps they had more to gain by pleasing the strong tribe which came out victorious.

The English themselves complain that, lately, they have not distinguished themselves by their usual *glorious* expeditions; that their war-ships and their fierce warriors are getting out of use, and that the late *Committee* of Government, made the name of England inglorious. This feeling at length got possession of the Lower House, and a new Committee appeared. These say that the attempt to carry on affairs with other tribes, upon the *moral* rules of the *Christ-god* worship, although the tribes are devotees, is absurd. That the late *Committee*, who had some slight notion of correct moral precepts, and thought possibly one might venture to trust the Sovereign Lord of Heaven, were *peace-at-any-price* men, milksops (a term of reproach equivalent to milkmaids) [kin-e-suk], and that, in their hands, the English Lion had been *muzzled*—made an object of contempt! (This blood-thirsty beast is the admired symbol of English power.)

This new Committee are pledged to seize the very first occasion which may offer to exhibit the *British*. Lion (as he is styled) with his muzzle off, his claws sharpened, and his frame well fed and strong. The taxes are raised and the most exact attention is devoted to all needful things to perfect this beast to the standard of his ancient might. And the present Government— *Committee*—watch with keen eyes for that opportunity, when they shall suddenly let spring this monster! It is supposed that the angry *growl* [heuien-ro] will sufficiently alarm; if not, the terrific roar [Zuung-luu] cannot fail! The only drawback to this ferocious pastime will be found in those members of the Lower House, who, themselves bearing a good weight of taxes without the emoluments of office, may oppose the majority and reduce the arrogancy of its temper. None the less, in the present brutal conceit of the Lower House and of the lower orders, a war may at any moment break out, if for no other purpose than to show other Barbarians that the British Lion is still a *Lion* in full vigour! The idea of a dull, toothless, blind old brute, which even a jackass (as one of the Barbarian fables has it) may kick with impunity, is too intolerable!

The morality of the present Loyal Court is said to be admirable—when you can once find the Royal residence. But this is quite a *myth*. There is, in this reign, no Loyal Court, only a domestic circle—a Royal Family—not kept up with so much splendour as some of the *homes* of the High-Caste. It is said that no suitor of an improper moral colour may approach any Princess, unless he be a cousin of the Queen, when the blood sanctifies the taint, and all is clean. If a real cousin be not of these suitors, one as nearly related among the poverty-stricken princes of the Barbarians from the Main Land as can be had, is selected. He must profess to worship the great Superstition of the English *Sect*, and detest the Roman Pope—at least, in public. His poverty is no objection—that is more than counterbalanced by the Illustrious obscurity of his race—that is, some family which ages ago contrived to live by plunder, and by making itself safe within the walls of stone castles, among steep rocks and hills. A family whose descendants feel more pride in these, now, old and ruinous wrecks of former insolence, than in any other possession—and whose alliance is acceptable to the English Queen! The poverty of these petty chiefs is, however, removed; nor do they marry a Princess of the English Queen unless they be paid for it. It is not the Queen who pays; the occasion is seized upon to obtain that *provision* to which I have referred.

And the paltry chief, and his new, royal bride, know poverty no more; they, and their children, and children's children, are provided for by the Lower House, who tax the people for this privilege, so much valued by them!—this privilege of succouring and enriching the worn out, useless and decaying chiefs of foreign Barbarians, who have any, the remotest, trace of kinship to the Royal House of England!

The more considerable events, therefore, in the present reign, as the Barbarians think, have reference to these marriages of Royal Princesses, births, christenings (baptizings), deaths, and the like among them. The Low-House readily takes these opportunities to profess its homage and devotion. The Queen follows the *Sacred Writings* with great exactness, which commands "take care of those of your own blood"—indeed, her devotion to this precept is, perhaps, more noticeable than her devotion in general.

Her Illustrious presence is rarely known among the people. When she does appear, she is hardly more respectfully and silently worshipped. She does not attract the *love* of the people—though she is (as a sly Barbarian youth of the Low-Castes once said to me, sarcastically), very *dear* [chean]. (A *pun* [phu-nsi] on the word; which may mean *beloved*, or *very costly*).

When, as rarely happens, to honour some Show wherein the Royal *presence* may bring money to a Charity, the Queen appears, surrounded by Royal guards, and in State, there is always to be seen a gigantic servant, dressed in the scarlet of the Royal household, seated immediately behind the *Sacred Person*, to watch over and rescue her from any danger. His body and mighty strength are always ready to be interposed! This favourite servant, it is said, assists her Illustrious, when, among the hills of the Far North, she visits the great, high rocks, and climbs the sides of mountains—his strength is so ready, trusty, and invaluable!

To her, and to her subjects, a great loss was inflicted when Death destroyed the youthful Consort of the Queen, when she was still young. He was one of ancient family among the petty Barbarian chiefs to whom I have referred; was near in blood to the Queen, and by her greatly beloved, it is said. He was never allowed any power in the State, and was a subject of the Queen, though her husband. It is whispered that he did not quietly submit to this condition of things—but it would not be worth the notice of a wise man to attend to this gossip. I could never learn that he was of any use; but, none the less, the Barbarians exalt him very highly, and have built lofty monuments to his honour. I said use—I forgot—he gave a very numerous brood of princes and princesses to the English Barbarians. Of these they are very proud—not because they do, or can ever do, anything useful, but because it adds to the number of the *High-Castes*, and around them very many poor members of that caste can cluster, and live upon the cast-off clothes and other second-hand things of these exalted!

On the whole, we may desire the long continuance of Her Illustrious' reign. If her will were law, distant plunderings would cease; and her influence is better than may generally be looked for. She cannot prevent, but she may moderate those expeditions despatched to subjugate the *Heathen*, extend trade, and bring under the dominion and worship of the Christ-god distant tribes. Great guns, fire-arms, gunpowder, and a poisonous liquor called Rum, would, perhaps, under other sovereigns, even more frequently be sent to prepare the way for the Prince of Peace (as the Christ-god is often styled).

Some respect for Justice and some regard to the rights of others have been shown under the influence of this Illustrious; but, as we have seen, this, the most honourable distinction of the present reign, is likely to be obliterated. The old predatory instinct of the English Barbarians again comes uppermost, and though caution and fear of taxes may make the Committee of Government tardy and unwilling to attack (unless some weak tribe, where victory would be sure and *its* glory conspicuous), yet, such is the prevailing temper, that *blood-letting* seems needful to cool those fierce and haughty Barbarians.

A ferocious war may be looked for; nor is it by any means incredible that the war-ships of these Christ-god worshippers and their murdering bands should again be directed against our peaceful Central Kingdom!

CHAPTER III.
SOME PARTICULARS OF THE INTERNAL ADMINISTRATION.

THE whole country is divided into districts, in general governed, like our Provinces, in the Sovereign's name, by viceroys and governors.

The heir to the Crown, if he be the son of the reigning Ruler, is Prince of Wales—a title bestowed upon his eldest son by an ancient king; and which, at the time, gave the administration of that Province to this son. The eldest son of the Queen now enjoys with this title also that of Duke of Cornwall. These lofty designations confer no power, although they carry with them high distinction and great revenues.

The Aristocracy in the case of the heir, as in that of the Sovereign, watch jealously anything which looks like *intellect*. They do not stint personal respect and ample revenues, but take care that upon coming to the Crown, the new Sovereign shall be a "puppet."

He is, whilst heir, not allowed to take any kind of share in government, but is surrounded by flatterers, flunkeys [pluc-ngi], idle young people of both sexes, and, from mere want of useful business, falls into every sort of sport and pleasure. He must, indeed, be strong in morality and in character, if, upon coming to his high office, he be not reduced to the selfish *imbecile* and puppet, desired by the High-Caste. Lucky if he have not become absolutely contemptible by his vices!

Ireland is governed by a High Viceroy, whose chief employment is to amuse the Irish with shows—the real power being in the hands of the General of the armed bands. Anciently, the Provinces were administered by Vice-roys, who possessed authority; but the pettiness of the Island and swiftness of communication have now concentrated all actual administration at the Capital city. The Provincial governors, however, keep up some show of the ancient order, and, nominally, command the Provincial *Militia*. This is a merely nominal force, composed of butcher-boys, farmer-lads and the like, who do not know how to handle a *fire-arm*, nor how to fight, unless in the Barbarian pastime of *the Ring*: a combat wherein the young Barbarians, two being pitted against each other, try each to hit the other a terrible blow directly in the eye. This, done with the hand doubled up, nearly destroys that organ. He is victor who succeeds in hitting both eyes of his antagonist, and fairly blinding him! This, a common and admired sport, is greatly esteemed by the English Barbarians, and considered an admirable training. It develops the ferocity and brutality required to make good soldiers (plunderers), and the powers of endurance indispensable in the distant forays. Even in the Halls of Learning, it is thought to be a manly *science*, fitting the young Aristocracy to match any man in personal conflict, and enabling him to be self-possessed and ready to fight his way through the world. As, in general, the lowest orders are badly fed and reduced in strength, and, though well used to brutal fights, yet are not trained to the *Science*, the young Aristocrat is expected "to pummel the brute" upon the slightest occasion of disrespect.

The provincial Magistracy are mainly employed in keeping the Lower-Castes in order, and especially in punishing trespasses upon the lands, or upon the convenience of the Higher-Castes. The most common form of trespass is that called *Poaching*. The High-Castes own all the lands, and the Low-Castes, who till the soil, are the ancient slaves—slaves no longer under any law, but nearly as much so by custom. Very poor, but little better than beggars, and really beggars in large numbers, and hungry, the temptation to knock over the abundant nearly tame creatures (birds, fowls, hares, and the like) everywhere around them in the fields and copses, is too strong to be resisted. To do this is to be a *Poacher*—a criminal most detested by the High-Caste; for he presumes to think, in some cases, that the right in these free creatures is *not* absolutely vested in the High-Castes. Yet this sort of property is most rigidly *preserved*, by the penalties of severe punishment, to the use of the High-Caste—for his sport in the shooting of them, rather than for food. The Poacher, who is merely tempted by hunger, and who abjectly begs pity and promises reformation, escapes in some instances lightly; but he who presumes to question the right to this wholesale appropriation feels the full wrath of the Law.

Petty civil and criminal offences may be tried by the Provincial Magistracy; subject, however, in cases involving any interests of importance, to revision at the Capital.

There is a sort of Provincial (and yet Metropolitan) Court called *Convocation* [Kal-ti-se]. In this, things touching the Christ-god Superstition are determined. If a Bonze has not worn, or has worn improperly, his neck-tie, or his *surplice* [ro-bsi]; if the table before the Altar (Idol) has been placed out of square; for things of this sort—or if a Bonze be accused of departing from the ordered rendering of some word in the *Sacred Writings*, or of having said something contrary to the orders of Convocation or of the *rites*—for these and other things respecting the great Idolatry, *Convocation* sits. It is composed of High Bonzes and a few delegates of High-Caste devotees, whose duty is merely to ratify the decisions of the High Bonzes—these regulate everything.

This High and Lofty Court was anciently styled *Star Chamber*, because exalted above mere mortal interests, and only concerned with the preservation of the Idolatry. Formerly it worshipped the Sovereign as Pope of the Superstition more devotedly than is the fashion at present, and burnt people to death for refusing to do so. Now it refrains from this severity, and is content (or tries to be) with depriving a Bonze who doubts, of his *living*, and all honours and emoluments.

It still convenes in the old hall of its former glory. A venerable moss-covered pile, vast and gloomy, with lofty towers and turrets of rock, with hewn cells and deep dungeons. Here may be seen, fixed to the rock, the rings and chains, worn and rusty with age, where the victims of superstition suffered beneath the decrees of this ancient Court. Slow and proud, along the dark stone corridors, and beneath the dusky arches of this great prison-palace, the High Bonzes and the devotees walk in state. Ushered with pompous ceremonial, and with the grand incantations to the gods and devils of the Superstition, into the lofty and obscure hall of the Star-Chamber, the *Convocation* sits. In deep alcoves around are stored the ponderous volumes, containing all the mysteries and terrors of the Superstition. In these are the horrid imaginings of fanatical Priests and devotees; the *dogmas* and *canons* of the Superstition; the dreadful arsenal, whence were drawn those frightful weapons of superstitious terror, whence issued the chains and bolts, and scourges, the faggots and the flames. One hears the groans of the tortured, the steps of the jailers, the clashing of the chains, when, in these long and resounding aisles and arches, the winds moan, the distant footsteps fall, or the old casements in the ruinous towers shake and rattle.

Nor is the arsenal wholly useless now; the weapons are not all rusty; *anathemas* may yet be found to terrify, and restraints to punish. *Heresy* [pho-phi], as any doubt concerning the Queen-pope and the *Superstition* is called, drives the culprit from Society, deprives the Bonze of all preferment, of his employment, and turns him ignominiously *adrift*, to live or to starve.

Convocation watches over the *Sacred Writings*, to see that no change, not so much as of a syllable, be made; not trusting to *Jah*, who may have himself, perhaps, grown indifferent to the matter. A curious thing, showing how irrationally men will act in respect of an irrational system. For the notion is that this Word of Jah (the *Sacred Writings*), being his *Revelation* (Word), have always been by Him exactly preserved through all the ages and the changes of languages, and of transcription, and of *everything to this hour*. Why is it to be supposed, then, that He will suddenly lose his power to preserve, or will be indifferent to preserve?

Punishments in the ordinary Courts are not very remarkable, only there is one so characteristic of the English, so comically barbarous, that I will try to describe it.

The offender is stripped naked to the waist, tied up with his hands widely extended, and with his face to a strong post; then a man takes a large strong cat, kept hungry and savage for the purpose, and placing the creature at the back of the neck, draws it forcibly down the naked back. Of course the cat holds on with teeth and claws. This is repeated till the culprit faints, when the cat is removed. The back of the man is washed with vinegar and salt, and he revives, perhaps to undergo the infliction again. This astonishing mode of correcting offenders is called *flogging with the cat*.

I may also make a remark upon another feature of criminal punishment. The crime of *treason*, not only insures the death, but the horrid mutilation of the culprit; and, not satisfied with this, reaches to the innocent wife and children. All the estates, titles, honours, properties of the offender are sequestrated to the State, and his blood is *attainted*; that is, made incapable of giving honour and employment to his offspring! Thus the innocent are disgraced, and reduced, not merely to beggary, but, as far as possible, placed in a condition of hopeless misery!

The Idolatry and Sacred Writings are, no doubt, responsible for this impolitic injustice and cruelty. For *Jah* is constantly made by the Priests to say, that he visits the sins of the father upon his child even to the tenth generation! A natural development of the moral sense would fall short of this vindictiveness; and in this false and horrible wrath, taught in their *Sacred Writings*, the fierce Barbarians are encouraged to outdo themselves!

The greatest of all the Courts, and which chiefly controls the others, is the High and Mighty COURT OF CHANCERY. It has many names—as Court of Equity, of the King's Conscience, and others—assuming as many styles and jurisdictions as the ancient *Proteus* of Egypt; who, as the Priests said, could take any form, or no form, be fire, or cloud, or invisible air. So this Court, feared by the Barbarians with a paralyzing dread, takes on any shape! It stands for the King's conscience—which, as the conscience of a Pope-king, must be a doubly divine thing. For, as remarked elsewhere, "*Divinity doth hedge a King!*" We, I think, should fear that this conscience would be as uncertain as the man. Its function is, therefore, to decide with *Equity*; to relieve against the inexorable hardness of the ancient rules; and give relief in cases of *mistake, accident,* and *fraud.* This looks admirable, but it is all *sham* (phu-dgi).

Not the least attention is really paid to equity, but only to the *decrees of the Court as recorded.* A Suitor petitions for redress. The petition is not examined to be determined upon the matters therein stated. First—The *Petition* must be in all respects in due form, according to the recorded rules. Second—The matter of it must be such as the Court will consider, and such as may come before the Court. Third—Are the Parties in the Jurisdiction, and are all the parties who may be interested, duly notified and present; or, if not present, accounted for. Fourth—Are the matters for the Court only, or must it be assisted by some petty judges to ascertain the facts. Fifth—The petition being at last before the Judge, he may not look into it, unless the Lawyers look into it with him; and, then, no opinion (decree) can be given until the Records are fully examined, to discover if anything of the sort *has been* relieved. If a similar case be found, then the petitioner is called upon to prove his case as stated in his petition; and, if he fail to prove his exact case (though he may make a stronger show for relief), he is ordered out of Court, and condemned to heavy costs (tin-tin). If the case be proved, then the Judge *reserves his judgment.* For he must very carefully compare all the cases, examine all the voluminous Records, besides examining the innumerable Papers which have grown up around the Petition during all the proceedings (often spreading over many years), before he dare to order the recording of his *decree.* For, this done, he has added another Case to the King's conscience; that is, to the highest form of Law and of human Justice!

He dare not do this unless justified by the Records; interminable, stretching backwards to the first King who pretended to have a conscience; obscure, contradictory—he dare not unless justified by the Records—*Precedents.* If he mistake, grossly, he will be certain to be called to account by the Lawyer-Caste, who make a business of seeking for discrepancies; in fact, he is bewildered—not by the case; that is simple, or *was* originally, simple enough; but, by the arguments of the Lawyers, the documents overlying and enveloping the case, *and by the difficulty of deciding according to the Precedents.* Could he merely announce his *own* judgment, there is no difficulty—but that is the last thing to be thought of—in truth, if reduced to *that*, he is bound to refuse any relief, however clear it is that *equity* requires it!

Thus the Judge, old and wearied; a man tottering over his grave, feeble, irresolute, takes the course which maybe looked for—and postpones, and postpones; other like cases accumulate on his hands; he dismisses some, "reserves" others, *refers* to another judge what he can decently, decides none! Or only those which are petty, or those which are really unopposed, or those exciting no interest.

Meantime, the parties to the *Petition* are dead, or absconded, or beggared. Years have elapsed; all parties are worn out or impoverished by the enormous expenses—at length, there is no one to pay Lawyers and the Court Officers—the thing *lapses*—dies. Term after Term (as Sessions of the Court are called), the Case is called. Some poor wretch struggles still to save something of the property *tied up* in the Court by the Case—he tries to call up from the mass of dusty and forgotten Records, a reminiscence of the lost Petition. In vain—the thing is a wreck, and has wrecked its builders!

The Case lies forgotten amid the interminable processes, affidavits, answers, pleas, replications, rejoinders, motions, applications, notices, subpœnas, summonses, commissions, bills of amendments, and of supplement; documents of all sorts, making up the *Case*, mouldering away in the stone alcoves of the huge Records; as the poor victims of it lie mouldering in similar forgetfulness! Not, however, without profit to the Lawyer-Caste; for some miscreant of this profession, perchance, discovering the Case, in his searches after means of spoil, sees how *he* may gain by it. He knows of an estate remotely touched by the matter of the old and forgotten Petition, and he knows quite well that there is really nothing affecting the property; yet, he sees fees and spoil. It is merely to frighten the possessor of the estate by an intimation of a *defect of title*, and refer to this old Case, never decided. The *bandit* [khe-te] sets in motion the machinery of the High Court of Chancery. One of its officers summonses the poor man to come into that Court, and answer to the allegations touching his right to possess the house in which, perhaps, he has lived for twenty years! and lived without objection from any source!

Now it does not matter at all that there is no sort of ground for this attack; the moment it is made, the title of the poor unoffending man to his own house is ruined—almost as completely as if by the sentence of the Court he had been deprived of it. The robber who attacks wishes merely to force the owner of the house to buy him off. To secure this spoil *he records his summons in the Court*, and from that moment no one will buy the house, nor will any one lend any money upon the security of it until that record be removed. If the victim of this oppression be in debt, or have but little money, or but little more than his house, or if he have borrowed money upon his house— in fact, unless he be a man quite rich, he is inevitably ruined! He is ruined, because the lawyer has, *by the Record*, practically deprived him of his estate. And this is done by a Petition to the Court, making allegations artfully and untrue. Yet, as they are not supported by any sort of evidence, and are merely bare *insinuations* often of anybody—it does not the least matter—is it not inconceivable that such a thing should be allowed? That merely upon the *Record* of a Petition, without any evidence, without any character, without any surety for its truth, without any, the least, inquiry, or any, the smallest deposit in Court to cover the expenses to which the summoned party may be put, should it appear he has been wrongfully summoned— this great injustice may be perpetrated, and perpetrated without risk of any punishment! "But surely the Court will immediately dismiss this iniquitous case?" Not at all; the Court cannot be reached; all the endless proceedings and delays already mentioned intervene. The fees and expenses are enormous—the decision far off. The victim cannot get a hearing. He borrows money and employs lawyers—in vain. He can do no more—he is bankrupt. The lawyer who has ruined him gets nothing in such a case, because the victim prefers poverty to gratifying the robber. He gets nothing, because he has no real case, and drops it as soon as he sees he can make nothing out of it. Should the party be very rich upon whom the robbery is attempted, he may fight it out and finally clear his property, and get a *decree* for some costs (only a portion) against the other party. But this *decree* is worthless; the party has no property and cannot pay. *He* has fought *for luck*, having nothing to lose, but all to gain.

Usually, however, as the Lawyer well knows, the party attacked will hurry to buy off the suit!

In this way, old Causes are Mines, which the Lawyer-Caste work to their own peculiar advantage. They have every facility, both from their experience and from the usages of the Caste. The very Judges of the Courts are of the same Caste, and give every assistance in matters of forms, continuances, motions, dilatory proceedings, and the countless processes by which Lawyers make fees and their clients are robbed.

Thus the Court of Equity, with a mocking irony, becomes a Court of Iniquity! and the very tribunal designed to do more perfect Justice is perverted to the most scandalous use—made an engine the most oppressive and destructive ever contrived for the misery of Society, short of one invented to destroy it wholly!

The Court was originally organised by Priests who had acquired the Roman learning, or some tincture of it, and endeavoured to strengthen their own Class, and to soften the barbarous harshness of the common Law, by erecting this Court. The laws of the Barbarians were savage, in civil as well as in criminal things; and the Priests, more cultured, endeavoured to soften and temper this harshness, or, at any rate, to get more complete control by it. They formed it, and administered it at first, and for a long time. But the Lawyer-Caste have now its administration, and they have not so much respect for the opinions of the general public as had the Priests, and have made the Court a *bye-word and a shame* [Kri-mi]!

The expenses and fees are beyond belief. A Lawyer who gets one good Chancery Case into his hands, lives upon it luxuriously. I was once shown a *Bill of Costs*, as these items of fees are styled.

I observed that one would be charged for a thing done and for the same thing not done—in other words, for the doing and for the not-doing. Thus, if one requests a thing be done, the Lawyer will charge for "receiving instructions," "for reducing the same to writing," "for instructing a clerk," and the like—then, having sent away the clerk on *another* matter, he will charge for taking new instructions and going over the same ground again. Thus, actually charging for the delay and obstruction caused in the affair.

Again, if you ask a Lawyer something, he will presently say, "I must take counsel," meaning he wishes to ask another Lawyer. When the *Bill* is examined you will find, say, "for being asked and not knowing, 6s. 8d.; for taking your instructions to counsel, 6s. 8d.; for attending upon counsel, £1 1s.; for fair copy made for him, £2 2s.;" and so on. Your simply unanswered *question* has thus served the following purposes:—If it had been answered at once the fee would have been, say, 6s. 8d.; but as it was not, but carried elsewhere, it has given the first Lawyer five times more of fees, and his *brother* in the Caste also a handsome sum! One may judge how ignorant the first Lawyer will be likely to be, and how often he finds it convenient to help his higher Caste brother, especially when in helping him he so greatly helps himself! We have some cunning rogues in our Central Kingdom, but such astuteness as this is beyond them!

I once visited this tribunal of Chancery to witness the proceedings—but they are so dull and prolix as to drive one away as soon as possible. The presiding Judge, and all the High-Caste Lawyers, wear wigs and gowns. The lower Lawyers, who are called Solicitors, sit in a sort of well, below and at the feet of the High, and have no badge of distinction. In fact, they are not respected, and only tolerated by the *bigwigs* (as the High Lawyers are often called) as the jackals who provide them with prey. They immediately act in matters with the victims of the Court, and do all the dirty work, extracting the fees, and the like—the High Lawyers taking the most of the plunder, although, for decency sake, they will not see the victims of their rapacity if they can help it.

The *wigs* spoken of are very absurd, and make the wearers seem to be engaged in masquerading, or fooling. (We have no term corresponding to the former.) The lappets of thick hair come down over the ears of the Judge, to enable him (as it occurred to me) to take his *nap* [qu-iz] with less danger of being disturbed.

No one can be a Judge, nor a High-Caste Lawyer, who does not wear the wig. It has a funny appendage behind, like a pig's tail, exactly fitting to fall upon the small of the neck; and is itself a curiously curled "frizzle" of horsehair, selected for uniformity of whitish colour. There is something *cabalistic* in this thing, which is carefully hidden from the outside world.

If a Judge take it off, all business immediately stops. A Lawyer instantly loses his power of speech if his wig fall off. It was told me in confidence, that the tail (like that of swine) had a peculiar significance, to say; the utter selfishness of the Caste and *greed*—another whispered a darker thing, referred to the Devil of the Superstition: that, anciently, this Caste struck a bargain with the Demon, and he made it obligatory upon the Lawyers always to wear this chief sign of *diabolism*! This may be merely the chaff [pti-ni] of these Barbarians. At any rate, something *occult* is attached to the thing; and a curious respect is shown to it, mixed of fear and contempt, even by outsiders.

The Judge sits so highly exalted, as to be out of the way of hearing the passages occurring among the Lawyers. He is generally half-blind, half-deaf; quite worn out with age, and the ceaseless wretchedness of his Court and the Lawyers, and incapable of vigorously dealing with anything. In this Court the most imbecile is most fit; for nothing is expected but imbecility (so far as the public is concerned), and fees for Officers and Lawyers.

When a Case is *on*, the Lawyers begin to talk, and to read from the big books, on one side, and then on the other. Neither tries to get at the truth, but each in turn does his best to mislead the Judge. Both read from the interminable and conflicting Records, and both find ample records which fit the precise Case, which each contends for. The poor old Judge, now and again, takes a note of these quotations from the Big Books of records—for he is to decide not upon the equity but upon the records, as we have seen. By the time he has found his *spectacles* [Qu-iei] he has forgotten the Book, the number, the Recorder's name, and the many other things, needful to find where the record is, and when he is again told, lifting up his wig-pallet, he only hears imperfectly, and *mistakes*. So, when, perhaps a long time after, he tries to make up a decree to fit the Case, the *record* to which he turns refers to nothing in the world like what was intended!

Hour after hour, and sometimes day after day, these speeches of the Lawyers go on. For the longer the talk the larger the *fees*—nobody thinks of Justice! The old Judge understands the trick of the *farce* going on, perfectly well; in his younger days he was famous for his skill in all the arts of the High-Caste Lawyers, and obtained his present position on that account, and because others wanted to get a formidable rival out of the way; he understands how very little (but fees) is involved in the endless talk and reading, and begins to nod—even, the gods would nod. The Lawyer observes, stops a bit; the unexpected silence awakens the wearied old man—he opens his watery, blinking eyes, fumbles his papers, or takes a pinch of snuff, and says: "Go on, brother Bounce, I'm with you"—meaning he is attending to him; and soon falls asleep again.

Perhaps one of the talking Lawyers is of the High Q.C. I am told that such is the dread of this Lawyer-Caste, that the Sovereign constantly flatters the tribe, and gives to them the *fattest* [phig-sti] offices. All Judges and the Keeper of the Sovereign's Conscience—this Court—and a great many other most important places, and exaltation to the Highest Caste of Lords [Tchou], falls to them by established rule—in truth, the Caste is chief in the Law-making Houses, and, consequently, in Government itself. The Q.C. is, however, a thing done to many who cannot, as yet, get fees from the public treasure, that they may get them from out-siders more amply. The right to attach these symbols to the name of Lawyer also gives him a *silk gown* (during the present reign) worked by the sacred hands of Royalty itself! The honoured wearer of this is a Q.C.—that is, Queen's Champion—and binds all its wearers to defend the Sacred Head (Pope) of the Superstition from the machinations of the Evil One, and those of their own order who, sold to the Devil, may possibly be put up by him to plot mischief, not only against the general outside world, but against "Crown and Altar!"

Perhaps, after days of this weary work, one of the Lawyers suddenly discovers that somebody, or something required in the intricate and dubious *processes*, is wanting; or in some document some erasure is detected; or something *to hang a point* upon is seized hold of—and at once a wrangle between the Lawyers ensues. The Judge fairly awakes; the whole *case breaks down* [kei-tz-se]; and everybody, but the poor victims in the case, anticipate more fees. The victims, however, who have already beggared themselves in it, suddenly despair; perhaps the case never again comes on, and the property involved in it wastes away in dark obscurity beneath the gnawing rats, which infest the Court.

Sometimes (as I was told) some poor man, or woman, who had scraped together the last farthings to pay the Lawyers (for they will in no wise act unless paid beforehand, feeling that such service as they render is not likely to be gratefully recompensed, and it being the severest rule of the order never to show any pity for outsiders), being in Court when they see all hope destroyed, and themselves and their children beggared, have fallen down and been carried out of Court with reason for ever gone; or with such a deadly blow that never more do they revive, but soon die, and are buried at the public charge!

You will see wretched creatures trying to look decent in well-brushed rags, darned and patched, with shoes through which the toes protrude, but over which the blacking [di-yte] is carefully smeared—you will see these victims of the Court, like ghosts, flitting about the passages, and watching for the entry of the Judge. One will attempt to address him—but he is conveniently deaf. He knows the *victim* is there, and though a party may speak, has the right to speak for himself, and the Judge is bound to hear, yet, such a thing is unknown. The mysteries of the Court deny to any *sane* man the attempt. These poor creatures are insane—or, what answers just as well, have been branded by the Lawyers as *Insane*. So the miserable wretch, trembling, raises his voice, "*My Lud*" (meaning my Lord), "My Lud;" here the Court-officer cries out *Silence*; or, if the man be, *for the first time*, attempting to call attention to his case, by the time he has got so far as to fairly say "My Lud!" what with the jeering looks of the Lawyers, his own ignorance of the mysteries, and his wretchedness, he either completely breaks down—or if the Judge, seeing a *new* face, asks him to "go on"— almost at once perceives that the man is only a "poor ruined suitor," and is entirely out of order, and *cannot* be heard! He says: "You must sit down. Case *Hoggs* v. *Piggs is in order.* Mr. Clerk call *Hoggs and Piggs*." Thus "My Lud" will be as far as any "poor ruined suitor will ever get!"

Besides the numerous, worse than useless, idlers (Lawyers) who fatten upon the industry of others, and the loss inflicted by their voracity and by the other expenses, this Court devastates upon a scale beyond belief. I was told by an English Barbarian that he once tried to obtain one thousand of money from the Court, which the lawyers said there would be no difficulty in getting, as it was clearly *his*; it would be only a matter of form, possibly *some* delay. "Well," said he to me, "I instructed my lawyer to go to the Court and get the money. He demanded fifty pounds to cover fees [tin]. To make a short story, he went to the Court, *but I never got any money*! After I had actually paid in fees more than half of the one thousand, the obstacles had grown to be so insurmountable that I merely dropped the matter." "But," I said, "the thousand—who has that?" "Oh, it is in the Court of Chancery!"

Another honest Barbarian told me that he had spent all his life (he was sixty) studying and endeavouring to awaken attention to the abuses of this Court—but in vain. The attempt seemed hopeless. The Court was entrenched in the very frame of the body politic, and nothing but *reconstruction* would answer; and that reconstruction is probably only possible after first *demolishing*!

This man said that a prodigious sum—sixty millions of English money— was *directly* locked up; and that of property of all sorts, subject to the *clutch* or injured by the processes of the Court it was incalculable, and, very likely, would represent a tenth of all the valuables in the whole Kingdom!

In my walks and in my travels, sometimes in the city, I would notice many houses, with windows smashed out, the walls tottering, the doors hanging loosely, or wholly gone, the approaches filthy, the whole place a *nuisance*, injuring and depopulating all about it, or filling the ever-spreading mischief with the vilest population. I have asked an explanation—"Oh, it is in Chancery." In the midst of a village, suddenly one comes upon a vacant space; it is an abomination; everything near catches the infection, all that portion of an otherwise pretty place becomes a *nuisance*. The character of the village at length suffers; it becomes known as a place ruined by the Court of Chancery. In fine, whenever one sees a wrecked building, or any property marked by neglect and verging to total destruction, the explanation is: "It is in Chancery." And the same thing is often said of ruined men and women: "Oh, they have lost everything in the Court of Chancery!"

To such an extent is the destruction of the Court carried, that the Law-making Houses are forced to interfere, or perhaps the Officers of Health. These may abate a *nuisance*, and sometimes mere filth and indecencies are removed. But nobody will improve a property to which he cannot have a certain and quiet possession. Therefore, when the evil becomes intolerable, the Law-making Houses make a Law by which a property of this sort is sold, under their *guarantee* that the buyer shall have perfect possession. This is a thing next to an impossibility; and nothing less than a great public evil too great to be endured, will ever induce the Lawyers who control the Houses to interfere with the legitimate work of the Court.

It is wonderful that the English Barbarians submit to this Court; but one must consider that, after all, it is not so inconsistent with Barbarian habits as it at first sight looks. Plunder is natural to all the tribes, and especially to the English. As nearly all plunder, the thing is normal. Lawyers must live; and the common English Barbarian makes a business to *keep out* of their hands. The Higher Castes enjoy so large a share of the gains, and are, in fact, so largely interested in preserving the Court, that *they* do not care to move. Then, to other causes, must be added the stolid conceit of the English Barbarians, who really think everything English so much better than what can be found elsewhere, that, in respect of this very Court, admitting some abuses, yet, after all, "Where else can you find such Judges—men who cannot be bribed?"

On the whole, therefore, with that conceited stolidity of character, more remarkable in the English than in any other Barbarians, they come to regard even the worst of *their institutions* as better than the best of the rest of the world!

CHAPTER IV.
UPON EDUCATION: A FEW REFLECTIONS.

IN our Illustrious and Central Kingdom, from times long before the Barbarians beyond the great Seas existed, or, at any rate, had any name or place in the earliest records, it has been the established rule that Learning (Li-te-su) should be the fountain of honour—that there is no nobility of birth. Under the Illustrious, the Son of Heaven, all were equal subjects—children—and that which made one more distinguished than another was *Wisdom*. This Wisdom, a knowledge of men and things; of the proper maxims [ri-te-es] of morality and government, and their proper application to human affairs. The *Central idea was to know oneself*, and thus to know others—to add to this, technical knowledge, and the knowledge of our Illustrious annals and customs.

The mandarins, great officers of our Illustrious, have no rights of birth. According to their class in the Schools of Examination, they are selected to advise, to administer, to govern in the Provinces, and order the forces for the keeping of due order. They rank in the degree of the excellency of their registration in the great Schools of Examination.

But it is very different with the Western Barbarians, where *birth* gives a right to exalted place in Government! Power, among the English, is wholly in the hands of this hereditary class—called *Nobility*—elsewhere called Aristocracy [Fo-hi]. Thus, learning has been unimportant, unless as a sort of accomplishment; and been mostly confined to Priests. With them, it was a means of increased influence, and added to the effect of the Superstitious pretensions. Force and fraud being the main agents of Government and sources of distinction, learning was not merely disregarded, but held in contempt by the High-Caste. What learning there was (chiefly confined to the Priests), busied itself with the Superstition, and with the ancient tongues; because with these Superstition had its *literary roots*.

Still, some grew more inquisitive, especially outside the Priestly order, and learning made some progress. Gradually, there emerged from the Halls of Learning, rules, which (countenanced by some Sovereigns), began to influence Society. For Sovereigns, and the High-Caste, had begun, in some measure, to affect a liking for learning—confined, however, almost wholly to the narrow range referred to. These *rules* were in fact DEGREES; which conferred upon the possessor a Literary distinction.

The *Halls of Learning*, which had been in good measure established by Sovereigns, out of plunder, upon the orders of Priests (who would obtain the money through the Ruler's dread of the devil, when apprehending or near to death); these, alone, could confer the degrees. No power accompanied them. They, merely, became requisite to any one who wished to enter upon, what is called, the *Learned professions*. These are of the *Superstition*, of the *Law*, and of *Medicine*. Soon, in these employments, the degrees became quite *Cabalistic*; and made these callings mysteries to the rest of the world.

What was intended to be evidence of fitness, was soon perverted to be a form of *initiation* into an exclusive Society; whose members insisted, not upon fitness, but upon compliance with arbitrary rules. This was made especially the case with the Law, and with Medicine. The *degree* was supposed to refer to proper qualifications for the practice of Law, and knowledge of Medicine, with its proper use in the healing art. It did nothing of the sort. It gave a *presumption* (but by no means a true one) that its holder knew something of the ancient Roman and Greek languages: not any presumption that, in the case of Medicine, there was any knowledge of the articles of Medicine, nor of their proper use; or of the human body to which they were to be administered. Nor any, that in the Law, there was any knowledge of the Statutes, laws and customs of the Realm, nor even of its Common annals! Medicine and Law suffered from this *Sham*; because men naturally used what little they did know; and, as to the Roman tongue, *some*, and the Greek, *less*, were in their heads; and the whole practice of Medicine and Law was in their ignorant hands; what could follow, but to muddle *these* with the useless obscurity and jargon of the unknown forms!

The Priests had also thrown around the Superstition the same jargon, and kept up the requisition for a *degree*—as if any true morality and worship were necessarily connected with a *literature*, denounced by themselves as impure and *pagan*! Notwithstanding these ignorant and selfish abuses, it was impossible to make the acquisition of even such narrow learning wholly useless. It was narrow, and even hurtful, by being perverted to selfish ends, and preventing honest and independent research. Still, it did work upon some minds to better use; and it gradually evolved a better learning, when the Ancient Literature really worked in free and broader channels. The High-Castes are less indifferent to literary attainments; and learning, in a more comprehensive sense, is becoming more esteemed. It is no longer limited to verbal knowledge; to ancient, dead forms—though these are still so paramount that, if a man were to be the wisest and most learned of mankind, and was deficient in these, he could not receive a *Degree*—he would be unlearned!

Useful, true and honest knowledge, outside the great Halls of Learning, is making some advance; though *in them*, the old, pedantic, and superstitious notions yet prevail. The new *Literati*, founders of a larger and truer teaching, endeavour with difficulty to get some respect and honour to attach to the *degrees* which they timidly register. The High-Caste, in general, disregard this better knowledge, and adhere to the old Superstitions and traditions—regarding that man only as learned who has the ancient badge; though, to any useful purpose, a fool.

The High-Caste also stupidly support the old preparatory schools; and will not, if they can help it, suffer any of the Lower-Caste to enter them.

In these, the barbarous customs continue; if one goes into them, he is at once carried backwards into the *dark ages* (as even the Barbarians call them); ages, when the Priests had all the Learning—wretched as it was—and when the *Superstition* coloured and directed everything. Here, the dead tongues are the chief studies, with something of the ancient *puzzles* as to Lines and Points—for the most part useless—with a style of administration fitted to the savage brutality of those times. The only part of the training cared for by the youths, is that which developes the forces of the body. The disgusting *Ring Fight*, referred to elsewhere, is a common pastime; and the lad is a milksop [kou-ad] who really avoids the rude crowd, and wishes to study. To be respected he must fight his way, and be feared. If, by chance, some lad of the Lower-Caste be entered, by the foolish wish of the father to bring the son into the *polished* circle of the High-Caste, he will be *polished off* (as these young Barbarians say), in a manner never dreamed of. The poor lad will be beaten, humiliated, and driven from the School; unless, indeed, he be strong enough to bully and beat his tormentors!

Very comically, in one part of these brutal fights, when one has got his antagonist completely in his power, and can bruise him as he pleases, the position is called *being in Chancery*! One of the fittest illustrations possible, of the universality of the judgment which places that Court among things the most repulsive!

The younger in these schools are the *Slaves*, for the time being, to the older and stronger; in fact, the whole effect of the training is really to make these youths selfish, quick of quarrel, hardy of body, and barbarous; to prepare them for the lives of predatory exploit, upon which fortune and all the best honours depend—learning being subordinate, and disregarded, unless it further the main purpose.

Force is still the god of these Barbarians, and *Jah* is worshipped because he, in this, fits them. The intellect is improved only that Force may be developed and disciplined to its most effective use.

One sees this everywhere. To invent the most destructive engines of war for the wholesale slaughter of the human species, to add to the swiftness of movement, to the durability and weight of action, to the means of assault and of defence, to bend the mind to uses based upon the idea that the normal condition of man is that of *a tiger with man's intellect*, to make the beast something inexpressibly dreadful!

The greater portion of the people remain sunk in the grossest ignorance—scarcely knowing (the most of them) much even of the Superstition, other than crude notions of Hell and the Devil. In this, probably, they are not much to be pitied; though in losing the precepts of Christ, and seeing around them the conduct of Christ-god worshippers, they are to be commiserated. They look with the contempt of ignorance upon foreigners, and call the people of distant seas *Heathen*, only fit for the Hell! As I have said, in another place, some attempts are being made to give this degraded populace, at least, the rudiments of learning. The task is hard, and made nearly impracticable by the stolid indifference of the Low-Castes, and their positive hostility to anything which interferes with their habits. They are very English, not different from their betters, and resent any sort of change as an interference with their individual freedom of action. To make these degraded beings *slaves*, you must not seize the individual—you must act upon them as a class—and they resent the attempt to teach them. Compulsion will be resorted to. The English Barbarians have a proverb [li-tze], "One may lead a horse to the water, but who can make him drink?" These people may be forced to the springs of learning, but who shall make them drink—unless *beer*? (This is the common drink, very muddling; used to an astonishing quantity.)

The women are not admitted to the Halls of Learning, though they are to be seen everywhere. Men do not wish them to be educated in those things admired by men—it would, as they think, make brutes of them. In this they are right; yet there is no consistency of idea in the general treatment of the sex, as will easily be gathered from these *observations*.

A learned woman—that is, one who has acquired the sort of education recognised by the *Literati*—is disliked by her own sex as well as by the men. The men will not marry her, unless she can buy a husband. This she may be able to do if she have money in abundance.

The things which may make them attractive and entertaining to the men, and be likely to secure a desirable husband, are the only things cared for. Some music, some drawing, a little acquaintance with the language of the chief tribe on the main parts, reading and writing, are the intellectual studies. But the engrossing pursuits are those which are supposed to add to female attractiveness. To DRESS, so as to enhance the delight of form; to cover, and yet to show with added suggestion; to move with grace; to carry the head; to use with tender, or arch, or modest, or haughty expression, the eyes; to turn the feet and arrange the limbs; to make the shoulders beautiful, and the neck and bust charming; to torture the hair and ornament the whole body; the ear-tips, the fingers, the eyebrows and lashes—to do these, and innumerable other things by which the sex shall be made *irresistible* [Kou-ket], these are the real cares. *Dancing* [ma-d-wo] is among the most admired of all accomplishments, and the game of *Waltzing* its most perfect development. In this art of dancing both sexes take part, and I may merely say to our Flowery Land, that we have nothing like it, and what little we have in any degree to represent it is confined to *licensed* girls, without, even with them, permitting men to take part! In this dancing the utmost female art (*blandishment*) is permitted, and it is the one by which, and in the intricacies of which the male is most surely expected to be ensnared!

Women are, also, particularly among the High-Caste, taught in riding on horses, in driving them attached to carriages; in running and walking; and even in swimming. Also in rowing in boats, in the use of bows and arrows, and many other things, which are very strange to us. But the sex like passionately the outdoor sports of men; and, in truth, show the barbarous instinct quite as clearly as do the males. They are attached to dogs, cats, and other creatures, which they fondle and *dandle* in the most disgusting manner.

The women of the Low-Castes, to the best of their ability, follow the example of their superiors; and make such copy as they can. They imitate the dress, the gait, the *airs and graces* of the High-Caste, often with a ludicrous effect! When they dance, they may not dance with the elegant *abandon* [lan-gu-tze] of the lazy and rich, but they can contrive to be quite as *effective*! The male of the Low-Caste feels but cannot escape the snare!

Accomplishments, directed to the one object of finding a desirable man, who will take them at the least cost off the hands of their relatives, are the things which occupy the time of women; the lower orders, in so far as possible, giving to the poor imitations that time which ought to go to useful objects. A poor and obscure girl prefers to be *something like* a lady (that is, a bad copy in dress and bearing), than to be really instructed in letters: because she sees herself more admired by the male, and more likely to dispose of herself to a husband.

The great pursuit among High-Caste families is man—a man who may be bought, and whom it is desirable to buy, to be a husband for a daughter, or relative. All domestic art and diplomacy are bent to this end; and, as men do not like learned women, whom they nick-name *strong-minded*, women do not wish to be learned. If from exceptional circumstances a young woman be well educated, and wish to marry, she carefully conceals her knowledge, and displays her accomplishments, and all "the power of her charms" (as the English poets have it). An educated female had better appear to be an *accomplished* fool, than a wise and learned woman—if she wish to buy a husband. For she must have a large sum, indeed, if she be known to be learned!—a *Blue-stocking* [Zu-re-to].

There are some women who have acquired knowledge, and look with disdain upon the *arts*, *airs*, and *graces* of their "weak Sisters." They appear in public Halls of debate (as talking-places are called); and, mixing with men, assume an equality of mental force and culture. They interest themselves like men, in all matters of general concern. They take in hand, or endeavour to take in hand, *the care of Women*; and demand an enlarged sphere for her action, and a reformed and proper recognition of her *rights*. Hence, these women are called, besides strong-minded, *Women's rights* women. They are nearly always old, ugly, and wholly and hopelessly incapacitated from longer pursuing men; even, in their inordinate vanity, *that* pursuit is abandoned.

There are some trifling exceptions—of women who like to astonish, and of others who, in *talking*, find a means of living—to whom all personal comeliness is not yet a tradition. But for these, the *Women's rights* movement would dwindle away; these sometimes commanding an influence either of money or family, draw into their circle a few men—remarkable, in general, for eccentricity of some kind, or led very often completely by a woman of the order.

The whole thing is inexplicable to our social usages; but is not an excrescence—only a natural outgrowth upon a diseased system. The position of women in the Barbarian Society is a feature very striking and very anomalous, and may receive attention in another place.

On the whole, one may see that education in its true and exalted sense is scarcely comprehended among the Barbarians. The moral function and the mind subordinate to that, and the body—its passions, its greed, its brutality, wholly subordinate to the morally trained mind—education, grounded upon this *central idea*, has but feeble recognition.

CHAPTER V.
OF THE LITERATURE OF THE ENGLISH.

THERE are innumerable books; and the conceit of these Barbarians attaches to them as to everything in their *Enlightened World* (Litz-i-ten). Nothing outside of the Christ-god worshippers is allowed to be enlightened—all else is darkness. This is true as to their opinion, strange as it looks; and all the Literature in every part of it shows this. The attainments and the experience of all to whom this worship is unknown, receive no other than a curious attention from a few of the literati. But we know that this conceit is absurd; ignorant and superstitious Barbarians really think that, without the adoption of their *Jah-Christ-Jew* superstition, with all the *Canons*, no true morality, no real civilisation, exists, nor can exist!

This I must premise; because we may dismiss at once the larger portion of the Barbarian Literature, inasmuch as it relates to the great Superstition. It is everywhere, striking into and permeating everything, to be sure; but I refer to works avowedly devoted to it. It makes the Books largely unreadable to one having no sympathy with the author; and it requires patience and a long use to get over the disgust caused by the offensive pretensions and ignorant references.

The Poetry of a people is generally placed *first* among the Barbarian *Literati*; and of this form the Western tribes are very fond. The English boast that in this they excel all others; though, for that matter, the same boast is made in everything.

The larger part of the Poetry may be called *trash* (ru-b-isti). Iterations and reiterations of the same conceits, the same shallow sentiments, the same metaphors, mostly of an amatory and indelicate sort. Poems, often tedious, verbose, strangely mixed with matters of the Superstition and of the ancient (Roman) myths; laudatory performances, *beslobbering* (spr-au-fo) great men with empty compliments, or giving lying exaltation to the fancied virtues of the eminently bad; dull and long-winded reflections from minds too obscure to reflect anything, unless with an added obscurity; an enormous *Waste* (Ban-s-he) which the English themselves never traverse.

Poetry with the Barbarians is far more esteemed than with us, although in our annals are found evidences of its immemorial existence. As with us, it takes many forms, and is reduced to an art. The two greatest names are Milton and Shakespeare. The first of these is esteemed as the most sublime of all poets, ancient or modern—but it is needful to fix the quality, the essence of the sublime! Of the gloomy grandeur of the man, and of his power of suggesting the vast and the intangible, there can be no doubt. Nor is he wanting in a mournful sweetness—the plaint of a beneficent being who feels an eternal despair! Nor can it be otherwise, for the grand imagination of Milton is wholly occupied with the devils of the Barbarian Superstition! With its terrible images—with the Hell in which they and lost men for ever burn in eternal fires, and yet are never consumed! He introduces the reader (in his great Poem) to Paradise [Kar-din], where man once lived in perfect wisdom and happiness—and here the Poet is full of that sad, that tender, that inexpressible, sweet despair! From this Paradise (as said elsewhere) man was enticed by Satan, who had been set free from Hell for the very purpose; and then follow all the surprising pictures, vast, terrible, indescribable—only possible to a mind fully possessed by all the *horrors* of the Jew Jah-god Idolatry.

Shakespeare, with a healthier mind, one not distorted by the Superstition, and with a human, natural vigour and feeling, writes in a manner to interest man. On the whole, the English Barbarians place him far above all others of any time or place—call him the Divine Shakespeare! This is very easy with a people who know nothing of the poetry of the great East, nor of that of our Flowery Kingdom—in truth, have but a slight acquaintance with the writers of the other Barbarians!

Disregarding this foolish conceit, we may admit that this man shows a broad and comprehensive intellect—he is one who knows something of himself, and that self is a manly self. And he simply exhibits *himself* in those creations of his fancy, wherein a great variety of men and women show the passions, follies, and changing interests of life. He has the power of vividly seeing and of clearly showing what in his mind he sees, and in language often low and uncouth, but frequently in fine and lofty tones. His certain knowledge of himself gives pithy form to his wit; and his expressions are the direct utterances of one who sees, not of one who does not nor cannot see. His, on the whole, was a very large and true manhood, which, in spite of unfavourable influences and some tarnish, manifested itself, and occasionally in grand and beautiful forms. In very garbage there are sparkling gems. He often offends decency, but is less indecent than his time—and when he is simply himself, the natural morality of a large man becomes conspicuous. Some of his minor things, based on the affectations of his period, and formed on bad models, which he weakly copies, are not without marks of his rich fancy, yet are so indecent that in our Flowery Land they would be suppressed. None the less, you will find these objectionable verses in the hands of the youth of both sexes.

This degradation of the moral sense is very common. It finds form in the versification of those poets whom the English style *Amatory*—chiefly with them, but more repulsively with the play-writers. Examples of this indelicacy and coarseness are lying about anywhere. It seems to us very strange: for to what good? No doubt, poetry very properly deals with human emotions and interests; but why should the poet dare to print what he would not dare to utter, unless among the shameless!

Some of these trivialities are not wanting in sweetness and tenderness—and some have a very refined feeling. The great blemish is *falseness.*

The Western Barbarians addict themselves always to a false and affected mode whenever they address themselves to the female: and the style is absurd. It is borrowed from the obsolete manners of ages ago, when it was the fashion [phan-ti-te] to pretend the most exalted reverence for the sex. They were addressed as goddesses, and there was a whole armoury of weapons of Love, from which these fantastic poets armed their divinities, and pretended to be pierced through and through, wounded, bleeding, at their feet! Dying, transfixed, and rolling their languishing eyes in death, imploring the goddesses to save them, even if by one glance of their bright eyes! The amount of this nonsense is perfectly astonishing!

I give a fair specimen here from a much admired writer of this class:—

"Sweet Phillis, idol of my heart,
Oh, turn to me those tender eyes!
Transfix my breast with Cupid's dart,
But listen to my dying sighs!

"I cling, imploring, to your knees;
Oh, cruel goddess, turn to me!
One kiss the burning pain will ease—
Thy lips give Immortality!"

The Elegiac [mo-un-fu] is, perhaps, the most cultured among the refined poets. The most distinguished of the English living writers of verse is very elegant in this form. He cannot emancipate himself from the habits of his people—for the wretched he can find no solace but in the Superstitions of the Christ-god worship. He demands a *Sacrifice* quite inhuman, when he suggests the only remedy for human grief. Possibly, he finds in this, a meaning of a different kind from what the language (used in the Superstition) itself implies. He may see a meaning common to all sorrowful and thoughtful men—*Self-Sacrifice,* demanded by the highest perception of justice, and, therefore, inevitable. In this department some of the minor poets sing very sweetly, tenderly—with a nice refinement. Generally, however, there is a sort of despair wailing in an under-tone of pathos. It would seem to arise from the gloomy spirit of the Barbarian nature, intensified by the terrible Superstition.

The comic poets are coarse, trivial, and not much esteemed. There is humour, but it is of the barbarous and unclean. It is frequently strangely fantastic, and delights in laughing at the terrific in the "*Sacred Writings*," or at the Priests, in a covert manner; often in *travesties* of the prayers, *rites*, and other *holy* things, which no one would dare openly to ridicule. Poetry is not much read, unless by young girls and lads, who, in the season of the sentiments, find food to feed their desires, or to print their tender epistles and speeches, in the Sentimental Authors.

Very rarely is there anything striking or true; and the mass of Verses, after receiving the *paid-for* attention of the daily writers, sleep a sleep of oblivion.

The Prose writings are innumerable—largely, however, mere *re-hashes* [mi-pi-stu] of existing works. It is a trade to make these new forms of old books—cutting down, working over, and revising. History, accounts of bloody fights, forays, commotions, massacres, and burnings, now by one Christ-god tribe and now by another; Biography, Travels, Lives of *Great men* (never heard of out of some Barbarian tribe); these are many, and read by the *Literati*. A few books, rarely read, devoted to *Science* and to *Art*, are printed, commonly to the ruin of the printers.

Of romances and novels there are no ends. With these and the newspapers the English Barbarians almost entirely occupy themselves, when they do read. The novels pretend to portray *life*, in its usual vicissitudes and with a natural show of the feelings. But the feeling depicted is that of Love, and the Life, the life of a Lover. In this curious creature, unknown in our Central Kingdom, the English young people of both sexes delight. I cannot describe him; he has no existence outside of a diseased brain. The great Shakespeare describes him, "Sighing like a furnace, with a woful ballad made to his mistress' eyebrow!" which will do as well as a more extended notice.

There are *Metaphysical* works. We have no term to represent it. It is a book which dimly suggests *phantoms*—things unseen, and not to be seen—mere words without bodies. Usually, making the matters of the common Worship still more inscrutable.

Close to these, and blended often in a confused mixture with them—a compound defying all reasonable analysis—come the Philosophical. This term is a grand one with the Barbarians, and embraces all knowledge. The Philosophical writers pretend to the most exalted insight and outsight—they measure the whole infinite and finite, mind, matter, and the very nature of moral and divine things. The Philosopher loves Wisdom, and Wisdom loves and teaches him!

Each philosopher, however, knowing everything, knows some things better than others; and usually exhibits to the world that *eccentricity* by which he is known. He parades this on all public occasions of the *Literati*; and feels happy and serene mounted on his *Hobby-horse* (again we have nothing to fit this word)—he appropriates the name of the ridden Hobby. Thus, some time since, one of these discovered and taught that man was an Ape—an Ape of high form. This discovery was not very well received; however, he was afterwards honoured by a title derived from his ancestor, and styled the *Simian* philosopher. In the old Roman, *Simia* means Ape. He is vulgarly and better known, however, as the Hobby-horse philosopher, from his own name, *Hobbs*!

Just now, this speculation has revived again, with but slight change. One Darwin dreams of immortality from the usefulness of *his* theory. In this, man no doubt is found in the *Simia*, but he *passes through* that type; it is well enough to find there the immediate origin, but the true *germ* lies further back among the *tadpoles*!

I do not know what tadpoles are, and did not think it worth while to inquire.

This philosophy, called Darwinian, is greatly admired for its profundity—especially by the select circle of Mutual Admiring Thinkers—but is strongly denounced by the Bonzes, and by the Halls of Learning and Literati of the Superstition. It makes man no immortal being at all, these say; and dethrones all the gods.

In our Flowery Land we may smile at these speculations and *eccentricities*—for such and similar vagaries are as old as Literature; and the special notion of Darwin, as to the *Origin of Species*, has not even the attraction of novelty. The *speculation of evolution*, by which all visible forms are developed from a form less perfect below it, and this from another below that, and so on, down to the beginning, is a clumsy mode of stating that original forms were few, and contained wrapped up in them, many—and that possibly there may have been primarily only *one*, containing all! The Sovereign Lord Himself! In truth, it is the immemorial *out of nothing* idea; for when a creator of worlds, in the shape of man, has got to a single form containing all, he has yet to account for that *Single Form*.

The few, most advanced of the Barbarian Philosophers, cut adrift entirely from the *Superstition*. They copy largely from the Greeks, Romans, and ancient peoples, who said, on such subjects, over and over again what these modern imitators say—and said it better. In *Physics* these moderns think themselves wiser. They may be, in the use of some things, but are not in the nature. Our Sect called *Taos-se* resemble these speculative writers in many things: the English may not directly teach the *Metempsychosis*; but in effect it is the same. Evolution may hold to an original germ which is fixed and indestructible; yet what matters if to the observer this germ takes on every possible shape! The Metempsychosis does not contradict the notion of an original germ—it is entirely consistent with it. This speculative inquiry into the nature of things is as old as man, who, even before he knows how to formulate his thoughts, has the deep shadows of them. The Old Greeks introduced *the Literature* of these fancies to the Western Barbarians, though themselves were no more than bright and beautiful dreamers of old dreams. The human intellect will always, as it has always, search into the unsearchable, applying to it whatever of sharpness, of imagination, of culture, it may have. There will be the inquiry, but never the answer. The mind itself finds its advantage; nor could the Sovereign Lord have designed otherwise, else the intellect would not persist in a vain task. Nevertheless, wise men rest satisfied with the *intuitions* of the moral and intellectual nature. The origin and essence of the Sovereign Lord and of the visible world cannot be known. The source, the purpose, the end, and the nature of Things are beyond the scope of man. He may ask, and he may find delight in the asking; for new ranges and glimpses of the infinite may flash upon him. But when he thinks he *knows*—that he has *discovered*—he is a fool!

Another department of what is called *Philosophy* deals with the mind, as the part just referred to more particularly affects to deal with matter. And writers upon the mind, when they speak of the moral function, call *that* by another name. Thus we have the *Intellectual* and *Moral* philosophers, with their many books. Very commonly this division is not sustained, and moral and merely mental evolutions run together. Indeed, there are those who deride this division, and assert that the moral has no real existence; that the mind itself is but matter *instinct* of life, and has no existence independent of material organisms. They say that man is an animal endowed with *Life*, and that this occult and hidden force is indivisible. That divisions of the faculties may be convenient to give exactness to mental movements, but are otherwise fanciful. They deny a "Moral faculty," asserting that it is only a peculiar refinement of the life-*instinct*; that the wish to do honestly is no more than this, and, educated to enlarged views, expands into all that man conceives of Justice. That you may just as easily train one to do dishonestly; and then an honest act gives pain. This proves the very proposition denied—the faculty may be misinformed—the pain demonstrates the existence of the faculty. An animal has the Life-Instinct or mind, if you will; but who imagines that the animal is ever pained by any remorse! To this, these philosophers reply that the pain does not really exist only as the remains of a *secondary instinct*, remembering consciously or unconsciously the penalty awaiting *disobedience*. The animal, they say, may be so trained that it will feel this pain or shame; and man, for ages disciplined, transmits to his offspring this *secondary instinct* of inherited fear; and, *here*, is the so-called moral faculty.

I may be pardoned in this tedious attempt to give the Flowery Kingdom some insight into the thoughts of the Barbarians on abstract matters, not for their novelty, but as a further illustration of that which is so well understood by our *Literati*—to say, the ceaseless activity of the human mind and its tireless inquiry into the things of the mighty world. A beneficent fact or it would not be. Perverted by vain thinkers, who do not think, because egotist; yet in humble men, conscious of ignorance, a solace. These reverence the Sovereign Lord, never comprehending other than His infinite Wisdom (and this by delightful flashes), nor His works, nor His methods, nor the use of Man, nor of any the smallest thing, nor the origin, nor the design! Enough that He is, and that by some inscrutable, though certain sense, man, with a grateful joy bounds towards Him, claims to be His, and feels Immortal!

The Barbarian *Literati* have often rested upon the Greeks as final in Metaphysics. Plato, whom they call Divine, was very generally followed in his notion respecting the eternal and independent existence of spirit and matter. But the newer men insist upon one substance only, and remove the Sovereign Lord so far back into the deeps of an Unknown, that he vanishes, or becomes an unintelligent and unconscious Cause. Here again reproducing the *Fate* of remote antiquity.

One school of Philosophers indulges in a curious form of materializing the mind. Pretending to fix all the mental and moral processes in the very substance of the brain, they declare that by a careful examination of the head, the exact qualities of the individual may be discovered! Some of these pretend to be teachers and *Indicators*—for fees, giving a precise chart to any one who wishes of the forces of the brain, so that he may order his affairs accordingly.

They profess to tell parents in what art or business a child should be placed, and in what manner certain good qualities may be made to grow and bad ones to shrink! They say that over each thinking part of the brain rises a corresponding *bump* [Ko-be], that these *bumps* contain: some thoughts of music, some of hate, some of love, some of numbers, some of place, and so on. They make charts showing these bumps and the thoughts which lie beneath them! These they sell, marking the bumps (after examination) to show the person what he is. If, for instance, his *acquisitiveness* (thoughts to take things) is a very large bump, he must develop a counteracting bump or he will assuredly become a thief! It is not quite clear how this development is to be brought about. Some carry this absurdity so far as to say that a man with bad bumps is not responsible—he ought rather to be regarded as an object to be cared for by the State. Before the bumps of the child be formed and hardened, *any* form may be given to them, by applying a gentle and continuous pressure. Government, therefore, ought to have all children examined in youth, and apply to the heads the proper moulds! In this way a perfectly moral society would be assured!

I refer to this nonsense as the only novel speculation among the Western Barbarians. And any one can readily discover in this, old notions moulded into a defined and material shape, to give charlatans [Qu-ak-st] an opportunity to plunder.

There are many books of the *Moral Philosophers*, who make a *Science* of certain movements of mind, and call it *Ethical*. But these books are to our habits useless or absurd—sometimes positively hurtful. The idolatries and superstitions colour and distort—distinctions are confounded, and a rational morality wanting. A merely Jewish ordinance from the *Sacred Writings* is made as important as a plain moral precept. The human conscience is overloaded with arbitrary and unreasonable matters taken from the *Superstition*, and, bewildered, despairs of well-doing. To offend in some priestly *dogma*, is more terrible than to break an established law of honesty. Disobedience in the false demoralises the conscience as much as disobedience in the true, when both are received as true.

In fact most of the *moral* books are merely books written to uphold the great Superstition, and the morality is debased by its injurious connection. By what strange perversion could the cultivated mind ever be brought to announce a principle like this, to say; "Belief alone saves man from eternal Hell; morality without it is only a snare of the Devil." *Belief* means an undoubting acceptance of all the pretensions of the *Superstition* (as explained elsewhere). What must be the effect of teaching so false and presumptuous an enormity? The Sovereign Lord will not deign to look with pity. He is a consuming fire! Heart and hands pure—a life of disinterestedness—worship warm, grateful. Nothing worse. First, BELIEVE—in the most monstrous thing which the diseased human imagination ever created—the Jew-Jah theology and worship!

When a system of morals is based upon such a pretension, it can only be hurtful; unless, as is largely the fact, the healthy human *instinct* unconsciously rejects the error. Still, great harm is done—must be done. And how much of prevailing licentiousness and barbarism may be placed to account of this false system cannot be defined. It is the immediate father of *Atheism*. Men reject the tremendous assumptions and believe nothing. But tender consciences, those in whom the divine faculty is large and clear, in general, directed by a true consciousness, simply disregard the horribly false things and attach themselves to the true. In this, vindicating the nobility of nature, which rises to its true recognition of the Sovereign Lord, *in spite* of surrounding errors. But, others, not so strong, delicate in conscience and feeble in mind, become the victims of this dreadful system. Thus it is also the father of *Idolatry*. For these victims, fearful of eternal destruction, place themselves entirely in the hands of the Bonzes, and adore all the gods and observe all the *rites*. They cannot be sure, of themselves, that they do properly *Believe*; a thing of a very mysterious nature, concerning which (as I have remarked) the contention is ceaseless. Nor can these victims of the Superstition, ardent *devotees* though they be, always obtain satisfactory *evidence* that their *Salvation* is sure. Then follow the self-imposed penances, and the sacrifices imposed by the Bonzes. They are *victimised* by the Bonzes in an endless variety of ways. Some build Temples; some go about begging, in mean garbs, to get money for the *poor* Bonzes; and the like; much as we see among our superstitious devotees. Superstition merely reproduces its natural effects, varied according to the circumstances. Still there remain those poor creatures to whom no escape is possible. They struggle in vain with the dark doubts which envelop them. They believe in all the horrors of their worship: that but a few are saved from hell; that goodness, charity, self-sacrifice, gifts to the Temples, to the poor, even to the Bonzes—*nothing avails*. Unless they have *believed* and been duly accepted and enrolled among the *Elect-few*, they are merely children of the Devil, awaiting death, when they become his associate in *Fires of the tormented*, for ever and ever! These poor wretches feel already all the *horrors* of the damned. They find no solace in a moral life; no peace in a grateful heart, turned to a benign, Heavenly Father. To yield to the natural emotions, to indulge in this peace, is vanity—is to be ensnared in the wiles of the enemy of Souls!

They catch sometimes feebly at a *hope* of Salvation, then fall again into a dreadful despair. At last the feeble mind gives way. They feel themselves already lost; they fancy they have committed the Sin which Jah himself will never pardon—(to use the words of the *Sacred Writings*)—the *sin against the Holy Ghost*, for ever unpardonable—they writhe, they cry, they beat their breasts, they fall down in unspeakable agony—"the pains of Hell have got hold of them!" This is again from the *Sacred books*. The scene closes in death, or worse, in a *mad-house*; where in chains or under vigilant keepers (to prevent self-destruction or the destruction of others), these wretches vanish from human hope and sympathy! The frightful Superstition in these victims has been a *reality*! And no human mind can bear that and live!

I will close these remarks upon the *Literature* of the English Barbarians, by giving some examples of the different poetic compositions.

From an Amatory poet, who refers to the conjugal endearments of the Roman Jupiter and his goddess—Queen Juno, on Mount Ida, where, according to the old traditions of the Greeks, these gods often resorted:—

"When Juno makes the bed for Jove,
And waits the god with blushing grace—
Soft music charms the air above,
And breathing fragrance fills the place.
Mortals expect the deep repose;
Ocean is calm, the Winds are still,
The heavenly rapture overflows,
And Nature feels th' ecstatic thrill."

I think our poorest poets could have improved upon "makes the bed." In cold England, however, bed-making is important. And for a wife of the Upper Castes to make the bed for her Lord, with her own hands, is to show a great love and devotion. It is laughable to think of the goddess so domestically employed, though the top of Mount Ida must be cold enough!

The poetry of the Idolatry has much of an amatory sort, very curiously mixed with its terrors. I give a rather refined specimen, quite free of the diabolic:—

"What grief, what darkness fills my breast,
That coldly I have strayed from thee!
Thou art my Love, my Life, my Rest;
All other love doth fade and die.
Oh, never may the joys of sense,
Entice my ardent soul again!
Thou art my only sweet Defence—
To love thee not is endless pain!"

From an unknown writer I extract the following, who refers to a great Sailor of the Western Barbarians. This man, repressing the revolts of his crew, with undaunted mind, day after day, and night after night, for weeks and weeks, still kept on, steering *westerly* across the infinite, big seas. Possessed with one great and fixed idea—that *Land lie beyond*. At length, when all hope had nearly died, far away like a cloud, the great *New World* was discovered! We know of this in our Annals, in the dynasty *Ming*.

"To be—this marks the nobler man—this Force,
This *visioned* soul, which sees the shadow cast
Of a great Object in its every course,
Urging it onward—common men will rest
With common things; such spirits are possessed
By greater somethings, which will not be hushed

With 'lullabys'—which are within the breast
Like inspirations—sleepless as the rush
Of world-surrounding waves, and which no earth can crush!"

This is a writer who takes the *Sea* as the scene of his poem. The style is affected; but much liked.

I add below an example of *Blank Verse*, a form greatly in use:—

"The Morn, exultant, on the mountain tops,
Leads in the Day—and over all the World
Delightful Joy spreads forth his glorious wings!"

This appears to be a parody of Shakespeare, who says beautifully:—

"Oh, see where jocund Day stands tip-toe,
On the distant, misty mountain tops!"

Very much of the poetry is obscured, and spoilt by the influence of the Superstition; and very much by artificiality and affectations. And everywhere there are poor or indifferent imitators of the ancient Greeks and Romans; upon whom the *Literati* mould their poetic conceits.

Of the Comic and common it is well to read little. Coarseness and indecency seem inseparable from all vulgar humour.

The Descriptive, tinged with the melancholy of the Superstition and Barbaric gloom, is often fine and smooth—sometimes tender and elegant.

I give an extract from an author of no repute, but agreeable; and the more so to me, because inoffensive. It is not defiled by the Idolatry of the Barbarians:—

"*Spring-time* of life, with open-eyed delight,
Wondering at beautiful earth and sky!
Budding in sweet expectancy, and bright
With smiles and charming grace, and blushingly
Unconscious of a Love, just to be born—
A trembling Joy, which smiles and tears adorn!"

From the same, written in the open country; which, though obscure sometimes, flows on finely, eloquently:—

"Stretched to the brilliant sky, on all sides clear,
Are hills, and dales, and groves, and golden corn—
Whilst in the peerless air, all things are near;
And far or near they each and all adorn!
Here, let us rest, on this fair, breezy hill,

Beneath the shade of this high, spreading beech—
And feel and see that we are Nature's still:
Her Peace and Beauty ever in our reach.
Her calm, majestic glory, harvest-crowned,
Fills heaven and earth, and blends them into *one*.
How vast and solemn bends the blue profound;
How sweet and strong th' immortal gods move on!
Move on, resistless, yet, with tender grace—
Inflexible, yet soft as summer rain—
Intangible—as where yon shadows race,
With nimble Zephyrs, o'er the waving grain!
Ineffable, though murmurs everywhere,
Swell into Anthems of delightful tone;
And smiling hill-tops, and the radiant air,
Rest in expressive Silence, all their own!
And there, by Avon's stream, are Warwick's towers;
And, here, is labour toiling in the fields:
For Lord [Tchou] or serf alike, the patient hours
Give back to Nature all which Nature yields.
Still human hope aspires and will not die;
Will rear aloft its monumental walls;
Informed by Instinct builds as builds the bee—
Mounting secure where stumbling Reason falls!
So Temples rise *Immortelles* of the race;
Where mouldering with the stones tradition clings—
Touching the landscape with ennobling grace,
And giving dignity to common things.

The day declines, and so my holiday;
Care slumbering by my side awakes again;
Grasps on my hand and leads my steps away—
So rudely rules the Martha of my brain!"

The *Martha* is a scolding, busy *house-wife* [bro-msti], taken from an incident narrated in the *Sacred Writings*. The writer refers to Temples in a pleasing way, and to the "mouldering stones," where, about the dead, innumerable legends survive. Burials are near to the Temples, and the graves are on *Holy* ground. His reference is comprehensive—meaning the universal *Hope of Immortality*, symbolized by the lofty Fanes.

I give below a few of the absurdities from the *Comic*, taken from a greatly esteemed author in this Line.

"Three wise men of Gotham
Went to sea in a bowl [tou-se];
If the bowl had been stronger,
My tale had been longer!"

The meaning of which is, I suppose, that when wise men do foolish things they no more escape the consequences of folly than others.

"I bet you a crown to a penny,
And lay the money down,
That I have the funniest horse of any
In this or in any town.
His tail is where his head should be—
'You bet! Well, come and see.'
And sure enough, within his stall,
The horse was *turned*—and that was all!"

Another, very ridiculous:—

"There was a man of our town
Who thought himself so wise,
He jumped into a bramble bush,
And scratched out both his eyes.
But when he saw his eyes were out,
With all his might and main
He jumped into another bush,
And scratched them in again!"

This would *seem* to suggest that a conceited man, having committed an egregious blunder, rashly undertakes to remedy it by one equally unwise. The folly of conceited impulsiveness!

Another, and I have done.

"Little Jack Horner
Sat in a corner,
Eating his Christmas pie;
He put in his thumb,
And pulled out a plum,
Oh, what a good boy am I!"

This is to encourage children with an idea that, if they be *good*, they shall have *plums*. It is very significant of the low culture. As if one were to imagine that the possession of a big plum (riches, or the like) demonstrated the moral excellency of the possessor!

Commentaries and parodies of these *Comic* trivialities have been written, and, forsooth, their beauties and meanings need exposition!

CHAPTER VI.
OF TRADE, AND REVENUE DERIVED FROM IT.

WE have ourselves, in our maritime parts, some experience of the English, as traders [Kie-tee]. Something of their moral character is known, not as traders only, but as representatives of the general civilization of their tribe. It will be a long period before the events of the *opium* war are forgotten—when these selfish and cruel Barbarians came with their big fire-ships and great cannons, and massacred so many of our province, Quantung! Nor will the slaughters of the people of our Central Kingdom, and the burnings and plunderings at the Illustrious seat of our Exalted, pass out of mind for many generations. Trade! yes, Trade is the *Moloch* [Kan-ni-bli] of the English; there is nothing (of character) which they will not sacrifice to this Idol. The god by which they mostly swear, and whose name they apply to themselves, knew nothing of trade, and his words, as recorded in the *Sacred Writings*, condemn every practice customary in it. This inconsistency is always found in the devotees of irrational worship; where formal observances stand for practical virtues. Perhaps dishonesty in trade is no more conspicuous, than immorality everywhere; only traffic touching on all sides, and affecting nearly every interest, carries with it an almost universal debasement. Blind and conceited, it is the custom to speak of our *Central Kingdom* contemptuously, and to brand our people as Heathen *thieves* [ta-ki]. We have thieves, and punish them. But how strangely to those of our people who know these Barbarians, this charge sounds! It is notorious that the vile stuff packed up as *Tea* by our knaves is for the gain of English traders; and that the horribly obscene pictures of degraded artists find a market with the Barbarians! We punish these plunderers when we detect them; but these Christians who would *convert* us encourage this immorality!

The Law-making Houses are continually occupied (and occupied in vain) to find remedies for the almost universal crime of *Adulteration* [Kon-ti-fyt] *of Food*. Scarcely an article of food, or of drink, medicine, what not, escapes this dangerous cheat. To make a larger gain some cheap admixture, often poisonous and rarely harmless, is added to nearly every article. It is not easy to understand how general the moral debasement must be, when a thing of this sort, striking at once at health, and even life, is so common as to be scarcely contemned! To be cheated is a kind of *comedy*—one expects to be cheated—cheated in his clothes, his wine, his horses, his dogs, his meat, his drink, his beer, his sugar, his tea, *his everything*! To have been honestly dealt with is a surprise—a thing to be remarked upon. To have been cheated—a *shrug* of the shoulder—an exclamation—"Of course!" In fact, almost always the cause of a hearty laugh, especially if a sharp trick—or at another's expense! The very laws of trade are based on dishonesty; and a people will not generally be better than their laws.

The High-Caste affecting to despise trade, do, occasionally, in the Law-making Houses (as I have said), feebly interfere with the general rascality. Yet, they are so dependent, indirectly or directly, upon trade or its gains, that they will not do anything to hamper it; and any law which touches the utmost freedom of action in *buying and selling*, in their opinion, has this effect. On the whole, they say, better a few rogues flourish, and a few people be poisoned to death, than that *commerce* (an *euphuism* for rascally traffic) be injured.

That man has a fine nature which traffic, in its best ways, cannot tarnish; and laws should take their colour from the best—not the sordid. The old Romans cultivated the land, and looked with contempt upon traffic. When riches and its corruptions lowered manliness, and Commerce spread through the provinces—still, the Roman jurisprudence based itself upon equity—it did not place trade upon a pedestal above Justice! They made no such Barbarous mistake as to suppose that any business of a people could be more important to its prosperity, than the maintainance of right principle!

The English Barbarians say the interests of the public require a disregard of right; and their famous legal maxim (in the Roman) is *Caveat emptor*—the buyer must take care—must sharply watch the seller. This is to say, "The seller is to be expected to cheat; and, if the buyer be cheated, let him thank his own stupidity!" The old Heathen Romans made no such immoral rule; they required the most exact good faith upon both sides. The seller could not sell a horse blind of one eye, or incurably, though not always visibly, lame, and to the complaint of the buyer answer, "Oh! I gave no assurance of soundness."

The High-Caste, despising trade of any useful sort, none the less delight in traffic of a high-caste colour. They deal in pictures, equipages, horses, jewels, sculptures, books, dogs, *nick-nacks* of all sorts; know how to bargain, and understand the *tricks*, especially in horses, dogs, paintings, and the like, as well as those whom they affect to despise.

The English are, doubtless, successful traders and plunderers. They are rough, and brave, and reckless; and in traffic are as unscrupulous as in predatory ventures. Their conquests abroad have been incidental generally, commerce being the immediate object. But they have never scrupled to use force when it has seemed fittest. The *plunder* of a people has been found easier, and the returns quicker and larger, than the slower gains of traffic.

For this shameful and cruel conduct, the English and other Western Barbarians find ample justification in their *Superstition*. For they believe that the peoples beyond the seas are Heathen, and under the ban of *Jah*. Their *Sacred Writings* so declare; and that "the Heathen are given to the Saints as a spoil, and their Lands as an Inheritance." Now, these Barbarians affirm that they are the Saints; that the people who do not worship their gods are Heathen; and that consequently they (these Barbarians) have a right to the possessions and lands of these distant and unoffending tribes! And not only this, that these tribes, under the wrath of *Jah*, and subjects of the Devil and hell, ought to be grateful for the inestimable boon of *the Gospel* (*the Sacred Writings*), by which they may learn the way to be saved; may, in fine, become Christians!

Thus it comes about that the intercourse of the Western Barbarians with peoples beyond the seas has been aggressive and piratical. From the earlier part of the dynasty *Ming*, when these Barbarous tribes first visited the great seas and distant regions in the far West and mighty East, the Pope (then worshipped by all the tribes) gave to two of them, very devoted to his worship and powerful in ships, the whole world of *Heathen*. This meant all the wide world but that small region in Europe wherein the Pope-worshippers lived. To the one tribe, called *Portugals*, he gave the whole immense East, and to the other, styled *Spaniards*, the vast regions in the West. Thus the two were possessed, by the gift of their god, of the whole *Heathen* world—India and our Flowery Kingdom being portions!

In their many ships, these two tribes, sailing East and West, landed upon the distant shores, and seized upon everything which they could. They thought it pleasing to *Jah* to put to death those who had offended him, and were already under *his wrath* and condemnation: the Heathen were justly extirpated, unless they *believed* and worshipped *Jah*!

Not very long after this gift to the two tribes, the English and Dutch, having quarrelled with the Romish Priests, refused to worship the Pope and denied his authority. The Dutch first, and then the English, growing more powerful in ships, made distant forays for plunder and trade; and, following the tracks of the Portugals and Spaniards, disregarded their pretended *exclusive* title to the *Heathen*. They determined to have a portion of this general transfer of the world to *Christians*; they were in their own judgment the better, the *Reformed* Christians, and far better entitled!

Since this enormous Blasphemy [Swa-tze] of the Pope, History, as known to the Barbarians, has been, to a large extent, an account of its consequences. Wars between the contending *Christians* for the distant possessions, and savage and cruel depopulation, plunder, and subjugation of the unoffending inhabitants. Whole races of men have melted away in the presence of these Christ-god worshippers; and the horrors of the dreadful Superstition, which in the regions of Europe had made man more like the Devil of his Idolatry than anything human, spread, with fire and sword, over the wide world! In the far West, beneath the setting sun, a beautiful and peaceful people, rich and numerous, suffered cruelties too shocking to tell; and in the civilised and populous East, the very name of *Christian* became a synonym of all that is detestable.

None the less, the English Barbarians, to this day, acting upon these Christ-god pretensions, will insist that this *Trade and Plunder* is the *handmaid* of Enlightenment, the chief agent in the preparing of the World for a knowledge of the true gods, and the ultimate salvation of the Heathen!

Trade is, therefore, a civilising agency and a powerful helper in the redemption of mankind from the awful Hell. A few poor Missionaries are sometimes added to the general cargo of *means of conversion*. The same ship which transports these Bonzes to convert the benighted *pagans* will, perhaps, have a few volumes of the *Sacred Writings*, some bad rum, worse muskets (more dangerous to him who shoots than to him to whom the shot is directed), gunpowder, flimsy articles too poor for home trade; to these, add the licentious and degraded sailors; and one sees how well the English Barbarians work to introduce their true worship and save the Heathen! But this is feeble: only a trade-ship. The great fire-ships, with big cannons, full of armed and fierce barbarians, which devastate the populous coasts, and burn and plunder the maritime parts—*these* are illustrious workers in the spread of the Christ-god *Salvation* and a lofty Civilization! Thus the very worship of the Barbarians has helped, by its cruel pretensions, to *ingrain* a wrong notion—one making them immoral and cruel. Taking the *Jah* of the old, huckstering Jews, as an object of idolatry, the whole people has, in trade, become *Jewish*, as in much else.

I have referred to petty cheating, and to that wholesale criminality of adulteration. But *fraud* is very common, and often on an enormous scale. Nor is there any remedy. In truth, it is so common, that, as all hope to have a turn at its advantage, none care to punish heavily him, who, by chance, has been too bold. The fraud must take the form of open robbery, or be of such grossness as to be hardly disguised, before the wrong-doer will be arrested. A man may enjoy unmolested, and even with respect, a great fortune acquired by notorious *trickery*.

So universal is this toleration of roguery, that the Plays and Pastimes are often enlivened by comical illustrations of the various arts, tricks, and deceptions practised. The charlatans, rogues, cheats, and the like, are shown in the Lawyer, the Doctor, the Bonze (low-caste), and other professions and occupations. Endless are the villanies of the Lawyer—the *quack* pretensions and impositions of the Medical man—the cant, hypocrisy and meanness of the Bonze.

Among the professions and trades, the teacher is a brutal *ignoramus*, who beats and starves the wretched children under his care; the nurse quietly drinks herself drunk and goes to sleep, leaving the sick man to gasp and die for the drink close at hand, but which he cannot reach; the milkman stops at the pump, and fills up his milk-cans with water; the teaman shows and sells you one sort, but delivers a very different; the grocer says his prayers, hurries to his goods, asks his servant if "the sugar be sanded," "the rum watered," "the tobacco wet down," "the teas mixed," "the *small* bottles filled," and the like; the tailor sells you more cloth than he knows will be required for your garments, and *cabbages* the excess; the cabman who knows you are a stranger demands quadruple fare; the innkeeper gives you the meanest room, and charges you the price for the best; and so on through every business of life.

The learned professions take the lead in this exhibition of roguery and immorality. The spectators never tire of these displays of the general rascality. The roguish landlord, the villanous horse-dealer, the artful, knavish servant, the Priest of Low Caste, and the Doctor, afford the most common diversion. The Lawyer is generally *diabolic*, the Bonze a hypocrite and knave, the medical man an impostor and dealer in medicines of infallible healing power.

Much of this may be referred to the love of coarse humour—but its real base is to be found in the *degradation of morals*. These representations are *types*, and would only produce disgust, were not the rascalities represented familiar. The excesses and exaggerations are of the Play—but the *types* are normal and common.

One great trading place is called the *Stock Exchange*—another, perhaps more important, styled the *Merchants' Exchange*. These places are established in every large town, and the *business* done in them absorbs the attention of traders and people who have any property, throughout the Kingdom.

The *dealings* [Keet-sees] of the former relate to *Certificates* and *Bonds*. These are *Pieces of Printed and Coloured Paper*, which represent in the words and figures a sum of money invested in a trading concern, or a sum of money which somebody owes and promises to pay. The *sum* may be quite a fiction, and is usually either never to be really paid, or paid at some very remote day. However, a small sum is promised to be paid every six moons, or in twelve moons—this is for *not* paying the big sum.

The business of the latter relates to the buying and selling of every sort of merchandise, whether on land, or on vessels at sea.

Other great trading places deal in money, or rather in bits of *Printed Paper*, which promise to pay money to him who has one of these *bits*. These places get people to sell them these bits at a price, and then resell at a greater price—or they *borrow* and *lend* these bits, paying less for the use than they obtain. Very little money is seen—business is in Paper—another of the ingenious *tricks* of these trading and gambling Barbarians, perhaps the source of more dishonesty and cheating than almost any other. As the like has no existence in our Flowery Land, it will not easily be comprehended.

The chief of these places for dealing in this money-paper is called the *Bank*. The Government shares in the advantages of this invention. Its object is to *bank up*, or hoard, all the real money (gold and silver) which it can get in exchange for the bits of paper. These promise that the Bank will always return the sum of gold which the bit acknowledges to have been received. The man hands the Bank his gold-money to be kept safely till he wishes for it, and the Bank gives him the *bit* of Paper (which is numbered and recorded in a book). He can carry this in his pocket, but the gold-money would be too burdensome and more easily lost. The Government pledges also that the gold shall always be safely kept, to be returned whenever the bits of paper are returned. This Bank-house is immensely strong and large, built of hewn stone, and is guarded by men armed with swords and fire-arms for fear of the savage and ignorant Low-Castes.

Ordinarily, only now and again, a few persons go to the Bank and wish the gold; because if one wishes it, some one of whom he buys, or to whom he owes, will take the money-paper and hand him the difference—consequently, the paper goes from hand to hand for a long time. Everybody takes it because it is convenient, and because he thinks the gold attached to it is safe in the Government Bank-house. The confidence in *Paper* is called CREDIT. To which I shall more fully refer.

Sometimes, when a great many demand the gold, it is suddenly found that the Bank-house has it not! The promise of *banking up* the gold till wanted in exchange for the Paper *has been broken*. Down goes *Credit*—every kind of value shrinks at once; for the Bank has *not* the real money, and values have been measured by the paper!

The traders and everybody connected with them have incurred debts—that is, made paper promises to pay, like those of the Bank, for property *valued on* the Bank-paper. It is found that this Bank-paper is too much by one-half—the property has been over-valued in proportion. Still the debtors are required to pay the amount of *their* paper promises!

It is impossible—ruin and *Bankruptcy* ensue—the whole trading world is convulsed, and tens of thousands are beggared!

The explanation is that the Bank is allowed by the Government (in consideration of certain advantages to itself) to lend out the gold for usury—that is, it lends a thousand pounds of gold to be returned in three moons, for which use the borrower pays twelve or twenty pounds! It makes its gains by thus using the gold which it has promised safely to keep. It is permitted to do this, because the risk of having *much* gold demanded at once is small, and from experience the Bank has discovered that if one-third part of its paper-promises of gold is in hand, it will be in little risk of having more demanded! Backed by the Government, it deliberately, for the sake of gain, runs the risk of being a cheat and robber!

Then follows a curious contrivance of these dishonest Barbarians. To save its own moneys and advantages in the Bank, and to save loss or ruin to the owners of the establishment, who are very powerful and numerous, composed of members of the High Castes as well as others—in fact, to save the general wreck of the *sham* paper-money (*Credit*) upon which values are falsely based, the Government issues a Law, forcing everybody to receive from the Bank its paper precisely as if it were gold!

Thus, having assisted in one fraud, it resorts to another, to remedy in some measure the evils of the first—extending and perpetuating the evil, which a wise man would remove!

Another remarkable thing is the organised *Betting*. The Houses where this is done are splendid, and the many people supported in them and by the gains, live luxuriously, and are greatly respected. The gains are, in small measure, also shared by those who put in money from which bets may be paid, when the House loses the bet.

The betting may be about anything. But the chief Houses are those where the bets have reference to length of life or injuries, to loss by fire, to loss by sea, and losses by fraud. If a man wish to bet that he will live say seventy moons, he pays down at once a small sum, and the House accepts the bet—that is, gives him a *writing, promising* to pay his heirs a very much larger sum if he die before the seventy moons expire. If a man have goods in a *shop*, he bets, say, one pound to 100 pounds, that they will not be burned during twelve moons—he pays down the pound and receives a writing (as before) that if the goods be burned during the time, he shall be paid the 100 pounds. So on, as to bets upon goods and upon vessels on the seas, upon buildings of all kinds, upon duration of life, and upon the life of another, upon accidents to body, upon honesty of servants—upon almost anything where the thing bet by the Houses is remote in time. This is the great point; for these never pay anything down by way of *stakes*, but always receive in money the *stake* (bet) of the other party.

One may readily see how corrupting all this is in its nature, and how falsely conceived. The rascally trader burns the goods, the possessor of a building burns that, the owner of a ship has her wrecked, to get the sums promised upon these events; and trade is promoted upon unsound practices. Even life has been taken by a wretched gambler, who has staked money upon the life of another. The *tendency* is to these crimes. Nor can there be anything but *loss to the public at large*; for these expensive Houses and their numerous and richly-living inhabitants are supported by the winnings made, without rendering any useful service. This must be true, even when all bets made by these Houses are *paid*. But another great mischief follows: they do not pay, and are often only *Swindles* [Kea-ties] on a great scale! There are those which pay—that is, have so far paid—but as there are bets for enormous amounts far in *the future*, no one can say that final payments are certain. The great object of all the Houses is to secure as large sums in cash as possible upon events a long way off. The more remote the event upon which the bet is laid, the larger the sum demanded from the individual who bets. *He* pays—the House merely promises to pay, and cannot be called upon to pay for a very long time! In this way, great sums of money having been got (some bets having been promptly paid to obtain confidence), the House shuts its doors! The rogues share the plunder and *decamp*. Decamp is to run away to distant parts to escape arrest and punishment. This is, however, rarely necessary; for such are the cunning contrivances of the Lawyers, who organise these Betting Houses, that very little risk is run—*forms* of law, slack enough at best, have been so well adhered to, that the rascals escape, though everybody knows that they have used those forms as a cover to more effectually defraud, and then as a shield to more effectually protect! These things are unknown in our *Central* Kingdom, and are only possible to a demoralised people.

The *dealing* at the Stock Exchange is mainly only another form of betting. It is hard of comprehension, unless by the *Initiated*. It is a distinct trade. Those who deal constitute a secret and exclusive *betting Ring*, or community. If by chance, when the doors are open, a stranger inadvertently enters, he is greeted with caterwaulings, howlings, "Turn-him-outs," and the like. "*Smash his hat!*" some one cries; and suddenly the stiff head-covering is violently driven down, completely over the face and ears, tearing the skin off the nose, and reducing the thoughtless and astonished stranger to a state of ridiculous helplessness!

Betting is a passion with the English Barbarians. The women, the children, the servants—everybody bets about any and every thing. Horse races, boat races, swimming races, all sorts of games and sports, attended by both sexes, afford endless occasions for the indulgence of it. Yet, after all, extensive, ruinous, and debasing as are the evils of it in these sports and games, the mischief is vastly greater in the Marts of traffic—in the Stock and Merchants' Exchanges.

In these, the dealings are, as I have said, either as to pieces of paper representing values, or as to merchandise in hand or at sea; and, I may add, as to *pieces of paper*, representing this merchandise, called Warrants and Bills of Lading.

The betting in the Stock Exchange concerns itself with the Paper of the former class, and the betting of the Merchants' Exchange with the Paper of the second kind. All this grows directly out of the Bank paper and the *Credit system*, before mentioned.

All values are founded upon these nominal promises to pay. But the promises themselves are ever undergoing changes, according to the varying circumstances. The promise *to-day* looks well—it is estimated at so much; *to-morrow* it does not look so well—and it is estimated at less worth. Besides, all the gold and silver in the world could not pay a twentieth part of these promises. Thus the fluctuations are incessant. The betting at the Stock Exchange has reference to *these* fluctuations. One of the *betters* is interested to have a rise, another to have a fall, of value. One agrees to deliver at a future day, at a certain price; all are interested to bring about a change either one way or another. The man who desires a rise may not be scrupulous as to any means which may produce the rise; and he who wishes a fall of price will eagerly second anything which will have that effect. Consider the consequences upon the honesty and good faith of those who engage in this betting!

The Merchants' Exchange is not so devoted to absolute betting; yet its largest business partakes of that vice. One buys a cargo at sea; another agrees to deliver a cargo three months hence. One sells what he has not, for a future delivery. Another buys what he never intends to receive, deliverable to him in the future. No money is paid, nor received. The buyers and sellers are merely gambling—betting (as in the Stock Exchange) upon the *rise or fall* of prices! And are interested—the one to advance the price, and the other to lower the price, of the thing dealt in!

Consider the temptation to unfair practices, the inevitable tricks, false rumours, lies, and deviations from honourable conduct involved in such transactions! Reflect upon the consequences to the honest trader, who is, in his very honesty, all the more easily tricked by the unscrupulous!

The stronghold of these various gambling Establishments, and the grand feature, in fact, of the English business life, is CREDIT—to which I will devote some space. We have nothing like it, nor had the ancient barbarians of the West. It is, perhaps, the most distinguishing thing in the Barbarian life.

As already hinted, Credit means that a Promise shall stand for performance.

It had its rise among the Barbarian tribes, not very long since, and grew out of their incessant wars. Particularly the English, finding they could not pay the armed bands, contrived to get the gold out of the hands of the people in exchange for the Bank-paper, and then, forcing the people to still accept the paper for gold, issued paper to such an amount as Government needed! From that period the people, especially the trading classes, making directly or indirectly nearly the whole, found an advantage in resorting to the same fiction—and the Government could do no other than give to the trader, who could not pay *his* promise, the same relief which it took for itself—for the Bank. It allowed him to pay what he could, and go on as before! No matter that he paid only one-third part—unless he had been guilty of some extreme roguery, he received a discharge from all his promises, and could begin to make new ones and go on in trade as before!

In this way, the Barbarian community is one wherein a false principle corrupts all. Boldness, recklessness, cunning, to say nothing of positive criminality, are encouraged; honour, delicacy, simple integrity, are driven into obscurity. Let him who would preserve his conscience smooth and clear, a mirror whence divinity be reflected, shun all the marts and ways of trade!

The Revenues of the Government are derived largely from the dealers in the great *Marts*, and it is immediately interested in the upholding of the *Credit* of the innumerable paper-promises of all kinds made by these and by the Betting Houses. It is, in fact, the chief supporter of the *whole sham*—it cannot be otherwise, for the English State rests upon it. The promises of the Government to pay gold can never be kept, and it forces an acceptance of a mere *fraction*, from time to time, as a *sufficient* redemption of its promises made generations ago!

Other sums are derived from taxes upon the tea, sugar, and other things largely consumed by the lower castes; whilst rich silks, laces, and costly things used by the High-Castes are not taxed. But then the taxes are levied by the High-Castes!

A great revenue is collected from the *excise*, a tax upon the beer, drunk in enormous quantities by the lowest Caste. To stimulate the consumption of this article and increase the revenue, *Beer-shops* are to be seen on every hand, and the drinkers everywhere. Drunkenness, wretchedness, riot, disorder— these flourish as the *Beer-shops* increase; these are the associates of those places! Yet in vain do good Englishmen try to remove these *evil dens*. What are the efforts of these few in the midst of a general debasement—a debasement which takes, without shame, a share in a traffic so vile!

I have spoken freely of the dishonesty of the Barbarian trade and business—a dishonesty to be expected when one broadly views the whole ground of their Society. Still, natural equity and its *instinct*, especially when the mind is more or less cultured, will always prevent absolute dissolution—thieving and roguery will be restrained in tolerable bounds. A man of genuine integrity finds traffic no good moralist in the best of circumstances. He needs the support of the State, or he will fight an unequal battle, and be forced by dishonesty to retire. The Barbarians are not yet sufficiently enlightened to raise the *measure* of honesty. The Government and the people are one in this. They do not perceive that the evils under which their industry, their peaceful pursuits, and all their interests suffer, are those inseparable from a bad superstition and false principles—these extend everywhere and into everything. Misleading in Statesmanship [Lan-ta-soa], in dealings with distant peoples, in due ordering and educating the people at home—stimulating wild speculation and extended confidence (credit) at one time, only to be followed by disastrous collapse, excessive distrust, and wretchedness, soon after! Giving, in fine, to Barbarian society that aspect of restlessness, that apparent but often vicious activity, that indescribable hurry and confusion, that unhealthy excitement, unknown to an orderly and industrious people, whose order and industry are grounded upon the simple and direct rules of reason and truth.

CHAPTER VII.
SOME REMARKS UPON MARRIAGES, BIRTHS, AND BURIALS. [HI-DY].

IN our Flowery Kingdom when a man marries *he* pays to the parents or relatives; but with the Barbarians the woman pays to the man. Women are such costly burdens that men demand some compensation for undertaking to keep them; and the relatives of women are glad to get them off their hands at any price.

There are in England four great Castes, which contain the whole population. The habits of the Castes differ, though you will observe certain characteristic features common to all. In order to understand more clearly the remarks which follow, it will be convenient to speak of the division of Castes.

The *first*—High-Caste. Those who do nothing useful and pass their time in mere self-indulgence.

The *second*—High-second Caste. Those who do but very little, and come as nearly as possible to the selfish existence of the *first*.

The *third*—High-low. Those who are obliged to work more or less, but are ever longing to attain to the idle selfishness of those above them.

The *fourth*—Lowest Caste (Villeins). Labourers, not long since serfs, and still so in effect.

The *fourth* Caste is so *low down* as to be usually disregarded altogether, in any account of the people, though included in the count taken of the population by Government. They may amount to nearly a half of the whole. They are rarely styled *people* at all. They are designated by many contemptuous names, of which the more common are *my man, navvy, clown, clod-hopper, parish-poor, boor, rough, brute*, and *beast* are frequent, especially when any of the despised Caste slouch too near, or happen to touch a Higher Caste.

When a man of the higher orders thinks to take a wife, he sees to it that she will bring him money enough to compensate the cost. He dislikes to part with his easy freedom and yoke to himself a being as selfish, frivolous, and useless as himself.

He may be broken in fortune and notorious for immoralities, yet, connected to the Aristocracy, he knows that he may demand a large sum if he will take for wife a woman a little lower in family than himself. She must be of High-Caste, but not of the highest.

The woman's relatives say, "Well, he is *fast*; but marriage will settle him. His father, you know, is second son to the Earl of Nolands, and his mother was a sixth cousin to the Duke of Albania, who has royal blood in his veins. I think we may make a large allowance for such a desirable match." It does not occur to the speaker, at the moment, that the royal blood coursed through very impure channels in the case cited.

It is an object eagerly sought by low rich to buy for their daughters a High-Caste husband; and men of this kind, ruined by gambling, loaded with debt, often degraded by vice, deliberately calculate upon this ambition to repair their fortunes, and get comfortable establishments.

The marriage ceremonies do not differ very much from ours, in some things; but it is very different before the ceremony. With us, the woman is unknown to the man; but with the English, the man has every opportunity of seeing her, and knowing her very well indeed. Our notions could not admit of this, but it has a convenience; it would prevent the disappointment occasionally arising, when, on opening the door of the *chair*, our new husband finds a very ugly duck instead of a fine bird, and hastily slams the door in the poor thing's face, and hurries her back to her relatives as a bad bargain! However, this advantage to the English husband is not so great as it seems; for the woman is too cunning to discover much till she has secured her game. Unless, therefore, the man be a very cool and practised *lover* [mu-nse], he is likely to be rather astonished when he sees his bride—and he cannot slam the door against her!

The Bonzes, generally, perform the ceremony before the Idol in the Temple. It is deemed to be important to have the marriage *invocations* pronounced. These are barbarous in the extreme; most indelicately alluding to those things which decorum hides, and calling the gods to aid the conjugal embrace—no wonder that the bride wears a veil!

The great bells ring in the lofty towers, the loud music strikes up, and the marriage procession enters the Temple; and any one may follow who pleases, so he be well dressed. In the great towns, the beggarly rabble—chiefly children and half-grown youths of both sexes, with old women and men—crowd about the Temple gates, but dare not enter. When the *cortège* leaves, this rabble clusters round the wheels of the carriages, turning over and over upon hands and feet, standing on head and hands, rolling and crying out, in the dust or mud of the street, begging for *pennies* (a small English coin). When these are thrown amongst them, they ridiculously scramble and tumble over each other, seeking amid the dirt for the coins, like so many carrion-birds upon garbage.

Arrived at the home of the Bride, a great feast is eaten, with wine and strong drinks. All make merry; whether because it is so desirable to be rid of a female, or because of the liking which the Barbarians have for eating and drink, I know not. The feasting over, all take leave of the new pair, the bride being addressed by the title of her husband. The Bride is kissed, the husband shaken [qui-ke] by the right hand, and good wishes given. On leaving the portal for the carriage, old shoes [ko-blse] and handfuls of rice are thrown after them; the rabble roosting about the areas and railings rush *pell-mell* after the old shoes, begin their *tumblings* about the street, and howl for more pennies. The rice-throwing is no doubt Eastern in origin, and has an obvious meaning; the old shoes refer to something in the *Superstition*— probably to appease the *evil imps*, who delight in mischief and are amused by the absurd squabbles of the beggars.

The *Honey-moon* begins at the moment when the pair enter the carriage and the old shoes are thrown after them. The horses start, and the newly-married are whirled away into the deeps of an Unknown! You may, perhaps, catch a glimpse of the bride, wistfully stretching her neck and turning her eyes, dimmed with tears, to the door-steps where stand those with whom she has lived—and whom she now, it may be, suddenly finds are very dear to her! But the husband has grasped the waist of his new possession, and is absorbed in *that*. He has before been the owner of horses, dogs, and the like, which have worn his collar—*this* is another and very different bit of flesh and blood; none the less, however, branded as his own exclusive possession, and ever after to bear *his* name! He understands so well the mere *fiction* of this ownership, that he is by no means sure that after all he have not made a *bad bargain*—it may prove *too* costly, and be by no means either useful or obedient! However, with his arm about his *wife*, just now he hardly realises these doubts, but feels, or tries to feel, *ecstatic*— as he ought.

The Honey-moon thus begun, ends exactly with one moon. It is a received opinion that the Incantations at the *rite* exorcise the Evil One for the period absolutely, though he may (as the Barbarians express it) "play the very Devil" with them afterwards!

I was told that the Honey-moon was so called because, during the Moon, the new couple fed wholly on honey and drank weak tea! There is some *mystery* attached to it, for my questions were always answered with a doubtful look. I had no opportunity of absolutely solving it—though my observation led me to judge that the honey diet did not agree with people—in truth, I wonder at its use. I have seen a bride after her return, thin, pale, peevish, who had left round and rosy; a bridegroom before the moon *jolly* [Qui-ky] and devoted to his bride, return taciturn, careless, forgetful to pick up a fan, or to place a chair for his wife, and even (on the sly) kick the very poodle which he before-time caressed! and when the wife *pouting* has said, "*Out again, George*," he has replied, lighting a cigar, "*Yas, I must meet the fellahs, you know*!"

The best hint on this subject which I ever got was from a married Englishmen, who to my query said, "Ah-Chin, my dear fellah, call Honey-moon *Matrimonial Discovery*, and think about it, ha!"

As the honey-eating and tea-drinking are to go on, whilst the new couple are quite retired by themselves, away from their friends and all usual pastimes and occupations, necessarily they have only *each other* to look at with attention. The honey-eating is trying enough, and needs, one would think, all the relief of gaiety and occupation possible! But no, it is only to eat and to closely watch each other!

I wonder no more at the changes which I observed. Nor do I wonder at the improved appearance of the couple when, after a few weeks of rational life in usual pursuits, something like the health and cheerfulness of old returned!

Yet I was informed that very many couples never recover from the Honey-moon (as my informant had it, Matrimonial Discovery), but from bad grew worse, soured and sickened entirely, could not, at length, endure each other, separated by consent, or sought the Divorce Court!

The thing, therefore, seems characteristic of the coarse humour of the Barbarians, who appear to find a comedy in an absurd, irrational trial of respect and affection, dangerously near the tragic at best, and often absolutely so! *Absurd and irrational after marriage*—one can conjecture its use before! However, it is quite of a piece with the general disorder, and want of knowledge and practice of sound principles.

When a child is born, the event is duly announced in the public *Gazette*, and relatives send *compliments*. When the infant is about eight days old, it is taken to a Temple to be baptised and *christened*. It is a singular *rite*, and one of the most astonishing in the Superstition. The Bonze who officiates before the Idol, takes the little thing upon his arm and *sprinkles* some water upon its face. At the moment he does this, he makes a curious Invocation to all the *three-gods-in-one* of the Worship, and pronounces aloud the *Christian* name of the babe, by which it shall ever after be known. This is called *Christening*, that is, making a Christian of the infant. The ceremony, it is believed, exorcises the Evil One, and makes it very difficult for him to get hold of the baptised (no matter how diabolically he may act) in after life—the water, duly made *holy* by the Priest, is a barrier over which Satan, with all his wiles, shall find it well-nigh impossible ever to get—some Bonzes say it is absolutely impossible!

Women, as soon as strong enough to attend the Temples, are *churched* (we have no term of the kind), a *rite* much like an ordinary *thanks offering*, for the happy deliverance and new birth. The Bonze makes *Invocations*, and refers to the various superstitions and barbarous pretensions of the Worship, devotion to which is inculcated under fearful penalties. However, on all occasions in the Temples, these dreadful intimations of Hell and the Devil are most frequent!

When a death occurs, it is also announced in the public *Gazette*, with honours and titles; and, if a High-Caste, with a long notice of the chief events of his life, and loud praises of his valour, as where he led, in his youth, a band of fierce Barbarians like himself to the plunder and burning of some distant tribe! His virtues are also proclaimed—to the astonishment of all who *knew* him!

The tombs of the High-Castes are something like those of our *Literati*—though, instead of being in the country amid the pleasing scenes of Nature, they are generally in the *holy* grounds of the Temples, and even within the Temples themselves—for the superstitious Barbarians think that, even *after death*, the body is safer from the Devil *there* than elsewhere! But the common people lie hideously huddled together, without distinguishing marks (or with so slight as to be quickly obliterated), and are soon totally neglected and forgotten—happy, indeed, if their despised dust may mingle with *holy* earth within the precincts of Temples.

The Bonzes pray and sing the usual invocations and prayers over the body of the dead, before it is placed in the tomb—but there is no real respect for the dead—it is not to be looked for in the rough, barbaric nature. In our *Flowery Kingdom* regard for the dead, respect for their memory, tombs carefully preserved amid the quiet groves of the country, tablets and busts set up in the *Halls of Ancestors*—these are ordinary things. With the English, in general, the dead is a hideous object turned over to the undertaker and his minions to be buried out of sight, as soon as decency allows! With us, the poorest will have the coffin ready, prepared, and carefully honoured and cared for. With the English, the thought of one is repulsive, and he looks upon it with loathing! No doubt the horrid superstition has much to do with this feeling.

The undertakers (a hateful crew) drape everything in black. They take possession of everything, and turn the whole house into a charnel. They place the *defunct* (as the Barbarians, with a kind of contempt, call the dead) in a black vehicle, drawn by black horses, and draped with black cloth—black feathers and scarfs, hideously flaunted, with men clothed in black, attend—the dismal Hearse, with its wretched accompaniments, disappears—but only to disgorge the body. Soon after these Vultures maybe seen returning, seated upon the Hearse, clustering there, like carrion birds, who have gorged themselves! When they have feasted and drunk at the House of Woe (woe, indeed, whilst deified by them), and generally spent as much money as is possible—they, at last, disappear—and the family breathe again!

An English Barbarian once told me that these creatures, in tricks of plunder and cheating, surpass the Lawyers; in truth, the fashion is to show respect to the dead by a lavish expenditure in *black draperies*, and is almost wholly confined to that. It is an object to speak of the *cost* as a measure of that respect! The whole thing being a *sham*, though a most disagreeable one, the Undertaker sees well enough that he might as well pocket a large sum as a small one. A certain sum is to be spent, *for respect*, not for any tangible thing. The Undertaker takes care to furnish more *respect* than anything more tangible—and to charge for it! In fact, the mode of plunder is reduced to a system; and it just as well satisfies the real purpose—which is, to do all that is customary, and to submit to all the customary cheating.

After the family have really got rid of the Undertaker, then comes the Lawyer, with the Bonze, to read the *Will* of the deceased. This is a new departure (as the English call it) in the family voyage of life. The Barbarian law is so erratic and confused, that no one knows what the dead man may have ordered to be done with his *money*. His Land goes probably to the eldest son, or nearest male relative; and, if it be all the property, younger children may be left quite beggared. The Will begins with some absurd superstitious *formula*; and, prepared by a Lawyer, is only intelligible to him. He, therefore, is present to read and to explain. For no one is supposed to comprehend its jargon but the *initiated*. The Will is read, therefore, to those who only imperfectly catch its meaning; and when a *name* is reached, the party listens with an eager attention. He may be one who, by nearness of blood, or by the nature of his relations with the deceased, expects to receive a handsome gift. When he, at length, from the mass of verbiage, dimly gathers only a *gold ring* or a gold-headed *walking-stick*, and sees some one, scarcely heard of, carry off the goods long waited for, he scarcely appreciates the *loving token of regard* ostentatiously bestowed upon him! Nor is his smothered rage extinguished by the satisfactory expression of other relatives, who whisper, "Well, *he* cringed and fawned to little purpose after all!"

From this Reading of the Will begins a new era in the family. Quarrels there may have been, but a common centre of influence and interest kept the contestants in order. But now, nobody satisfied (or only those who expected nothing, and *got it*), all are in a mood to attack any one, to charge somebody with meanness, with treachery. So bitter animosities spring up. Lawsuits, hatreds; families are severed; old friendships sundered; the lawyers stimulate the broils; and, at last, very likely the Will and all the property covered by it get into Chancery! When I have said this, I have said quite clearly, even to the Barbarian mind, that *here* all are equally wretched and equally impoverished, excepting the Lawyers!

The power of the dead man, by a *Will*, to cut off a wife or a son with a *shilling* (as the Barbarians express it), is monstrous. Then the unjust law, by which the next of kin takes all the Lands of a deceased, works endless misery. Think of younger brothers and younger sisters being forced to depend upon the *cold charity* of the oldest, who, by mere accident of birth, takes every thing! And not only this, but some distant *male* relative may cut off the very means of subsistence from females very near, and throw them helpless, and too poor to buy husbands, upon the world! A disgrace and shame too shocking for belief.

Then, too, the wife's relatives may have paid to her husband the very money which, by the Will, is coolly handed to a stranger!

Such anomalies are unknown to the customs of any well-ordered and civilised people.

The new Widow usually remains shut up in her house, inaccessible to all but her children, her servants, her Bonze, and her Lawyer, for twelve moons exactly. During this time she devotes herself to the prayers and invocations of the *rites*; and will not so much as look at a man, unless the exceptions named. She is wholly draped in black; her children, her servants, even her horses and dogs, are *in black*. She entirely quits all the *vanities* of life; she only allows her maid to *smooth* her hair. She suffers her hands and face to be washed, but never paints her cheeks, nor tints her eyelashes. If she go abroad, it is to the Temple to pray, or to the tomb (in some cases) of the "dear departed," covered from head to feet in thick black, followed by a tall footman, all black, bearing the *Sacred Rites*. If a man come too near, he is waved, with a solemn gesture of the hand, to remove away: this is the special duty of the *flunkey*. If, by any chance, the widow in her march happen to lift her thick veil, and catch the eye of a man,—ah! how dolorous must her prayers be!

Precisely at the stroke of time, when twelve moons have gone, the widow drops all the *habiliments of woe*, and is herself again!—that is, a woman in search of a husband!—*if she* have not, from clear, sheer desperation, and want of anything better to do, already pledged herself to her Priest or to her Lawyer. Now, free and at liberty to choose, she may wish to look further; but it is probable that "the inestimable services" of the Lawyer, in her time of misery, hold her to recompense; or that the Priest, attentive to the precept of the *Sacred Writings* (which commands that *Widows shall be comforted*), has so well obeyed, that the Widow, completely solaced by the *dear, good man*, gladly rests with him!

The great book of *Rites and Customs* regulating the conduct of widows, of widowers—in fact, the observances of *Society* generally—I have never been able to see. It is in the care and under the constant supervision of a High-Caste of exalted state, from whose authority there is no appeal, styled *Missus Grundy*. I think a stranger can in no case be allowed to see this Illustrious, nor the Book. Indeed, I was told that no one, not even Royalty itself, could inspect the Book, nor challenge this authority. It is hereditary in the mighty Grundy family; and the head of the House is believed to be infallible in social observances. Another remarkable thing is, there is never a failure in the succession—a Grundy is always on hand!

Now, *Missus Grundy* speaks with more tolerance as to Widowers: they are not absolutely liable to decapitation if they marry again in less than twelve moons. Widowers, for reasons I do not know, are favourites with the Barbarian females; and young women with money will give all they possess to get a Widower, even when he have many children. It may be because of the love for the "*pretty dears*," as the young ones are called; but, whatever the cause, the fact is certain. To gratify these gushing females, *Missus Grundy* allows a Widower to marry in a less time than twelve moons: it is so desirable that the *pretty dears* should have the tender care of a new (step) mother!

As the Barbarians have no *Halls of Ancestors*, where the family preserve with dutiful care the records of the virtuous dead—inscribed on tablets of brass or polished stone—and where, arranged in due order, stand the marble busts of those more distinguished—they soon forget the dead.

The High-Castes sometimes set up monuments in public places; in Temples and the Temple-burial grounds; and inscribe thereon lofty panegyrics, as false in fact as they are bad in style—and no more thought is given to them. In truth, these monuments are always considered to be to the honour of the *living*—who take the occasion to display their own wealth, characters, titles, or taste.

The Lower-Castes do but little more than hurry to the grave the dead body, and dismiss the "unpleasant topic" as quickly as possible—imitating as well as they are able the High-Caste, by setting up a *Stone-slab*, carved with a ruder but not truer description. Couplets in verse are often added; and, as giving an idea of the humorous and coarse conceit of the Barbarian mind, I will insert some of these *Inscriptions*.

Often the slabs are flat upon the ground, and the tombs ruinous and neglected; in fact, very generally the burial-places, though *holy*, are in a wretched condition—tombs fallen, stones and tablets prostrated, graves quite worn away by the careless feet of passers; the whole place wearing a sad air of utter neglect and forgetfulness. One discovers a better culture making some progress, by curiously regarding these stones, inscribed with memorials of the dead. They have slowly become less uncouth, less barbarous, and less devoted to the wildest vagaries of the *Superstition*. However, this observation is to be taken in a very general sense.

Often, in the country, I have stumbled upon a singularly-built old stone Temple—standing quite alone, with the tombs and the tablets of the dead, clustering beneath the shadow of the lofty, square tower of hewn stone. Upon the hill-side, with a lovely view of hills, and soft vales, and rich fields of ripening corn, and scattered groves—with green meadows divided by flowering shrubs, where the flocks and the cattle fed. Near by, orchards, white and pink in blossoms; and all the air fragrant with a delicate perfume. At my feet, a few houses nestling among lofty elms—far away to the West, the sun shining above with slanting rays across a wide expanse of beauty—sitting upon a stone bench, beneath the ivy-covered Temple-porch, I have looked upwards to the serene sky, and outwards upon the tranquil and lovely scene; and I have known no Barbarian rudeness, felt no Barbarian Idolatry. The solemn Temple, eloquent in silence, the unbroken rest of the dead, the calm and delightful presence of Nature, these were here, these are there; man unites his grateful worship across the wide world—the Sovereign Lord *is* worshipped, though darkly, by these Barbarians! And in this worship (in time to be purified) we are one!

But I must give some specimens of Barbarian Inscriptions—by them called *Epitaphs*, when written to the dead—taken from tablets in places of burial.

"Here lies an old maid, Hannah Myers;
She was rather cross, and not over pious;
Who died at the age of threescore and ten,
And gave to the grave what she denied to the men!"

Another:—

"Poor Mary Baines has gone away,
'Er would if 'er could but a couldn't stay!
'Er 'ad two sore legs, and a baddish cough,
But 'er legs it were as carried her off!"

Here is one which refers to certain mineral [zi-kli] waters, prized by the Barbarians for curative properties:—

"Here I lies with my four darters,
All from drinking 'em Cheltenham Waters;
If we 'ad kept to them Epsom Salts,
We wouldn't a laid in these 'ere waults."

Here seems to be one, not uncommon, which covertly shows its disdain for the gods of the *Superstition*:—

"Here lie I, Martin Elginbrod—
Have mercy on my soul, Lord God!
As I would on thine, were I Lord God,
And you were Martin Elginbrod!"

The following is most absurd:—

"Here lie I, as snug
As a bug in a rug!"

And some equally *funny* relative placed near, but not probably pleased with him, adds:—

"And here lie I, more snug
Than that t'other bug!"

A slang term for a low, brutal fellow.

The following turns upon the word lie [pha-li], and the word lie [pu-si]:—

"Lie long on him, good Earth—
For he *lied* long, God knows, on Thee!"

This is ridiculous in manner of quoting from the *Sacred Writings*; and adding, without proper pause, the death of another person:—

"He swallowed up death in victory
And also Jerusha Jones
Aged sixty!"

Here follow references to the Superstitious horrors:—

"Whilst sinners [kri-mi] burn in hell,
In paradise, with Thee, I dwell!"

Another:—

"When the last trump doth sound,
No more shall I be bound
Within the earth;
My soul shall soar above,
To shout redeeming love,
Which gave me heavenly birth!"

This I fear will be scarcely intelligible. The *last trump* refers to a statement in the *Sacred Writings*, where it is said that a great Trumpet shall awake the dead, and so on. Probably, the remainder may be guessed by attentive readers of these *Observations*.

The next intimates that the couple had been quarrel-some, but had, at last, silenced their bickerings in a common grave:

"Here lies Tom Bobbin,
And his wife Mary—
Cheek by jowl,
And never weary—
No wonder they so well agree:
Tim wants no punch,
And Moll no tea!"

These refer to occupations. By a cook:—

To Memory of Mary Lettuce:—

"If you want to please your pallet,
Cut down a lettuce to make a salad."

By a sailor [ma-te-lo]:—

"Here lies Tom Bowline,
His timbers stove in—
Will never put to sea ag'in!"

"Below lies Jonathan Saul,
Spitalfields weaver—
That's all!"

Spitalfields is a famous place for silk-weaving [tni-se-ti].

I need not make any criticism upon these things. They would be impossible to our better culture and refinement. Our *Book of Rites* would not suffer such low conceits to see the light if, by any chance, any one should indulge in them privately.

It may be said in fairness that these are specimens of the *low*, and with *these* there is less indecency than formerly. There are, however, abundant samples even among the Higher Castes, of things in really as bad taste, though in neater language—quite as *offensive*, but to the feelings of right reason rather than to those of literary delicacy. They refer to the *canons* of the Idolatry, and seem, to a stranger to that Presumption, quite incredible.

However, one must reflect upon the effect of superstition, long ingrained, and "born and bred" till its *enormities* are as familiar as the most harmless images; and its blessings appropriated, and its curses distributed, with an equal equanimity!

I have not referred to the great Pageants when High-Castes are buried who have been famous as Braves, either in distant forays with armed bands upon the Heathen, or among *Christian* tribes of the Main Land. Or, perhaps, some high chief who has ordered the great *Fire-ships* in burning and plundering beyond the Seas. I have not referred to these, because they *are* merely shows, and do not in any sense apply any especial characteristic. One thing I have remarked—there seems to be no respect for the dead, they are immediately forgotten, and the very *monuments* ordered to be set up probably never appear; or after so long a period, that a new generation wonders who can be meant by the *figure* which rises in some public place! And when these *are* once placed on their pedestals, neglect falls upon them in a mantle of indescribable filth. Even *royalty* cannot have the royal robes of marble so much as washed by the common street hydrant [phi-pi].

It is impossible not to feel that the cold and coarse feelings of the Barbarians are, in respect of the dead, rendered more repulsive by the horrid features of the Idolatry. In this there is so much to brutalise and render callous, that it is only as *it* is disregarded, that the natural human feelings come into play, and tenderness and delicacy find expression.

CHAPTER VIII.
OF ART, ARCHITECTURE, AND SOME WORDS ABOUT SCIENCE. [KRI-OTE].

UNTIL recently the Barbarians had no proper style of Architecture, unless in Temples, Castles, and Ships. The dwellings, even in cities, were as ugly and inconvenient as it is possible to conceive.

When the great Roman civilisation disappeared, the barbarous tribes for many ages so slowly improved, that the aspect of common life remained savage. The Priests of the Superstition, however, saved some tincture of Roman learning, and brought from Rome some of the older knowledge. These, however, directed their minds to the erection of Temples, and edifices designed for the objects of Priestcraft.

Then arose those structures, truly wonderful, in stone, which exhibit so clearly the character of the gloomy Superstition: at first like those of Rome, but in time added to and changed, till at length the vast Temples, truly gigantic, called *Gothic*, arose.

These are like huge *phantasms* of carved stone, rising into the sky. Huge walls, buttresses, turrets, immense clusters of columns, vaulted and lofty arches, long aisles, lighted by strangely-tinted windows, carved masses of stone in prodigious strength, leaping, flying upwards, upwards, in grand confusion, and yet upon a strange, wild plan!—giving expression to an imagination only known to these dark and strong Barbarians. Externally, on all sides these Temples are monstrous idols in stone, stuck most curiously upon corners, high up in niches, on turrets and battlemented [trit-ti-sy] walls, over the sculptured, grand portals, everywhere—chiefly *diabolic*, exceeding all the dreams of a mad and dreadful frenzy, yet borrowed from the Superstition and illustrating it! Others surmounting these dreadful things, *angelic* and serene—as if, after all, the human instinct spurned all the low and horrible intimations of things too foul for expression, and yet so frightfully *attempted*, in ghastly and grinning stone!

The Roman-Greek types knew nothing of such—how clear and beautiful these stood out, cheerful and *clean*, in the pure sky!

As art found this sort of expression in the structures devoted to the Superstition, so in the buildings for the chiefs of tribes the same spirit directed, though modified by the object. In these art found pleasure, and the barbaric mind delight, to pile up lofty Castles of huge stone—dark, menacing—where all was for strength and to symbolise *Force*, and nothing for refinement, nor even comfort. These great structures are now, for the most part, crumbling away; not from change of barbaric spirit in the love of *Force*, but from the uselessness of the Gothic forms in the presence of big cannons. The Roman Architecture, somewhat altered, is generally revived in buildings of importance. Yet the Priests build much as before—dropping off, however, the more hideous of the grinning idols. In this unconsciously giving a sign of the decay of the Idolatry itself. For when all its *horrors* shall have disappeared, the morality and the simple worship of the Lord of Heaven may remain. The improving condition has improved dwellings, particularly of the Higher Castes. The poor still grovel in huts and hovels, often too offensive for the healthy growth of anything but pigs. Among the Low-Castes, in great towns, the filth and stench are quite insupportable.

In ships the English Barbarians pride themselves to be foremost. Upon this subject we may fairly give an opinion. There are others quite equal, and those of the *Starry Flag* often superior.

At present the style is changing, and from wood are becoming iron, with such massive sides of thick steel, that no shot fired from any cannon shall be able to break through! So these English think to sail with these huge iron machines into the waters of any people and force submission. For the mighty cannon, shooting out vast fiery balls of steel, are expected to knock to pieces any Castles and utterly burn and destroy any city. And sheltered in these impregnable, swift, floating fortresses of steel, these Barbarians expect absolutely to dominate over all the Seas, and to sink everything which dares to oppose. This supremacy is already vaunted; and all the taxes which can be got from the people, from the tea and beer which they drink, from the tobacco which they smoke, from the letters and papers which they write and use in affairs, and from a share of their daily toil, are devoted (after handing a certain portion to the Queen and the High-Castes for their pleasures) to these big, floating machines of war, to the huge cannons, and to arm and pay the sailors and soldiers, that this domination be absolutely assured! Still, so far, none of these terrible vessels have proved of any use, as they can neither float nor fight; or, if they float, turn bottom upwards at a small breath of wind, and, if moved to act in concert, are so unmanageable as to be only terrible to each other! The sailors, therefore, dread them as unfit for the sea, and as *Iron Coffins* to poor Jack, who is forced to go into them!

The introduction of *Steam* has only rendered the Western Barbarians more conceited and more miserable. On nothing do they pride themselves so much as upon the tremendous *Force*, which they have acquired in the various Arts, by the use of steam. They, in this, as in other similar inventions, mistake the nature of the thing used and its effect. They think themselves *wiser* because they move faster—as if the hare be necessarily wittier than the ox; and more civilised, because more powerful—as if the rhinoceros were to be preferred to the horse.

At this moment, the Barbarian tribes of the West are devoting all their energies to this single notion of Supremacy. FORCE is absolutely the most coveted thing—to be strong, the only desirable thing. And the acme of that civilisation of which they boast, glitters only with polished steel, towering high, bristling with terrible weapons of destruction!

There are canals not much used, and not commonly of good depth and width. The High-roads are nearly as good, in some parts, as those in our Flowery Land; but more frequently quite inferior, being either very dusty or muddy. They have none of the conveniences for the shelter or rest of travellers, provided everywhere by our Illustrious; nor are the signal towers and fine shade trees, which give such beauty to our roads, to be seen, excepting occasionally, and quite by chance, the latter.

The Bridges are insignificant, as a rule, owing to the littleness of the rivers; but they are handsome and strong, built of stone, in the Roman style. They span the rivers, the canals, and form *viaducts* [pa-se-gyt] for roads of *Iron*. Upon these roads, passing sometimes over the dwellings and streets of towns, move rapidly the long chain of carriages, drawn by steam-engines, conveying many people and much merchandise. These iron roads are numerous, and the works and buildings connected with them very great and costly. The Barbarians greatly vaunt the usefulness of these roads; but the rightfulness of their opinion is by no means apparent. They break up the quiet and the accustomed industries of the people; excite agitations, produce restlessness and expense, accumulate too many *here*, and depopulate and render meagre *there*. They crowd the cities with the poor, and leave the rural districts empty; the towns are overburdened and the fields untilled. They foster the extravagances of the rich and add nothing to the comfort of the common people. It is said that in the saving of time is a saving of money. But it is to be considered that this ease and rapidity of movement is not always usefully directed. It may be, and it is, largely used only to waste and dissipate money and time. It is said to save material measured in relation to effect. *This* is not clear; for, although a *ton* be moved far quicker to a given point, who shall say that the ton moved by usual means would not, all things estimated, be as economically moved, and with as good result to the common weal?

The real question is not considered, which is—Have Iron-roads added to the useful means of the people? Consider the cost, and say whether such vast expense in other mode or modes of outlay would not have produced means more beneficial.

How much more numerous and better roads, vehicles, buildings for the poor, improved culture, tools, larger areas of recovered lands, new fertilisers, new and numerous schools—innumerable details of improvement—had the intellect, time and money directed to these roads been directed to the many needs of a people! The good, then, is rather the good which activity of brain and outlay of money naturally effect—possibly that activity and expense have not been most usefully employed in Iron-roads—indeed, very probably *not* to the good effect of a more naturally ordered expenditure. But the English, seeing the *effect* of a prodigious activity and employment of money spread over many years, place it to the credit of a *thing*—STEAM; never considering at all whether the thing has been necessarily the cause, or only the accident. To what effect, during the same time, might that same energy and money have been applied! The new power stimulated energy, and possibly misled it. It may be said that steam did its service by giving this stimulus. Probably not so. The question is, Has Steam after all *misled*—fallen short, in fact, of those effects which the usual and less novel forces would have produced? This is an unanswered question.

In the industrial arts the English are not remarkable. They are good in fire-arms and curious in weapons, as may be expected. They are expert in making barrels and vessels to hold liquors from wood; *need*, which they call the mother of invention, made this art a necessity; such is the prodigious quantity of *beer* which they consume. In dress-fabrics, in tools, in furniture, in metals, they show no more skill than our artisans, and in many articles not so much. We have arts, useful and beautiful, unknown to the Barbarians; they have things of mere show and luxury for which we have no use. In what is called *Fine Art*—that is Painting and Sculpture, particularly—we have but little to compare. By *Fine Art* is meant what is impossible to us; it is for the most part intolerable to us.

Think of the Illustrious of our Flowery Kingdom crowding into Halls, glittering with gilt and showy colours, to see there, arranged upon the walls and standing upon marble tables, great pictures of women and of men, often naked or nearly naked—wholly nude figures, mostly of women, in all attitudes, carved from marble, or made of a fine baked clay! Not only so; but the illustrious mothers, wives, daughters, and female friends, accompanying the men to the spectacle! The young man and the young woman together gazing upon the nude and flesh-tinted voluptuous female, glowing in the picture! No; we give no such encouragement to fine Art! Yet our painters compare favourably with those of the Barbarians, in such proper use of the Art as is allowed by us.

For the same reason, as Sculpture with us is only permitted where useful or innocent, it does not reach after such effects as with the Barbarians; where a naked figure of a young woman, done in marble to the luxurious taste of a wealthy High-Caste, will command a great sum. None the less, our Artists can execute with fidelity, as our *Ancestral Halls* will show.

Copying from the ancient Romans, in their most wanton and luxurious period, the kind of painting and sculpture referred to is most highly esteemed by the Christ-god worshippers! Many of the Roman works have been discovered, and serve as models; thus the *ancients* are imitated in their vicious taste, though condemned as very children of the devil!

With the decay of the darker terrors of the Superstition, the mind, rebounding from *asceticism*, swung to the other extreme. A rational morality and worship would have preserved a due medium. But with ancient letters revived a love for ancient art; and the indecencies from that source were condoned to the excellency of the work—or pretended to be. The Priests took no care to repress this outburst of voluptuousness; in truth, moulded its nude forms to the embellishment of Temples; and, holding the warm fancies of its devotees, strengthened their influence by a new device. This zeal for the voluptuous in Art and reproduction of Roman types, began by the Roman Pope, spread everywhere. Thus the *Superstition* itself sanctions this taste, which to us appears so unseemly and immoral.

In Parks and Gardens the English Barbarians are not surpassed. We have no equals in horticulture; but in gardens the English are fine artists, and in parks have caught the true *instinct* of Nature. When in these, I have felt conscious of a fine civilisation. The lovely parterres of blooming shrubs; the grand vases, rich in brilliant colours of delightful flowers; roses, festooned, trailed in arches over smooth walks; green spaces, where the sunlight lay warm and cheerful; noble avenues of lofty trees; sweet arbours, embowered in blossoms and verdant vines; shady walks, meandering among the trees; groves of evergreens, musical with cascades, gleaming in marble basins; and fountains, ornamented and sculptured in shining stone. Little lakes, where the breezes awoke the sleepy waves and chased them to the shore, and where the aquatic birds of many forms delighted to sport! The whole place eloquent and still in beauty! *Here*, no force, nor barbaric rudeness, nor worship of brutal strength, nor of hideous forms, nor of lighted altars! *Here*, the English Barbarian was a civilised man, and here I could love him!

Ah, when shall he, so strong, see his *true* strength, and know how to use it! Arm no more—teach the other Barbarians the proper use of Force! Dreaming no harm to others, fearing no harm to himself, and using the revenues of his great tribe to render it invincible in virtue—how then invincible in all!

One day one of the High-Caste took me under his Illustrious protection, and conveyed me to his grand House, built of hewn stone in the ancient Roman method. It stood among fine trees, a long and glistening *façade* [phr-not] of white and ornamental marble. He presented me to his illustrious wife, who graciously saved me from the too great embarrassment of her presence; for, as I shall hereafter explain, the custom of the Barbarians in this respect shocks all our notions. Hanging upon the gilded walls were the costly works of painters—among them naked women, coloured and tinted, in most voluptuous forms, smiling down upon us—upon sculptured pedestals, stood white statues, in rich marbles, of exquisite maidens, nude, and attractive in every graceful attitude and personal charm! All this was surprising, if not pleasing—but when this Lord [Tchou] took me into the gardens and Park, there, indeed, all was calm—the agitation of my spirit subsided!

Walking with him, he took me by the arm, and said, "Ah, my dear *Chin-le*, how little we know of each other; you do not understand *how* many things can be with us, nor can we understand many of your customs; but *here* we are not unlike—in *this* art we meet on common ground." I expressed my grateful sense of his goodness, assented to his happy reference, and then ventured to observe, "Your illustrious treats me like a relation—a brother." "In what respect—I do not know." "Ah, you presented me to the exalted, the *lady* [da-mtsi]—with us that is to say, *this is a son, or a brother*." He smiled. "Well, perhaps you are right. I rather think you are, in respect of women, though her Ladyship would not assent." I delicately hinted my embarrassment. "The pictures, the ———." He laughed good-humouredly, and replied, "Doubtless to eyes unused, such things look dazzling, and so on, but it is really only a matter of habit." But then, I suggested, "Is not Art misdirected when so employed." "Well, possibly; but an elegant thing, a beautiful thing—why not give an expression to that beauty which is the most interesting, the most charming?" "Does not *that* imply a purity above experience and above nature?" "I see; you lead into an ethical maze—look there?" I followed his hand, and the noble Park extended on all sides; yet, I said to myself, in our Flowery Kingdom, if a point be *doubtful* in morals we lean against the doubt. But is there any doubt as to these *nudities*? However, turning with admiration to the well-trained flowers, the spreading lawns of soft verdure, the beautiful vases of brilliant shrubs, the fine trees, with here and there a modest statue, or a marble fountain, I exclaimed, "How perfectly satisfactory and pleasing are these effects of an elevated Art, where nothing is suggested but what calms, cheers, refines, and makes generous!"

"Ah-Chin, my dear fellow, your enthusiasm is admirable; but we need more than the serene, the cheerful, and the generous!" As he said this he smiled at my look of bewilderment—for I was puzzled. Since then I have understood better. Art among the Barbarians must be suited to the restless eagerness of their nature, which demands excitement. And the passions which ought to be severely repressed, Art, in a hundred ways, finds itself best rewarded to covertly gratify. Thus, all the strong emotions are most coveted, either as shown on the canvas or in the marble. Male figures, nude, writhing, wrestling, and in attitudes of force, or expressing hate, or pain, or fierce contention, or, if in repose, lapsing into the languor of desire. Female figures, for the most part, so managed as to stimulate those feelings, or to suggest those incidents which a wise man likes to ignore; or in such methods as to suggest emotions of shame, of terror, of suffering, or of crime—often debasing or evil in tendency, and rarely to any good purpose. Pictures of bloody fights, of burning cities, of great ships sinking, or *blowing up* with all on board; of wretches tearing or cutting at each other, or struggling in blood and fury amid the waves. Statues distorted by agony, or paralysed by terror—in such, Barbarian Art greatly delights. In this, as in the sculpture of the Temples, showing, in another form, its fierceness and love of strong excitement.

In the cities, there are occasionally statues to men who have been famous; and, in some of the great Temples, Sculptures of High-Castes are sometimes set up. They are, as a rule, strange exhibitions. Many of the great pieces consist of a crowd of figures in marble—an astonishing jumble. There are figures blowing great horns; other impossible ones representing huge human birds hovering about; chiefly, however, naked women, with wings awkwardly fastened behind the shoulders, transporting the dead; and others (again females) with rings of leaves held in their hands over the head of the dead or dying man! All this is done, or attempted to be done, in marble; and involved in it will be a great ship burning, or great guns being fired, and men and women being killed by hundreds; or other dreadful scenes wherein the great man took fearful part! Memorials or huge paintings, in honour of persons famous in fight and plunder, are thus exhibited in the Temples and public Halls. They are, in general, very astonishing!

In the street corners are sometimes placed, on pedestals of huge stone, carved effigies of a King, or of a Queen, or of some High-Caste man. Of some Brave, who has cut off more heads than usual, or who has seized more plunder, or carried fire and sword over the lands of distant tribes. He is sometimes on horse-back; sometimes naked, with shield and sword, and very terrible; sometimes so far aloft, on top of a high stone column, that nothing can be descried but a *cocked hat* and a pigmy figure under it. Rarely there may be a statue to some High-Caste, who has been distinguished for wringing more taxes from the common people, and, by this means, keeping large armed bands at work abroad—to the glory of the English name! more rarely a statue to the memory of any one renowned for a life useful to mankind.

As works of Art, these things are not to be criticised. They are works of *money*—that is, paid for by weight; merely meant to compliment a *party* or faction in the State, and not to honour, particularly, the subject of the Work, or to give a noble expression of human genius or skill. No purpose, perhaps, in the sordid workman other than to pocket the large sum for the big show! Nothing wherein a grand imagination, inspired by a fine enthusiasm and full of a noble conception, glows and breathes in the stone, and makes it imperishable!

Whether an unconscious *disgust* leave these public statues and monuments alone in their ugliness, I know not; but they are totally neglected, begrimed, covered with filth—often made the roosting-places of the unwashed street *Arabs* (beggar boys) and *loafers* [na-sthi]. Even the statues of living Sovereigns are so totally forgotten and deserted, that the nose of *Majesty* may be a small pyramid of dirt, and the ermine robes more defiled and foul than the rags of the street mendicant!

The Western Barbarians are very fond of *Science* [kno-tu-ze]—(this is the nearest word in our language, though quite defective)—and consider themselves in *this* to be far superior to the ancients and to all the peoples beyond the great Seas. I have never been able to comprehend, nor do I think the Barbarians themselves comprehend very accurately, the meaning of the word.

They will say of a man who is almost a fool, "Ah! but he is very scientific." Of another, constantly blundering, and who has been famous for prodigies of mistake, "His science is astonishing." A builder of a great ship, or of a great bridge, sees his ship upset or his bridge fall down; none the less, he demonstrates to his admiring countrymen that, upon *scientific* principles, the ship should have stood upright and the bridge been as stable as rock!

A doctor kills his patient [vi-zton] scientifically; a dentist cracks the jaw in extracting a tooth; a surgeon breaks the leg which he cannot set: *Science* is satisfied—"all was scientifically done!" A man spends his life in looking at the stars; he is a man of wonderful science. Another keeps a List of fair and rainy days during twelve moons; his scientific attainments are respected and his *observations* recorded, as if the fate of the harvests were involved.

You will hear of a man of marvellous science, before whom ordinary scientific men stand uncovered in silence; he has discovered a new kind of *tadpole*, and added another to the already interminable *terms* of natural Science.

I have heard one of these learned *professors* [pho-phe-sti] say wisely, "He is a benefactor of the race who makes two blades of grass to grow where one grew before;" "but," he added, "he is a greater who teaches mankind how to do this." In this way, wishing to show that an *idiot* might chance to find a way to double his growth of grass, but would be incapable of discovering the *cause*; so that, probably, the accident would die with the finder. A wise man would, at once, look for the reason, and finding *that*, be able to secure the benefit for all time. This knowledge of cause is the kind called *Science*.

The explanation is familiar to us. In our Flowery Kingdom, the master teaches the rules, and the artificer puts them in practice. We call him an Artisan who has knowledge of an Art: we call him who knows how things ought to be done, and who examines into things so as to comprehend the best modes of doing, simply a teacher, or master. We do not see that his knowledge, without actual performance, makes him a great man—a man of Science (as the Barbarians have it). Indeed, if a man do a thing merely mechanically, as a horse turns a mill, no doubt he is an ignorant artisan. Still, this stupidity does not exalt, in any degree, the nature of the knowledge of a brighter man: this one is only an intelligent artisan. On the whole, then, it seemed to me that the Barbarians, for the most part very ignorant, were easily imposed upon by those who, having leisure, mastered the multiform *terms* (or some of them) used by the teachers of Natural History in its various departments. These, too, idle and with some ambition to be known, easily fancied that the dry knowledge of words *was* knowledge; and discovering with surprise at first, but soon with great complacency, how very little one need to know to be ranked with men of *Science*, at length prided themselves upon the very trivialities which otherwise would have been unvalued. In fact, finally imposed upon themselves as they imposed upon others, and really believed those trifles *to be* important, because confined to those who paraded them as Scientific. These busy, idle triflers in words become *the men of Science.*

This is very laughable, and shows how mankind, everywhere, constantly repeat the same follies. In our Illustrious annals men like these have appeared and disappeared; founded schools, been admired, had disciples, then passed into oblivion; their works, often voluminous, never met with; or occasionally dug out of mouldy bins and reproduced in some parts to show up the pretensions of a *new* charlatan—to show how much better the same things were explained, or the same terms used by an old and forgotten author, 5,000 moons ago!

These men, as with us, constantly overrate the value of their labours; the world really can get on without them. Getting together in *Congresses* [Bed-la-mi], they pay (or affect) great respect to each other, and put on an *air* of abstraction; they are supposed to be pondering upon the care of men and things, and feel the weight of responsibility. Other men may be trivial; but to those upon whom rests the due ordering of Nature, Care should be a genius and Dignity a presence.

In these Meetings, nothing is worthy of debate unless it be *Scientific*. A plain paper, directed to a simple, useful object, and stating in ordinary and intelligible language the rules useful to the end, is not satisfactory. There should be something novel and obscure, or it is unlikely to come within the desired category. In truth, high and mighty *principles* on which man and the gods exist and move and flourish, or upon a disregard of which decay and dissolution follow—these are alone the proper objects of philosophers and men of Science; and involved in the profound investigation of *principles*, the Congress disappears from the common eye, and is lost even to itself!

On the whole, the value of these scientific men to the world did not seem to me to be considerable. I mean as *scientific men*—without any of the pretension or cant [Bo-zhe] of their class, individuals may be useful, and would be more useful without the false glamour of class-vanity. A man of brain and who really thinks and examines, if he have anything to say will say it, and it will be judged by its merit. But when men having *time* and not knowing what to do with themselves, and having some knowledge of words and but *little brains*, see an *opening for imbecility*, and are received and praised and dubbed *Scientific*, because they devote time and waste a large quantity of paper to give the world *their thoughts*—it is doubtful whether the more harm or the more good be done. To be sure, the idle and empty man may be rendered supremely happy in his vanity, and may have been saved from some personal degradation or vicious inclination—but the world could have been well spared his *Catalogue of the Parasites* on the Lobster, or his *Notes on the Habits of the Barn Swallow*, or his *Suggestions* as to the proper use of smoke, or his *Hints* upon the hybernation of Eels. No great harm is done, for nobody reads these things but the men of Science, who are obliged to keep up to the work of busy idleness, in reading for debate with each other and at the *Congress*.

This body professes to teach the proper rules for physical improvement, and its members are natural philosophers. They do not, however, confine themselves to the investigation of natural phenomena—they range over the whole broad field of speculation as well, demanding to know the cause of all things, and the very essence, object, and end. Those who take upon themselves this wider inquiry, assume a dignity far above the mere *Scientists*—these deal with mere visible *forms*; but those with the *laws* which underlie the forms, and with the source of Law, its origin, its object, and its end! These are PHILOSOPHERS! and when a man is a man of Science *and* a philosopher, then no more is possible to human exaltation!

I have sufficiently referred to the *works* of these in another place. They cannot be wholly useless, if there really be a *brain*, honest and strong, at work. For to such patiently, humbly, earnestly, full of grateful recognition and conscious of the limitations of knowledge and of inquiry; seeking and looking out, with sad eyes, upon the vast world; to such, some new evidence of the grand order, some new and brilliant ray of divine illumination may come—*not* to show *cause* nor purpose, but to delight and tranquillise, to give new assurance of the Beneficent and Infinite Wisdom!

The English Barbarians have true men of Science. They are those to whom the people are indebted for nearly all of the useful discoveries and inventions. Men, who, engaged in some pursuit, apply a patient investigation and thoughtful experiments to see if they cannot *improve* the existing *means to ends*. In these investigations, they discover a new source or a new *way* of power; and, in the experiments, new applications and uses of it. When these men fall into the hands of the *Scientists* and Philosophers, and, leaving their work-shops, *shine with the gods*, at the Congresses—they usually end in that *glamour*—their light is no longer an illumination!

Of the musical Art, some things may be said. There is a wonderful variety of instruments—not many at all like ours.

Some of the stringed are similar to our *Che*. There is one, so enormous a structure, as to equal a house in size. It is made by a wonderful combination of hollow, metal pipes, ranging in size from a flute to a big cannon; and in height from a span to the lower mast of a ship. Its sounds are many, single in melody, or astonishing in a wild, clanging harmony (the Barbarians think); but to me, discord. All the combined noises are terrific; and surpass what the effect would be of our *Che*, *Yuhnien*, and *Pieu-king* all sounding at once!

In Singing, the men often roar like bulls, and the women scream, making hideous contortions. A handsome woman does not like to sing.

There is a Theatre—play—where all the parts, men and women, are sung. The passions of love, hate, jealousy, and so on, are sung and screamed at each other by the players in the most absurd manner. The woman will sing and shriek out the most astonishing *gymnasts* of voice, the man shouting and bellowing back, and then both together bellow and scream; the woman, at last, falls into the arms of the man, or the man throws himself in a passion at the feet of the woman—both singing and screaming all the while—and the curtain drops! Then arise the noisy plaudits of the spectators—demanding a repetition!

The barbaric music is, for the most part, like themselves, rude and noisy. There are some exceptions—and in simple melody often sweet and tender. The *flute* and the *horn* are pleasing—the former is much like our *Cheng*.

Occasionally, one or two thousand singers, and as many performers on instruments come together, and give a grand *Musical Treat*. Judge what this must be, when you add to this vast combination also the prodigious *House of Noise* (called Organ)!

Oratory is an Art much admired among the Western tribes, and the English think themselves to be prëeminent. I can hardly judge; one needs to be a perfect master of a tongue to follow a speaker as he ought to be followed. Barbarous races commonly produce effective Orators; the imagination is vivid, the passions strong, and there is enough culture to make the forms of speech at least tolerable.

In the Law-making *Houses* speeches (orations) are often delivered. For the most part dull in manner, insignificant in thought, poor in illustration, very ineffective. The members go to sleep, or withdraw, or rudely interrupt— sometimes *coughing* down the speaker. Very rarely are to be seen any flashes of eloquence, to be felt any thrill of its power. Unfortunately the same conceit, here as elsewhere, leads many to believe themselves to be Orators to whom the ability to speak properly is denied by nature. Yet these insist upon "airing their eloquence" (as it is styled) on every occasion possible. Generally these men have some subject, nick-named by the other members as a Hobby, which must be spoken to whether the House will hear or not. Then occurs one of those scenes so characteristic. The Hobby-man rises and tries to speak. He waxes eloquent (at least, he intends to be) on his favourite topic—perhaps the Pope at Rome; or the *rights of women*; or the *purification* of mud-streams; or the poor man's *beer*; no matter what, when the other members determined to drown the speaker, break through all the rules of the House, the orders of the Head officer, and more, all the ordinary decencies, and *caterwaul*, and *cough* and *howl*, till, from mere impossibility of hearing his own voice, the poor, *squelched* orator sinks into his seat.

Now, the House prides itself upon the *liberty* of speech and of debate; it is *one* of the palladia of English Freedom; and this is a forcible illustration *of the liberty*. Anything obnoxious to the majority, or even to a noisy minority, may be silenced—such is the freedom of debate!

The English Barbarians especially boast that the Great Council (Law-Houses) is not only the foremost of all national councils, whether ancient or modern, in character and in wisdom, but also in dignity, and the extreme care with which is guarded that most inestimable of all *Institutions*, the Sacred *liberty of Speech*!

There is a kind of oratory, sometimes contemptuously called Pulpit-oratory by the English, which may be referred to, because it forms a considerable part of the literary entertainment. Once a week, on the *Holy* day, ten thousand speeches or more are uttered by the Bonzes from a high place (called *Pulpit*) within the Temples. From the place of delivery the name mentioned is given to this kind of speech-making. The speech is known by one name—*Sermon*. These sermons form a part of the *rites* in the Temples, and are therefore numberless and never ceasing. As ought to be expected, they are as dull as such a formal thing must be. Some Bonze, new to his office, may attempt to give a little life to the performance. But the High-Caste do not like to be disturbed by any novelties; they prefer comfortably to sleep in the soft seats with high-backed supports, where their fathers have slept, Holy-day after Holy-day, for generations before them. They will not have the Bonze, therefore, thunder the terrors of Jah in *their* ears, nor affright *their* wives and children by painting Hell and the Devil. Eloquence, therefore, in the Temples, if it exist, must be content to glide softly over "green pastures," murmuring drowsily with "meandering streams."

The *lower-sects* are not so disposed to neglect their duty. With these the Bonze is expected to be "instant, in season and out of season," in the work of Jah. His *terrors* and the awful Hell; the wiles of Satan; the agony of the damned; the danger of neglecting repentance; the need of Salvation; the glorious Gospel; the blessedness of the redeemed; the worthlessness of good works; the absolute loss, here and hereafter, *of failing to Believe*; all these *canons* are vomited forth from the pulpit with an energy, and, sometimes, when directed to *unbelievers*, with a vindictive ferocity, startling and overpowering. The hearers do not sleep; even the boldest tremble, and the timid and weak sometimes go into convulsions of fear.

There are itinerant Orators, who go about the country making speeches (and trying to make money) upon all sorts of subjects. They are rarely effective, though occasionally, when they happen to seize upon a popular fancy, or to stir up some popular feeling, they gain a certain attention from the Lower-Castes. Whenever effective, it is by blending some of the strong points of the Idolatry with the prevailing agitation. If there be some matter concerning which the populace presume to have any opinion, then the itinerant speaker has his chance; and he is doubly influential if he mix in his discourse a good proportion of matter taken from the *Sacred Writings* and the *Canons*—this he distributes, to damn opposers and to reward adherents, with a combined Priestly and Lay vivacity and force!

We have, and have always had, ample specimens of these self-elected teachers and speakers; and they receive with us, in general, about the same neglectful consideration accorded to them by the Barbarians.

On a review, it must be admitted that the Western tribes are ingenious in domestic arts, and not wanting in invention. In the fine Arts they are sometimes effective, though immoral—merely imitating the ancient Roman-Greeks, whom they call *Masters*. Their architecture, when worth attention, is Roman. But they have produced one novelty, *the Gothic*—a wonderful outgrowth of the Barbaric mind, formed by its great Superstition. In painting, when confined to natural scenery and objects, they are sometimes very pleasing and correct. But in this department, where they are not immoral, they are often repulsive, seeking for startling effects, caught from the strongest passions. True Art elevates, refines, and pleases. It never lends itself to *deformity*, to the bad passions, to baseness. And it cannot sully *itself* by tampering with impure things. It recognises the twofold nature of man, and addresses itself to his *moral instinct* and love of divine beauty.

CHAPTER IX.
OF AMUSEMENTS, GAMES, AND SPECTACLES.

WHEN the lowest-caste takes a *holiday*, decent people keep away from the place of resort, as they would from pestilence. The coarseness, indecency, and uncleanliness are too revolting. Not that they really differ in the ways of enjoying themselves; but from their personal brutishness.

The remarks following refer to those above them, and to the great body of the *people*, when at spectacles and public resorts.

To me, unaccustomed to it, the presence of women everywhere perplexed and surprised. In days of sports, eating, drinking beer, gin, and other drinks, romping of the sexes, and an incessant restlessness, are very noticeable. In the open grounds, all kinds of sports and games are going on; women and men dance, whirl about upon seats, rush after and chase each other, swing in swings, all in a wild revelry! There will be games where the woman is now pursued, and now the man; and now shouting, screaming, giggling, struggling and kissing, men and women rush after each other, catch each other; and then, reforming in ranks, go through the same wild pranks again.

The chief out-door sports are horse-racing, boat-racing, hunting upon horseback, bats and balls, foot-races, and the like. In-door: the theatres, the dancing-halls, the circus, and a great variety of shows and spectacles. Women attend upon all, and take a part in all—or nearly all. In the theatre, the circus, the dances, and many other places and things, they take the most conspicuous parts.

Horse-racing is esteemed as the greatest of all spectacles; and ranks as worthy of a national support. The Highest-Castes—even the Sovereign—attend. The Law-making Houses, the Great Officers of Administration, and the High-Bonzes, leave the duties of their exalted rank, and postpone the making and ordering of the Laws, to attend the *Races*. The Illustrious wives, daughters, and female relatives—even royalty—hasten to them, and esteem them as the best of all sports.

Every Caste—thieves, beggars, jugglers, the very *scum* of the cities; *loafers*, vagrants—rich, poor; men, women, children—every description of person, rush or crawl to the *Races*. Every sort of vehicle, every mode of conveyance is used: on horseback, on foot; in any way, the enormous multitudes crowd to the *Races*—it is the English Saturnalia (as an ancient Roman festival, noted for its licentiousness, was called)—I have heard the word *punned* [joakd] *Satan-ail'ye*, by jesters—meaning the *Devil is in it*. Not a bad notion, having reference to the evil effects of the sport.

On both sides of the space where the horses are to run, immense numbers of carriages of all descriptions, booths, stands and seats, are arranged, where the vast crowds stand, or sit, pushing, elbowing; whilst the horses are *trotted* out, and the *race* is duly prepared. At length, a great many horses, ridden by little men, looking like Apes, rush off at a signal; spurred, whipped, urged by the riders into madness, with eyes bloodshot, and nostrils distended, and every cord and muscle starting out and straining—whilst the multitudes of men and women stand up, shouting, leaping, screaming with excitement—sweep like a whirlwind along the course, and pass the goal! And thousands of gold are lost and won! By as little as a head, or a neck, one of the horses is declared to be winner! The name of the horse is sent all over the Barbarian world, and the *event* is watched for by millions—because bets are made, not only upon the ground, but in every part.

I can hardly explain to the people of our Central Kingdom, the excitement and the confusion of this scene. The most illustrious men and women are present; the great Bonzes are there—all classes, the lowest and highest, jumbled together, if not in contact, all carried away by the same wild passion. About the splendid equipages of the rich, mere human vermin crawl and fight for the crumbs and bones which fall, or are thrown from the feasting women and men, carousing in the carriages. In these, beautiful women laugh and bet with the men, drink the wines, and exchange a hundred smiles and jokes. Betting books are opened, and the women take bets and plunge into the vortex of the phrensy. The race is over, and thousands are impoverished, many utterly ruined.

With us the Theatre is merely a public, out-door spectacle, of no importance, amusing the ordinary crowd, and free from immorality. Women take no part in the representations—boys, dressed as females, playing for women. But with the Barbarians the Theatre is an organisation of government, and receives the highest support. Women act, and are more popular with the spectators than the men.

The first in estimation is the *Opera*. In this representation, as I have said in another place, the action goes on, all in *Singing*. To me nothing could be more ludicrous, more in defiance of all reason and nature. The most terrible emotions—fear, hate, envy, as well as the tender; love, affection, friendship—all sung, and not merely sung, but bellowed, screamed, shrieked, in every contortion of throat and mouth!

In the Tragic performance the fierceness of the Barbarians delights in dreadful murders, plots, assassinations; in things which tear and lacerate human feelings, and bring despair and death!

The Comic is as coarse in loose *buffoonery* [Kro-sen-to-se] as the tragic is for an extreme of agony, based upon crime and baseness.

But the most astonishing of all the representations upon the Stage is the *Ballet.* I should not dare nor desire to refer to this, were it not to illustrate a point in the Barbarian character, only too prominent; and to give further cause to the people of our *Flowery Land* to be thankful to the Sovereign Lord, that He has not permitted such mark of degeneracy to stain us.

The Ballet is supervised by a very High-Caste Lord. It is composed of a band of young women, selected for beauty of form and of limb. They appear in public nearly naked, or so clothed in tightest hose [ki-i-e] and draped in thinnest diaphanous fabric, that what is concealed is half disclosed and more piquant than if left uncovered. Troops of these appear—dazzling in white or pink—upon the stage-floor. Before they show themselves to the public, however, they parade, one by one (as I was truly informed), before the High-Caste Supervisor of the Ballet, who, with his assistants, duly examines the legs, arms, busts, and drapery, to see if all be in due order. The drapery is carefully measured to see if it be of the required length, and, if too short, must be extended to the knees. Not to cover anything, but to satisfy a pretence. For these transparent fabrics, aside from *that* quality, are so contrived that they float off from the body and limbs with every movement—and the motions studied are those which produce this effect—twirling around rapidly being a chief feat. When the High-Caste is satisfied that there be nothing to offend the most delicate, and that all the demands of a pure *Christ-god* morality are satisfied, he sends the young girls to the stage, and they appear in the *Ballet.*

This is a dance—why should I say more. But consider this dance is before the highest and best—in an immense and brilliantly lighted, lofty house. There are vast crowds, seated upon a level with, or just below the stage—in rows, one row above another, forming a grand half-circle, from the floor to the dome; so high, that the faces cannot be distinguished. Then the rich and glittering decorations; the paintings, the sculptures, the music!

The music of innumerable instruments strikes up. In come the troops of half-naked girls; their busts, their legs exposed. In they come, leaping, dancing, twirling, whirling, flying! They twirl around on the toes like tops. They spin on a single toe, sticking out the other leg—and, in this attitude, revolve about! They retreat, advance, stoop, go backward, forward; twisting, twirling, throwing themselves, their arms, and particularly their legs, into all possible positions; whirling about on one leg and extending the other, being the most admired feat! This is (very faint) the *Ballet*!

Mothers, wives, husbands, daughters, sons, lovers, maidens, look upon this spectacle—and pray for the benighted Heathen!

Englishmen often remarked to me, jocosely, "Ah-Chin—no like the Ballet—why, the Theatre nowadays *stands* on Legs!"

It is a fact that, in those times which the Barbarians call *dark*, when ignorance and brutality marked the whole aspect of common life, the *instinct* of decency prevented women from appearing on the Stage at all. It is quite a modern invention.

The Circus is another favourite show. In this, women appear, ride the horses, fly in the air, walk upon ropes tightly drawn above the spectators, and form a main feature. They make the same study of exposing themselves, and are undressed like the women in the *Ballet*. They give to the performance the same kind of stimulus, to which is added the further excitement of danger. For in leaping, flying through the air, vaulting, and walking upon the tight-rope high above the spectators; the probability of a broken back, or neck, gives a new sensation.

In the warm weather, the English Barbarians find great amusement in crowding to the Sea. Here, little houses placed on wheels are trundled into the waves. From these, women, men, and children wade, and plash and dive into the water. The women, and even children, often swim very well— the men nearly all. The two sexes bathe quite near, or together, in full sight of the people on the shore. Here, on the sands, thousands are walking, sitting, and lounging about, amusing themselves in the idlest sports. The men in the water are, with the exception of a mere loin-cloth, naked. The women, though tolerably covered, yet so carelessly that, with the motions of the bath and waves, they are sufficiently exposed! In these sea-bathing places you will see Barbarian life in all its rudeness, and love of boisterous fun and frolic. The men, and women, and children, abandon themselves to eating, drinking, bathing in the sea-water; to sports and games; to dancing, sight-seeing, and *match-making*. The last is the pursuit of husband-catching, which the free-and-easy life at the sea-side greatly facilitates.

Boat-races—sailing boats, and boats rowed or paddled—take place at these sea-side places, and are greatly admired. They are unobjectionable, and natural to a maritime tribe.

A strange feature is to see women go fearlessly into boats, and, hustled with the men, enjoy the excitement of the wind and wave, to witness these races, or merely for the frolic—but women are everywhere!

The Cattle Shows are characteristic. Here, fat cattle, sheep, fat swine, fine horses, poultry, tools used in tillage, fruit and vegetables, are shown; and the best receive prizes. Only a few of the High-Castes attend these, and then merely as a form. The real support comes from the farmers; and from the *Lower-Castes.* These crowd to the show, paying at the doors, merely for frolic and fun. Open to late hours at night, with music, lights, and places for eating and drinking, the mixed crowd of men and women delight in the hustling, crowding. The usual beer and other drinks are ready; the usual giggling of women, surging, and elbowing, and pushing about! One wonders much, whether the fat animals are not more respectable than the animals which crowd about them! But I can hardly fairly judge of the real *character* of the crowds, for they are too novel and too offensive to the habits of our Flowery Land. It is certain, however, that the Barbaric element always perverts the most useful things; and a Cattle Show must be debased and turned aside from its proper objects. What have the women and men, who push and surge about the brutes, of interest in the thing? Nothing. They may know and care for sheep, when *roasted,* or for fat swine, when in the shape of a *rasher* [fri-ie-tz].

The most curious, and, perhaps, most important of out-door scenes is the *Hustings.* When there is a vacant place in the Lower-Law-House (of the great Council), the Sovereign commands a new member to be chosen by those who have the right, in the town entitled to send. A sort of stage is put up in the market-place, and here those meet who are to be *hustled* for. Hustings comes from this word, and means *to shake together in confusion.* There are some who wish to send A., others who wish to send B. Accordingly, these are seized by their struggling supporters; each side endeavouring to put upon the stage *its* man, and each trying to put off the man of the other side! One may judge of the *hustling.* Each candidate submits to every sort of indignity. The *hustlers* (voters, generally called) are chiefly of the Lower (not Lowest) Caste, and enjoy this privilege mightily. Beyond the immediate actors are the associates of the two parties—not having a right to *hustle*; but, none the less, aiding in the general struggle, by pelting with rotten eggs, garbage, or other harmless (sometimes not harmless) nastiness [phu-fo], the man whom they dislike. Finally, one of the men is got upon the stage; entitled to be the new member for having had the larger number of *indignities* put upon him, and come out a-top! These are—to have the head-covering driven violently down over the face—to be befouled with stinking eggs and garbage, and all the time to say, "*Free and independent voters,*" accompanied by bows and grimaces, intended for *smiles*!

If the Lower-House, however, find on examination that some one has hustled twice—that is, thrown two missiles, then the scene must be rëenacted! For it is thought to be too dangerous to allow of this unfairness. If one could do this on the one side, then it would be done on the other; and in the excitement, things harder than mud would be thrown, to the danger of life! As to the outside throwers, the police take care that they do not exceed mud, filth, rotten eggs, and vegetables!

When the new member is chosen, he is called upon by his supporters to thank them in a speech. He rises to do this, and, bowing, says, "I am powerless to express my grateful sense of the honour. *Free and independent voters*"—at this moment a half-drunken supporter of the defeated man gives the signal. The rotten egg has fairly hit the new member in the face; the crowd on the one side and on the other rush in *pell-mell*; the stage is broken down; stones, sticks, clubs, brickbats, are used and fly about freely; noses bleed; heads are cracked; oaths and yells arise! The new member, surrounded by his supporters, finally conquers; and, placed in a chair, is lifted by strong arms to the shoulders of sturdy men, who bear him to his illustrious house, where his exalted wife and noble friends receive him with delight. The tumultuous crowd are feasted by the Servants; and, finally, yelling and shouting for *my Lord*—the new member—he appears at a lofty window above them, thanks them once more, and disappears. The rabble leave the place, the gates are closed, and my lord and lady can congratulate themselves and be congratulated that the *farce* is over. Power and influence remain with them—*the indignities are all washed off*—it is merely English humour.

In these Hustings the Illustrious wives and daughters, as well as all male relatives, take part, and are obliged to take their share of the *indignities*. The dirty child of a low-caste (who happens to have a right to *hustle*) will be taken upon the silken lap of *my Lady*, and feel boldly in my Lady's pocket for pennies; and the daughter of my Lady sits down upon the stool and feeds the hungry *old hag* of aged poverty. The old hag being ill, and mother to the *hustler*. In this way, and on these rather infrequent occasions, the bold Englishman of Low-Caste vindicates his manhood and shows his power in the State. But it is a mere form. The High-Castes understand the Barbaric temper, and consider this mode of amusing it the cheapest and least inconvenient. There is a struggle sometimes for the new membership between individuals, but these are always of the High-Caste connection and order. Actual power does not exist in the hustling rabble—*that* is in the High-Caste. Nevertheless, sometimes the *Hustlers* can determine which of two shall be sent; and, therefore, it is necessary, when more than one desires to go, to submit to the *hustling*. Nearly all the worst *indignities* are omitted when only one person is named. In this case, all the hustlers being of a mind, they do not inflict more than the *accustomed* indignities, which are moderate in comparison; though one would think sufficiently humiliating.

In the civic processions, which occur when a new magistrate is appointed to a city, one observes how the old barbaric features still predominate. Like children those things are most esteemed which grown people disdain or laugh at. Rude force and the emblems of it; men absurdly accoutred in old, fantastic arms and armour; banners which once marshalled trained men to war; gilt and golden vehicles, conveying priests and officials; these carrying glittering baubles in their hand; loud music and bands of curiously dressed braves; these things delight the multitude, which comes swarming out from every hole and corner of the city. Such crowds of both sexes, with children even in arms! Nowhere out of these Barbaric and populous tribes can such a spectacle be seen. The vast throngs rush and push about, and woe to that decent man who gets entangled among them! Often the selfish, reckless hordes, rushing through some street with a new purpose, overwhelm and crush every moving thing in the way.

Women, children, strong men, are often thrown down, maimed; even killed outright! Thieves, beggars, the indescribable *scum* of degraded humanity, mixed with the crowd (in its own character but little removed from lowest debasement), give it an air of unspeakable disgust!

Of these Civic Spectacles, *a Coronation* is supreme. This only takes place when a new Sovereign is crowned. No one is admitted to the actual Ceremony but the highest of the High-Castes. The common people, who bear nearly all the taxes to pay for the enormous cost, must be content to get such glimpses of the passing pageant, as is possible to them, at the risk of limb and of life. The whole thing is so guarded by armed bands, on horseback and on foot, with fire-arms ready, and swords drawn, that it is only by rushing close to the horsemen, and pressing upon the foot-braves, that any glimpse can be got by the common multitude; and for these mere glances—under the bellies of horses, or between their legs, or through some iron railings, or the like—the devoted barbarians will risk their lives. Such is the admiration which this great show attracts!

It is thus admired, not only because of the awfulness of the CROWN, but also because the Idolatry plays so large a part in it. The new King is always crowned by a Highest Bonze, in his costly priestly robes, and anointed with *holy* oil; whilst the *Sacred Writings* and Incantations are duly read and uttered! The worship of Christ-Jah and the other gods, are all pledged, together with all the Canons and beliefs, including the Divine Revelation of the Jewish *Sacred Writings*; in fact, the ceremony, in the Priestly part, is Jew throughout!

The scene is characteristically barbaric. Force, and glittering display; all the jewels, the gewgaws, the golden rods, orbs, bowls, sticks; the spears, swords, steel armour, helmets; the robes, furs, silks, velvets; jewelled garters for the legs; ornamented chains in gold, for the neck; coronets, for the hereditary *nobles* [Hi-fi]; cassocks, gowns, mitres, staffs; scarlet and crimson cloths, cloaks, and waving plumes of the great braves; men in steel, on horseback—all these things, and a thousand more! With the grand women, and the High Lords! all are present. All is show and glitter; and childish! In the midst, out there rides a man, all covered with steel armour, with a long and flashing spear, who, sitting proudly on his horse, looks defiance! A trumpet sounds; another dashes forward, and proclaims the new Monarch; then the first, with a loud voice, defies to mortal combat any one who dares to challenge the right of the proclaimed Sovereign—and, thereupon, throws down a glove [kang]. If any one should pick up the glove, it would imply an acceptance of the challenge. No one takes up the glove. The trumpets sound, the music strikes up in a hundred places; the vast multitude cry and shout, "*Long live the renowned, the exalted, the Illustrious!*"— and the new-crowned man is King!

In this barbaric display, the money expended is enormous in amount. The jewels and mere inanities are so costly that, put to proper use, poverty would scarcely exist. Nor is this all; the High-Caste get all the honours and emoluments, though they bear but a small part of the expense. Many of this Caste hold *hereditary* offices connected with this Show, from which they derive revenue and high honour! One may be hereditary *sword-bearer*, another *cup-bearer*, another *towel-holder*, another *bottle-washer*. Nor is this sort of sinecure (*name* for frivolous, useless Service) confined to males; females may be hereditary *folders of the Queen's night-cap, washers of the baby-linen, keepers of the robes, maids of the bed-chamber*, and so on! Still, such is the ignorance and debasement of the common people, and even of the better classes, that, although they pay for these expensive whimsicalities and barbarisms, and never by any chance share in the personal benefits, *they admire them*; and believe them to be, in some mysterious way, connected with their *glorious constitution and privileges*!

I scarcely like to speak of the displays by the *braves*. These are those on horseback, those on foot, those with horses, and cannons mounted on wheels; and some who march partly, and partly ride. Our *Flowery Kingdom* knows these armed bands, and how rude and disorderly they are. How they plunder and kill the defenceless, and burn and destroy! How fierce they are, and how reckless of order, even to their own chiefs!

But I will refer to the main display of these armed bands. Once or twice in twelve moons, all the bands being assembled, are divided into two parts. Each part has a great Chief at the head, with horsemen, footmen, and those with the wheeled-cannon.

One of these Divisions is sent to a distance, and the other is kept at hand. Then the one near is commanded to act as if the distant force was an enemy, who, having landed, was marching into the country to subdue it. In this way, it is intended to teach the armed bands to march, countermarch, hide, seek, advance, retreat, get into ambuscade, get out of it, rush up hills, rush down hills, cross rivers, make bridges, construct roads; *pretend* to blow up and to construct earth-forts; *pretend* to charge, to fire, to shoot, to rush with horses, to swiftly move and fire the cannons, each against the other; to skirmish in small squads [kong], and fight in large bands—in fine, to carry on a *Military campaign* (as the Barbarians term this prodigious nonsense). Some one said to me, "A very *sham pain*." It seemed to me no sham to the soldiers—so far as *toil* is concerned.

How, in carrying out this tomfoolery [hen-di-ho-ty], bands of armed men may be seen scattered over a wide range of country. Smoke of fire-arms and reports of the cannons may be seen and heard, in different parts—and a quiet traveller may be surprised to see suddenly a band of men, armed, rapidly approaching, with the bright steel glistening in the sun; and, levelling these steel-spears affixed to the fire-arms, see them rush, *pell-mell*, upon a row of bushes, firing and shouting—then, suddenly recoiling, rush back and hurry to shelter behind some *other row*! Then cannon will bang, and smoke will rise from among trees near the place; and the horses will be seen advancing rapidly, dragging after them the cannon, which, being planted on a hill, fire and bang away; then, all at once, some great braves, with feathers flying, and swords flashing, will rush directly upon the cannon, even right into the mouths!

Then *pell-mell* other horsemen, cutting and slashing with long swords, and firing off little fire-arms, will be seen; and soon long lines of foot-braves will appear among the trees and bushes, and some will rush upon the others, and others rush upon them, firing and banging away, in a manner very surprising; and this is a *sham-fight*. Sometimes the braves get so excited that they really do fight in good earnest. As there is nothing but powder in the fire-arms, the danger is in the swords and spears, which are sometimes so used in the heat and excitement that many braves are really hurt.

When all is over the head braves of the two forces make Reports of the doings of their respective divisions, complimenting the braves and the head men upon their discipline and order.

On one occasion the Royal Prince and his attendants rode directly upon the mouths of a battery of cannon. Now the whole idea of the *Sham* is that everybody is to conduct himself precisely *as if* the doings were real. Any head-brave who forgets this is disorderly and liable to punishment. What would have been the fate of the Royal party had the cannon which they rode directly upon, been charged with balls as well as powder! It is not to be found, however, that the Great Brave in his Report referred to this extraordinary exploit of the Royal Prince.

With an enemy, real, deadly, strong, advancing into the country, then indeed the braves would have work which would stir all their wits and nerve all their strength. Marches in rain and mud; toilsome nights; work in the ditches; cold and biting winds; wakeful and wearisome watchings; all endured manfully, and hardly noticed *because it is real*. Even a pauper disdains make-believe toil, and takes the pittance tendered for it as an insult. To the common man all this labour and exposure is very hard and very real—all the more so, because it is mere noise and smoke. No wonder that he is careless and indifferent; no wonder that he curses the nonsense which wearies him without giving him any satisfaction. Show him true, honest need; where the enemy of his tribe lurks, and he is alert, active; calls up all his intelligence, looks to his arms, looks about him, and feels no fatigue. But this—he loses discipline, and is really demoralised by a *Sham*.

Still the Barbarians greatly admire all this noise and blustering; and the Head-Braves fancy that the bands are improved in order and in knowledge of arms; that they would really understand how to meet a genuine enemy more skilfully, by having *made-believe* to fight a friend. All human experience shows the opposite of this to be true; for the *sham* is certain to *entail* some of its mischief and injure the very qualities which it is supposed to improve. In the nature of things this affair cannot be good. The object is a sham— everything, therefore, about it is sham. The fight is a sham, and the fighter is a sham-brave, and, therefore, worthless. Who doubts that he is injured by this pitiful work?

When these armed bands march in the displays made on public occasions, then, knowing that they are doing true work with a true object, they enter into it with spirit. Every man feels himself to be a part of a fine whole, and interests himself to do his best. These displays of the numerous armed men, marching with banners, bright swords and spears, with cannon, great troops of horses, long columns of glittering steel flashing in the sun, with brilliant coverings and gay colours, and the loud clanging music—these attract great multitudes. Whilst the High-Caste Braves, on grand horses, clothed in bright armour and steel, prance about and order the bands of braves. All are quiet and orderly, and preserve due restraint. One would not know that these are the same turbulent, untrained, reckless, and cruel plunderers and murderers, who devastate the homes of peaceful people beyond the seas.

I did not see the big fire-ships, for it was not permitted to me. Or rather it would have been very uncomfortable indeed, for the rude and insolent Barbarians in the ships know nothing of ordinary politeness and civility.

They jeer my illustrious country and people, and mock at us with the brutality of conceited and barbaric ignorance. I was told that the big ships perform a great many movements, firing off the great cannons, and moving about each other, and pretending to fight—in this way to teach the head officers and the men how to manage the vessels, and how to fire the enormous guns, and how to shoot the big balls and fire-bombs, and other horrible things, in the most destructive way. Sometimes an old vessel is allowed to float on the waves, and the fire-ships shoot off the cannon balls against the hull, to see how soon they can destroy, burn, or sink it. Sometimes they send against it a curious machine filled with gun-powder, which, sinking under the old hull, suddenly blows up, raising the great mass entirely out of the sea, and utterly destroying it! So ingenious are these fierce tribes of the West in all contrivances for the destruction of mankind!

CHAPTER X.
OF THE EMPLOYMENTS OF THE PEOPLE,
AND ASPECTS OF DAILY LIFE.

I HAVE spoken quite at length of the English Barbarians as *traders*—these form a large portion of the whole. Below these are the lowest caste, workers, beggars, and thieves. The tillers of the land make a great part of the workers; then those who toil in the mines, shops, and great factories; lastly, mere day-labourers of all sorts.

The tillers of land are wretchedly poor. In the years of their strength they just keep from starvation, living in hovels hardly fit for a brute, and not so good as the *Master's* dog-kennel. When strength goes they become idle, paupers, and die in the poor-house [do-zen-di].

The mine-workers delve in the dark bowels of the earth for coal, iron, copper, tin, and other minerals. No beast works in more dirt, nor under more brutal circumstances. Out of the light of day, far below, in pitchy blackness, illumined only by the faint light of a lamp fastened to his head, the *serf* toils—exposed to death from suffocation, by the falling-in of earth, from great outbursts of water, from accidents of many kinds, and from the fearful *explosions*! He gets more money—but in the light of day, when he has cleansed himself from some of his weight of filth, the gin and beer shop give him the readiest and only resource! The lives of these toilers and of their families are scarcely imaginable. An explosion sometimes destroys nearly a whole village!

The vast numbers, men, women, and children, who labour in shops and factories of all kinds, present a very uniform appearance of misery and degradation. They swarm in the great towns, amid the *débris* [kon] of coal and iron works, and in the *purlieus* of the places of labour—dirty, noisome, barbarous. No High-Caste, unless by mistake, ever goes among them; and even the lower avoid them. Worked by their task-masters all the day, from early morning till late at night, for such pittance as may keep them *at work*, what can be expected? Young girls and lads work together; there is no decency (there hardly can be), connections are formed, children come; but who is to care *for them*? What can describe truly the actual state of things?

When work is over, weary, without respect from others, and feeling none, therefore, for themselves; no decent home, wife and children draggled and wretched like themselves, where else to go but to the warm and brilliant-lighted drink-places? Here is warmth, shelter, comforting drink. Is it surprising that these, *the only homes*, take nearly all earnings; and that the small remainder gives to the bare rooms, ragged garments, and squalid wives and children, that aspect of misery and brutishness? Whole quarters of towns are given up to this degradation. The portals of Temples, the porticoes of grand edifices, the very steps of public charities, are crowded with these victims of ignorance and selfishness—a selfishness peculiar to the cold nature of these Barbarians, and which receives its finest and most exquisite polish among the High-Caste. I speak of the steps of Charity Halls, where relief is supposed to be given to the starving; but on the very steps misery may find its last, wretched repose.

It seems to be accepted as *inherent in the nature* of things that this abounding debasement and wretchedness, wherein *crime* breeds by an inexorable law, *must be*. The crime must be watched and kept within bounds, and guards must carefully repress the disorders of this foul *shame*, but the thing itself is inherent and ineradicable. It may be so to the barbaric nature.

The ordinary labourers of all descriptions, in the street, in the shipping-docks, in waiting upon the artificers, in the digging, toiling, manual employments, differ not much from their *congeners* [re-la-tsi] in the factories and mines. Their habits are the same. All are alike really *serfs*, taking no notice of the refinements and the enjoyments of the higher-castes, and being everywhere rigidly avoided by them. On a sunny day, if you walk in a public garden, you will see some of these miserable beings lying about on the grass, stretched out in the sun, asleep. By no chance will they occupy any place which is usually used by the upper castes, nor will any of these, by any chance (short of dire need), ever speak to or notice one of these low creatures. Sometimes an open green space will present an appearance like a battle-field after a combat. These *serfs* scattered around, here one or two perfectly still, there some just turning or raised upon elbow; sometimes an old crone resting upon a recumbent man; most, perfectly still and flat, give an aspect of dead and dying strewn over the field. Occasionally men and women will be cuddled close together for warmth; in truth, this grassy, sunny couch, is to them a luxury.

The aspect of these day-labourers as they lounge, or slouch [gr-utn] idly about the streets, is repulsive and curious. They seem unable to stand up. Whether from the nature of their toil, or from mere shiftlessness, I know not. But they never do stand erect, and slouch along from one beer-shop corner to another, till they can *lean* or *lie down*. They cluster about the corners by beer and gin shops, rarely molesting any one, but frequently noisy and quarrelsome among themselves. They carry their strong passions and strong drink to their wretched haunts where crime and violence are rife. Women and children of this class are also at these drinking places, and give a feature to the degradation of unusual repulsiveness. These beer and gin shops, in low quarters of a town, are prolific of riot and crime, but abounding everywhere, in parts more decent, the police [ta-pki] are forced to be more watchful. A striking illustration of the callousness of the High-Caste is, that they derive their own revenues largely from this very degradation of the *serfs*—for an immense tax is paid by them upon the beer and gin which they consume—and this tax enures wholly to the benefit of the High-Caste. In the Law-making *House*, therefore, whenever some good man wishes to moderate this excessive evil of drink and drunkenness; pointing out how *Crime* takes root and flourishes, and vice spreads from these drinking-places; how the whole community suffers; he is laughed at and pointed at, and made odious to these miserable creatures, as one who would deprive the *poor man* of his Beer! In this connection of the serf with the rich man's revenue, it is convenient to say "*the poor man*," on ordinary occasions, the "*drunken beast*," or the "*brute*," would be more likely.

There are parts of great towns where decent people never go unless by sheer need, and where in the night they would not go unless accompanied by a policeman. Nothing can describe the aspect of the dark courts and streets, of the mean and filthy buildings, shops, and dens! Nastiness, foul smells, dirty shambles and garbage; doors and windows smashed and stuffed with rags; gutters festering with impurities; and the human vermin swarming like maggots in rotten flesh! Upon *this* foundation the palaces of the rich and the vast stone Temples rest; one wonders that they do not sink into it.

It is a great boast of the English Barbarians that "a slave cannot breathe in England." At first, when I heard this, I supposed that it meant that he would die under the conditions of life awaiting him—he would not be able to *breathe*—and therefore slaves were unable to live in the land. But the boast merely means that it is not permitted to add *black* slaves from abroad; they cannot live in England; nor do I think they could. I do not comprehend the boast, unless on the ground that it would be an expensive as well as useless cruelty to land even *blacks*, merely to have the trouble and cost of burying their carcases.

I have called these low-castes *Serfs*, disregarding the barbarian *fiction* which calls them *free*. Not long since they were slaves under precise law; now they are so by universal custom. When they were legal *slaves* they had some care and protection; there was *a tie* existing between master and servant; hearty service and affectionate concern rendered the relation not merely supportable, but positively advantageous. The tie is severed; there is neither hearty service nor affectionate concern. The master possesses everything as before, but he is no longer *obliged* to maintain his labourers. These are numerous; they must work or starve. Whilst they *work* they get enough perhaps to live; no longer able to work, mere pauper-life in poorhouses and the pauper's grave await them. Nor do the masters even pay for these; they have cunningly contrived to have the expense borne by all who have anything to be taxed. Thus the severance of the ancient tie has only enriched the High-Castes and freed them from all obligation to care for the labourer, and sunk him into a condition of hopeless and debasing poverty. The freedom is all on the strong side; the *slavery* more abject and less softened by humane sentiments.

Now there are a few, who have some dim perceptions of these so obvious features to a disinterested spectator. They see that it is a poor compensation to the wretched misery which holds thousands hopelessly in its grasp, to point out an occasional accident of escape—where some one, more gifted and more fortunate than his fellows, happens to rise into comfort and slight esteem! These noble men, the harbingers of light, who try to see and to act honestly, in spite of early prejudice and habit, perceive that there is no hope for these *serfs*, unless they can be moved with a higher interest. They think they discover a chance to move them by offering them *knowledge*, without, or nearly without, cost. But it is doubtful if they be not too low, too brutal, to care for *knowing* anything. Then, "they must be forced to send the children, to be taught—*they must be whipped to School*." This is resented as an outrage on the *freedom* of the serf—as an invasion of his family rights—as a positive, additional, tax and burden. For he gets *something* from the petty work, or from the begging or thieving of the children, and now the Master takes *that*! Yet, probably, this is one needful thing—to take the children into the hands of the State, in every case where the natural guardian is unfit to properly care for them. But the State cannot *half* take them. It cannot take anything of the present pittance, and claim to have compensated by giving words instead. It is cruel to say to him who starves in body, "Starve—I feed the mind!" A poor parent cannot receive even knowledge in exchange for bread. And it cannot be asked of him, in his low estate, to exchange the little added support of the child's wage for the, to him, useless words of knowledge. In the face of want one cares only for bread! Therefore, the State which teaches must also feed the poor—or see to it that the honest poor be first fed. If the parent can only feed by the help of the child, the State must not arbitrarily assume to be Master and Judge—saying, "Come to school—and starve, if must be."

The High-Caste, secretly, clog and obstruct all attempts to raise the low. Learning belongs to the master—ignorance to the serf. It is enough for *him* to obey and work. There will always be poor, and vicious poor. It is better to merely watch and guard against an *Evil*, for which there is no remedy. To give instruction to the low-orders, is to arm demagogues with a dangerous weapon. "'A little knowledge is a dangerous thing'—it only enables the multitude to see just what it suits the purpose of the *Agitator* to show! There is nothing but evil in these grand measures. All must be left to individual effort; and to the Priests. These must work as comes in their way; instructing those who wish, and encouraging those who dutifully obey, and attend to the labours imposed upon them by divine Providence" (Meaning, that *Jah* has ordained, from all time, that some must be "*Hewers of wood and drawers of water*"—a quotation from the *Sacred Writings*).

In this manner, the High-Caste, when it condescends to the subject at all, dismisses it. Indeed, this Caste, the Master-Caste, really feels no other concern in the low orders, but a concern for their peaceful subjection. To this point they direct so much care, as to have always trained bands of braves, and strong, picked, well-ordered men, called *Police, ready at hand*. So, in case the wretched, degraded, and despised serfs and thieves, should dare to raise any stir, disturbing the ease and enjoyment of the luxurious High-Caste, they may be shot down without mercy!

Necessarily, the elevation of the low-classes will be very gradual. Many of the Priests, wishing to enlarge and maintain the influence of the *Superstition*, actively exert themselves among the honest and industrious poor. And some of these Bonzes are as benevolent as the traditions of their Caste and of their Idolatry will permit.

It is doubtful if the present condition of the masses of the English Barbarians be so manly and independent as ages ago—when they were sufficiently intelligent to move in their own cause, and were really of some importance in the State. Unfortunately, they did remove from their necks the pressure of immediate, personal service, only to accumulate upon them, *as a Class*, the whole weight of the landed and trading interests. As a whole, therefore, they are more servile, more abject, and more dependent; and the few individuals who may raise themselves above the level of their class cannot even flatter themselves in this to have gained. There never was a time when these individuals did not exist—it is not clear that their numbers have increased.

CHAPTER XI.
OF THE HIGH CASTES: SOME PARTICULARS OF THEIR DOMESTIC AND SOCIAL CUSTOMS.

IN this chapter I shall try to show some of the peculiarities of the opposite extreme of Barbarian life. From ignorant poverty, verging upon crime, crime and vice; we are taken to luxury, also verging upon crime, crime and vice—though under very different forms. The All-wise and Sovereign Lord knows how to judge each class of offenders!

The High-Caste is very exclusive—it will not, if it can avoid it, notice one of a lower order; and never will do so unless it has some selfish end in view. This cold-bloodedness characterizes all Castes. When the Barbarians, therefore, chance to meet, and being of near Castes, cannot be distinguished by dress, they never touch or address each other—but stare rudely up and down the person, to see if it will be *safe* to be civil, the one to the other.

In general, however, the two Higher-Castes present so many features in common, that a spectator may regard them as one. Both look upon all useful occupation as shameful; and whilst it is hard to call up a blush for anything mean, detection in any honest work covers with confusion!

The women of this Caste appear everywhere in public, with the same boldness as men. They dress in laces, silks, satins, velvets; richest furs, feathers, shawls, and scarfs. Are so addicted to these things, and to costly jewels, and ornaments of gold, precious stones, and the like, that a fortune is often carried upon and about a fine Lady. (*Lady* is for the female like Lord for a male). In truth, a Lady only lives for two purposes—*to dress*, and *to marry*. I ought to add another, but whether it be subordinate or chief I know not; in fact, I hardly know what it is. We have no very near word. It is a *something* of which you hear constantly—*to flirt*. To dress, it is necessary *to shop* [keat-hi]. This, is to buy the innumerable articles which make up a fine Lady's wardrobe and personal appointments. Heaven and earth, and all the lands beyond the great seas, are ransacked to gratify the insatiate demands of Barbarian High-Caste women. The finest paints for the cheeks and eyelids, the most precious stones for the ears, the neck, the wrists, the fingers; the most delicate perfumes, the pure gold, the richest furs and feathers, spices, oils; the laces, scarfs, silks, embroideries;—an endless variety. Shopping is, therefore, the serious occupation (subsidiary to husband-catching and *flirting*) of ladies. Many ruin themselves, or their fathers, their husbands, or relatives, in this expensive luxury of idle vanity.

High-Caste women show themselves in public, sometimes on foot, but, more generally, lolling, with poodles in lap, within open, grand carriages, drawn by great, high-stepping horses. (Poodles are nasty dogs). They attend the Temples, waited upon by *solemn* servants, clothed in showy colours, and bearing ostentatiously the *Sacred* books. They are conspicuous, when at the Temple, for audibly accompanying the Priest in the Invocations and Confessions: "*miserable offenders*" seeming to be a phrase rolled like a sweet morsel, and having a savour of repentance and humility, very edifying!

The men do not appear very numerously with the women—leaving them to do as they please. The men going off to their own exclusive pleasures: gambling, betting, racing, boating, hunting, and other things equally useful and improving.

All through the night, which is the time of High-Caste revelry, the streets where the great live resound with the noise of the carriages, constantly busy with the transporting of the High-Castes to and from the Theatres, the Dances, the places of Amusements, the Dinners, the Parties, Routs, and visits. To mark the difference of the Upper from the Lower, time itself is reversed; night is taken for life and sport, and the day for rest, gossip [Quen], and *shopping*. In nothing could the difference be more striking. The luxuriousness of mere self-indulgence, which takes no heed of the usual order of nature, and does not suspect that day has any better use! When in the country, there is the same round of busy nothings. Visits, feasting, drinking—dancing, routs, and parties. Women taking the lead everywhere and in everything. Here, as in town, the business of life with women is to flirt, to marry, to dress—the last should be first.

The men add to the follies of women some things more robust, but not more useful. Betting, horse-racing, riding over country with dogs, pursuing timid creatures—or gambling, drinking, and feasting.

When I first arrived in England, I was amazed, and supposed all women were *shameless* [ba-tsi] that I saw, whenever I went in public. In our Flowery Land this class [ba-tsi], under the strictest survey and care of the magistrates, are barely tolerated, and forced to the most scrupulous decorum of dress and conduct. With us no modest woman of any rank ever appears in public. Therefore my surprise and astonishment may be imagined. Afterwards these were moderated, and I could make allowances for the force of custom. None the less the custom is remarkable, and will receive attention elsewhere.

The mode of dress is simply wonderful. It is ever changing and ever indelicate and monstrous—especially for women. When I first saw one of these with a huge *hunch* on the top of her back, I thought the person was afflicted with an enormous *tumour*; but when I observed the same thing on all hands, I saw my mistake. The great hunch was no more than a machine placed on top of the seat, under the outer garments. The effect is something amazing. The women in walking also wear the robe drawn as tightly as possible back and over the hips, so as to display the whole form from head to foot in front, and also in rear, excepting at the back-seat where the protuberance is. Here the clothes are clustered, and hang down in a trail upon the ground! The feet are thrust into very high-heeled shoes, or boots; so, in walking, the woman stoops mincingly forward with short, unsteady steps, as if pinched at the toes, rattling her heels upon the pavement, and tossing her back-gear and headdress, and showing off to an astonished observer (unused to the apparition) something to be remembered! On every little occasion taking up her *trail*, and discovering legs and ankles.

At home, when receiving male and female friends to dinner, the women do as they please—also in dances, routs, and the like. I was invited, soon after my arrival, to dine. I had looked at a *Book of rites* and ceremonies for the great, and hoped to get on tolerably well. On arriving, my first mistake was to address the servant as Illustrious, taking him for the master. In many houses the servant, dressed like the master (being much more of a man in appearance), may well be taken for him; but in some houses the servants are made to wear *badges and colours* of their station. Women are very choice about these men-servants, and will not have one unless he have very large, well-formed *calves* [fa-tze]. I have heard that the rogues supply this requirement by adding so much fine hay to the leg as will give due swell and figure!

Upon being shown up to the room, where I was to address myself first to the *Lady*—the Illustrious wife—I made my next blunder. The lady was large, full of flesh, rather red, with bright eyes. Another lady, just moving away, trailed her long robe suddenly before me—my foot caught and held her. She turned her white shoulders upon me, frowned—at the moment I stumbled, and recovered myself awkwardly, with open hands full upon the ample bosom of the Illustrious! Ah, my confusion! I could not recover my composure. I could see nothing but necks, shoulders, backs, bosoms of women, and eyes flashing at me—heads, and feathers and jewels—lights, noise, confusion! I got away—never knew how.

Women, when undressed in this indelicate way, are said to be in *full dress*. I think this is a sly sarcasm of the men. The men, however, dress in a manner not at all better. When in full dress, they put on a ridiculous close garment, slit up behind, and very scant, with two tails, which pretend to cover the hinder parts. The *trowsers* (an "unmentionable" article for the legs), no more than the *under* garment worn by us, is the only covering for the legs and lower part of the body! Imagine the indelicacy! In this style of *full dress*, the women and men of the High-Caste Barbarians meet and mingle together everywhere, and at all feasts, revelries, and dances.

In the shows within-doors the same mode prevails. At the public spectacles, in full view of thousands, ladies sit exposed to the gaze of men, who often level at them the magnifying glasses taken for the purpose! Critically examining the exhibition before them from a distance of twenty feet [tu-fai].

The dress of women on horseback is as follows:—The head is covered with a man's head-gear, round, hard, high, black in colour, with a narrow rim. The bust and body are just as tightly fitted as possible, the hips and figure exposed in exact shape (how much *made up* no one can more than conjecture), and the legs covered by the dress falling over them long and full. The woman sits on a side-saddle, one leg well up over a horn of the saddle near the front top, and the other supported with the foot in a steel rest. She is lifted by a male servant, relative, or friend, into her perch. And when she, with the little whip in hand, takes up the long strips of leather by which she guides the horse, and starts off, there is a show the most curious! Up and down, with every motion of the horse, she *bobs* [Ko-bys], exposing, to any one looking after her, the most precise model of herself! but in an attitude and costume so remarkable, that I never saw even the accustomed Barbarians disregard an opportunity to see *this show*, however indifferent they may usually be. Nor do I think that the Barbarian women esteem any exhibition of themselves superior to this.

In the country you will see several apparitions of this kind, urging their flying horses after men and dogs, all chasing *pell-mell* some poor hare, which, running for cover, is pursued by a crowd of men and women on horseback, with dogs, yelping, barking, men blowing horns and shouting; the women on the horses leaping over fences, ditches, and urging their horses as wildly, boldly as the men—and sometimes in all respects as skilfully and well! This Sport is considered by the Barbarians to be very manly—nor do they consider a broken back, or even neck, as any objection to it!

The *Rout* is a favourite amusement with the High-Castes. So named from the confusion of armed men when *routed*—put to flight. It is to get together just as many people of both sexes as possible. With no sort of regard to the size of the house, but only to show how many of the High-Caste will respond to the invitation.

In full *undress* the ladies and *gentlemen* (Barbarian style for any High-Caste man) crowd into the house. Every stairway, every hall, room, chamber is filled. Refreshments are provided, but the flux and reflux of the people render all eating and drinking very difficult. The women flash in jewels, pendants in the ears, sparkling brilliants on arms, busts, ornaments of flowers and gems in the hair, jewelled fans in hand, perfumed laces and scarfs, tinted, and flushed, and adorned, exposed to bewilder and intoxicate the men—in fine, in the pursuit of husbands, or bent upon flirtations! These entertainments are designed for the very purpose of excitement and match-making. "*Society* is kept alive—life is made endurable by these things," the High-Caste women say. They have no other business but to attend to such matters; and to them *Society* looks to save it from dissolution and despair!

In the *Rout* all is confusion and opportunity. The young people, the old people, the highest and the lowest (permissible), are thrown promiscuously together. Women and men mingle, jostle, jamb, crowd, wriggle, and writhe together as best they can. The young lady suddenly finds herself quite in the arms of the young man who has saved her from a fall; and he, in turn, "*begs pardon*" of some woman, into whose lap he has almost been thrown by a sudden press.

Acquaintances may be made, *flirtations* begun, ending in something or nothing. But *Society* has had its excitement, and its members their chances for mere idle display, gossip, sensual gratification, or the more serious business of High-life—*fortune-hunting* by men and *husband-catching* by women! The *Waltz and Dance* are, however, the great game (for they are really one) of Barbarian life. Every Caste, according to its ability, dances—the low imitating, to their best, all the "*airs and graces*," dress and *flirtations* of their superiors. In the Waltz, when the music strikes up, the man takes the woman about the waist, standing with the other dancers in the middle of the floor, and she leans upon his shoulder interlocking the fingers of her disengaged hand in his. In this close position, they begin to wheel around, around; one couple follows another about the clear space left for them, till many couples are seen twirling, whirling about, around to the sound of the music—ever in this wild, whirling sort of a gallop, following one after another, rapidly! The long trails of the woman are held up, the embroidered skirts fly out, the silken shoes and hose flash; she is held close and more closely in the supporting arm, her cheek almost touches, her bust, neck, and face glow with excitement, the eyes and jewels sparkle, the man and woman whirl about, till intoxicated, dazed, and nearly exhausted, she sinks upon his arm and motions for rest, and he half supports and half leads her to some soft bench or chair! Such briefly is the Waltz. The dance is the same thing nearly, only more variety of movement is introduced. The whole object is to bring the sexes together, and keep *Society* alive, as before. *Flirtation* and match-making being main elements of social life.

The manners of the High-Caste are not really more refined than elsewhere; only there is a cool tone. Nothing must surprise, nothing confuse, nothing abash. A blush must be as rare as a laugh. A young woman seeing a young man gazing at her with bold admiration, must coolly *look him down*—if she please. His is an action of mere rudeness, or *should* be, when directed to a virtuous woman: but no, "a man may gaze upon what is everywhere exhibited *for* his admiration—may he not?" And yet, with strange inconsistency, a woman has a right to complain if a man, captivated by the very means designed, too rudely express his pleasure. And one man is required to chastise another for the rudeness to his relative, though he know that, in the nature of things, the female should expect what she encounters—and more, the complexity is further involved, that though one man must call another to account for this sort of rudeness, yet every man indulges in it!

Young people, in public, of the two sexes, without shame appear in close intimacy—and will look upon statues and paintings of naked women and men, talking and criticizing, examining the works and looking at them in company, without confusion, or appearance of there being any indelicacy. As if, in fact, in the bosoms of the High-Caste there did not exist any of the passions of ordinary mortals!

There are very numerous galleries of Art, where statues, paintings, pictures, models, and the like, are shown, which are always crowded by High-Caste women, children, and men. And shop-windows are made attractive by displays of pictures of nude, or half-nude, women and men, who act in the Plays, or who are notorious in Spectacles. This sort of indecency prevails; and strikes one, not used to it, with an unpleasant surprise. He knows not what to think of its significance—have all his ideas of decency been indecent?

I am not able to say much of the interior life of the family. I was told that a happy family was rare—quite an exception. It is only *where the wife rules* that any peace is secured. The wife is allowed to do, generally, in Society and at home, as she will. The husband goes off to *his* pastimes and pursuits. Children whilst young are committed to the care of servants, and when older sent away to be educated and trained by hirelings.

The daughters, when grown, often move the jealousy of the mother by attracting more attention from men—they are often *snubbed* and made to dress unbecomingly, so that the mother may shine.

Marriage among the High-Caste is an arrangement for an *establishment*; and to secure the succession of family name and title. To these ends great care is given to the money question. The man demands money for taking the wife. Domestic happiness is hardly thought of; unless, occasionally, by very young people, and they are laughed out of their ridiculous romance.

In the marriage ceremony, the wife, in the presence of the Idols, and following the Invocations of the Priest, solemnly promises to obey the husband. But this is regarded as a mere form. Any husband who undertakes to enforce obedience, finds himself branded by *Society*, as a "brute!" Much of the infelicity in marriage rests upon this false basis. For, with the virile instinct, man naturally expects obedience; yet has, in his unmarried days, fallen in with the false notion of woman's superiority in delicacy and moral virtue. This peculiar affectation colours all Barbarian intercourse with the sex. It has its root in the *Superstition*, possibly; where an immaculate virgin gives birth to a *Son* of god-*Jah*! who is the Christ-god. Thus, woman came to be mother of God!

From this, very likely, followed all the false worship and gallantry of the barbarians; who still, keeping up this mode of treating women as superior in excellency, could scarcely deny to them a superior place in the family. Assumed to be absolutely chaste and pure, they are to be implicitly trusted—nor *to them* is there impropriety! Hence follows the *fine Art* exhibitions—the undress dress; the waltz; the mixed crowds—the *everything*, where women, according to the ordinary feelings of cultivated men, should not be, or be in a very different way. But the man before marriage, and afterwards, too, (excepting to his own wife), pretends to look upon woman as a divinity—as something far above him in moral goodness! *After* marriage, it is difficult to dethrone this divinity—the man has not a divinity at the head of his family; but all his friends (male friends) pretend to think so; Society says so; and he is *himself* compelled to *pretend to the same thing*. Under these circumstances he will never be likely to get much obedience. None the less, a struggle commences; the man persistent, strong; the woman unyielding, crafty; the family divided; the children demoralized; a false and wretched farce of conjugal *Play*, so badly acted as to deceive not even *Society!* and finally ending in the Divorce Court.

This is the tribunal where *Causes Matrimonial* are settled; and, if one may judge from its Reports in the *Gazette*, conjugal contention is exceedingly common. For the public cases must be few, compared with those where publicity is avoided by private arrangement.

Doubtless, a fine man and an excellent woman may unite, and live happily together, in spite of the unfavourable conditions. But, more commonly, the high-minded man, really believing in the superior purity of the sex, and her greater moral delicacy, finds his *Ideal* to be too high; and without absolute cause to quarrel; in fact, seeing that his Ideal was *itself* only an error of the prevailing delusion; ever after struggles to bring himself into harmony with the existing fact—to love and respect a woman and only a woman, with a woman's vanity, love of excitement, frivolity and caprice—a very weary work. The woman, too, still flattered, and exacting the devotion which her *lover* (now her husband) gave to her in his days of delusion, thinks herself treated with coldness; and, gradually, by her unreasonable complaints, estranges altogether the husband, whom she, too, tries to forget, in the admiration, flatteries, and excitements of Society!

The affectation and falsity, therefore, respecting woman, tends to a fundamental error in the relation of the sexes and the ordering of the family. It is a strange and almost fatal error to give this exaltation to woman. No doubt, a real trust and respect tend to secure, in some degree, the virtues accorded; and this true respect of an honest man, who places his wife, or his relative, before himself in purity, challenges the best of nature in the female. But man has reversed the true order, and run counter to the true instinct of the race (quite as strong in the female as in himself), when he thus puts woman before him, in anything. What authority is there for this reversal of the natural order? Why is woman more moral, more chaste? There is nothing in the nature of things, why the man, here, as in all things, should not be, as he is, the superior—the master. In morals he should be her guide, her teacher, her best support. That Society is, indeed, unsound, wherein the man may be low and sensual, and fancy, or pretend to fancy, that the woman is better than himself—it is a delusion. Man gives the real character to any Society—the woman will not be, cannot be better than the man. The English Barbarians, in spite of the absurd falsity of their customs, must have some tolerably happy families. The innate perception of the eternal fitness of things will cause many couples to arrive at a proper method. The wife, without exactly admitting it, even to herself, submits to her husband; and the husband, without exactly commanding (except in rare instances), feels that he is really the head of the house—and the family gets on pretty smoothly, because living in the natural order. But, in general, the struggle for mastery destroys either the existence of the family, or all attempts at affectionate ways of living. To avoid public scandal, the members do not actually separate; but all harmony and true domestic life are lost—and life is a dismal and disorderly rout.

The exaltation of the sex and the complete freedom allowed to them belong to a state of society, if any such there be, where man is still *more* excellent. There, indeed, a bright and beautiful ideal is made real, and men and women know how to love and to obey; and love is as true as the respect and the obedience. The Barbarians, full of immorality, of rudeness, of strong passions, of selfishness, controlled by a false conception founded in their Idolatry, act, in respect of their women, as if purity, cultivation, generosity, and the highest morality, everywhere existed! This, so false, is well-nigh fatal to them. Yet, it is only an illustration of the uncultivated and confused state of mind, even in the highest, that so simple a thing as the natural order governing the relation of sex and family is not comprehended;

and that their Society is saved from absolute wreck only by the strong and controlling instinct of nature, which, in spite of obstacles, does bring the female into subjection to the male—at least to an extent sufficient to make life possible!

None the less the disorder of households is dreadful. Sons and daughters, as they grow strong, assert themselves [Quan-hang-ho]. They act and speak (and in this follow the wife and mother) as if the sole business of the father was to give the means of selfish, idle indulgence. This would not be so unjust among the High-Caste, but it descends to all grades, and the middle orders are content to see the father toil at his business till overworked, or ruined altogether, in his efforts to supply these daily exactions. No doubt he himself is a victim to the whole vicious falseness—yet the cold-bloodedness of this conduct on the part of children and wives is remarkable. "Obedience," or "gratitude!"—Words sneered at, laughed at!

The daughters, directed by *Mamma* [na-ni-go], are taught to dress, to *look* modest, to practise all those arts by which they may attract the male and secure husbands, and are exhibited in public places and in Society accordingly.

The sons are sent off to be taught. In the *Halls of Learning* they acquire but little of the knowledge paid for in the *Lists*, but a great deal of that which does not appear there. A youth may have entered, at least, honest, moral, and generous—he still leaves unlearned, but dishonest, corrupt, selfish—he has acquired that knowledge most sought for (even by his parents), a knowledge of the *World* [Quang]! In truth, the youth instinctively feels that it is better for his success in life to know the World than to know Letters. He acts upon this feeling, which thrives in the demoralised atmosphere which he breathes. Father is called *Governor*, and is regarded as a sort of creature to be made the most of! The money allowed (perhaps too ample for really useful purposes) is spent in things foolish and hurtful. Money and time are wasted. The latter is valueless, to be sure, to these youths anywhere—but the money may be wrung from relatives, who put themselves on short diet to enable the son or brother (who is defrauding them) to appear well in *Society*! To perfect himself in the learning which he feels to be effective, he devises *new* methods of wringing more money from the *Governor*, who begins to protest. To drink, smoke, lounge about with easy and cool impudence; to stare into the face of women; to bet, gamble; to get in debt, and curse the creditors who presume to ask for pay; to make, or pretend to make, love; and generally to lay broad and deep that moral and cultivated *elegance*, to take on that exquisite *polish* [gla-mshi], which shall dazzle society; shall attract the silly butterflies (women) who have influence or money; shall, in fine, shine in the Grand Council, or at the head of armed bands, or to the illumination of the Courts of Law! Noble ambition, based upon manly principles! With the Barbarians to be a moral and wise man is to be a *milksop* [Kou-bab]; to be *a polished man of the World*—admirable!

The English Barbarians who are fathers, generally consider it rather a *joke* to have their sons trick them and poke fun at the "*Governor,*" only it must be marked with some pretence of deference. If the "*young fellows*" do not positively disgrace the family—that is, marry some poor creature whom they have first debauched; or actually forge, or rob, or descend to improper friendships with inferior Castes—the parents esteem themselves to be fortunate. If he have acquired no knowledge of letters, nor of anything but vices, yet he is a "*fine, manly fellow*, who will make his mark in the world." That is, he is a tall, strong, active *Barbarian*—just fit for the armed bands!

The infelicities and disorders of family life, which only prefigure the inevitable confusion and evils of the whole Society, are more intolerable among the Middle Castes. In the *Highest, secured revenues* enable the wife and the husband each to see as little of each other as they please; and so long as the husband is not stirred up by *Mrs. Grundy* (who is not severe with this Caste) he cares but little what his wife may do. *He* goes about his sports and his pleasures as he pleases; and his wife, not wishing to be looked after, does not look after him. On this free-and-easy footing, with no want of money (*Mrs. Grundy's decorum* being observed), they get on well enough, and may even form quite a friendship for each other. But it is not possible to establish this condition in a family of small income—and here it is that the wretchedness of false principles has full scope. The husband and father, honest and good, finds himself mated to a woman, weak and vain, with children moulded by her. He, misled by false notions and ignorance, took to his heart one whom he fully trusted as simply true and modest; he took her for herself and without money, and flattered himself that she would be a helper and solace. She and her children have made him a miserable *slave*, who finds no quiet unless he satisfy all their clamorous demands—*to shine in Society*! If a good man, he tries to obey and live, even under exactions beyond his utmost efforts; for he has learned to see that his wife, though weak, is no worse than the Society which she loves, and which he also cannot escape; he is merely in a false position, and must largely thank himself for having heedlessly entered upon it!

But this kind of man is not universal, and one may judge what follows, where there is a man who will not yield, or yields only because he no longer cares for anything but his personal ease and indulgence—seeking for pleasure, though unlawful, abroad, as the only recompense attainable for the loss of happiness at home!

Such a man feels that life is insupportable, where he makes so wretched an object—to be merely the *mute beast* of burden for the family, without receiving so much tenderness and consideration as is accorded to the dogs lolling in the lazy laps of the females of the house! He seeks, therefore, abroad for some means of enjoyment, though illicit!

This sort of picture is to be seen everywhere in the Barbarian *Literature*, and is constantly shown in all its minute and miserable exhibition at the Courts of Divorce.

Adultery, which in our *Flowery Land* is punished by death, is not so much as a crime among the English Barbarians. And, as it is the chief cause for which the bond of marriage may be wholly severed, one may judge whether the Court do not encourage the immorality. For when parties wish to live apart, here is a way to secure it, lying directly in the path of desire and opportunity. Then, too, the *seduction* of a maiden, which with us may be punished even to death, receives no sort of reprobation in the Court, and scarcely in Society. If the ruined girl be of low caste, her relatives feel no disgrace if the seducer be a High-Caste—rather an honour; receive from him some paltry sum (not so much as he lavishes upon some favourite dogs), and buy with the money a husband for her from her own Caste!

With us a guilty *intrigue* is almost unknown; with the Barbarians it is almost a pursuit.

None the less, there is too much vigour in the organism; too much moral, intellectual, and physical strength, to suffer total decay. As is always the case, where the mind is active, even Idolatry itself has intermixed a pure morality, and the Barbarian nature, still unformed, untrained; still rude and stirred by passion and by force; wrestles with the divine *instinct*, and, unconsciously, often moulds to its light.

Away from the glitter and *sham* (sometimes *in it*, but not of it), there are quiet families which live lives of honour. The father works honestly and cheerfully; the wife, in her house, finds the beginning and end of her aims, of her love, and her duty. The husband-father is head; on him rests all responsibility, and to him belong *obedience*. This is not exacted; it is not questioned. It is founded in love and respect; love and loving obedience spontaneously arising from uncorrupted natures. *His* whole being responds with unmeasured joy. Whatever is pure, high, tender; all are for these—his wife, his family; so true, so trusting, so helpful, so delightful. He feels no hardship; there can be no sacrifice, for these; all that is done is in harmony with himself. *Everywhere* he is in accord. The very ills and misfortunes of life touch him not, for he is living in the *divine order*.

And from such a man, the inside-life being serene, outer ills fall away. He is so clear and simple; so *whole* that nature smiles for him, even in pain and sorrow; he lives in the presence and calm of the Sovereign Lord.

These families are the *Salt* which saves. Among the Barbarians they are generally obscure, and as wholly unconscious of the service which they render as are the glittering inanities which ignore them. This should be reversed, and the *Inanities* sink into obscurity.

I will now say a word or two as to the personal appearance and demeanour of the Barbarians. There is no standard of best-looking, and each tribe will judge from *its* best type. In general the eyes are too prominent and open; the nose large and irregular; the teeth bad or false; the height indifferent; the figure either too lean or too fat. The hair all colours; red and light most common. The women are so made up, judging from the articles openly exposed for sale, that one cannot speak of them with any certainty. The hair, teeth, complexion, bust, outline of form, are all false or artistically got up. The eyes are too bold and open. The feet long, and hands large. Too tall, and either too meagre or too stout. The youth are sometimes pretty. The women are often brilliant under gaslight (a bright, artificial light). I have spoken of dress, but I may mention that the women, not content with every sort of *made-up* thing to add to their attractions, pile upon their heads an enormity of false curls, bands of hair, laces, and high sort of head-ornaments; it is truly amazing. Some of these gewgaws are hung upon big pig-tails of false hair, and some are stuck high a-top. Nothing really can be more absurd, unless the false, mincing steps, and protruding back. Some women are beautiful; but to my unaccustomed looks, even the brilliant eyes could not blind me to so immodest an exhibition—or, to *me*, not modest—so instinctively do we demand that especial quality in the sex, as the crowning grace of true beauty.

One thing of a personal kind in the habits of all, high and low, I remarked, which would be intolerable to us. A lady or a gentleman, whilst conversing with you, or at the table of feasting, will suddenly apply a handkerchief [mün-shi] to nose, and blow that organ in the most astounding manner; and this may be continued for some minutes, even accompanied by *hauks and spits*, and closed by many nice attentions to the orifices not worth while to describe. Surely this strange thing disconcerted me very greatly at first, nor do I understand how any people above savages could do it. A fine *lady* will interrupt herself in the very midst of speech, or of eating, with spasmodic effort, to clear her head; emptying into her fine pocket-handkerchief the obnoxious matter, and then returning the article to her silken pocket.

However, we should not expect refinement in a Society where the women may boldly mount a horse-back, and follow men and dogs over ditch and wall, urging her steed with the best, to come in to the death of the poor hunted creature. And this, a noble sport, fit for a lady! Nor this only, but will crowd to public spectacles, and be hustled and crowded promiscuously, forgetful of all delicate reserve. These habits are only to be criticised because of the boasted prëeminence claimed in all such matters. But what would be thought of our *Literati* piling into the mouth huge morsels of flesh, or of guzzling [kun-ki] (with a gulping noise in the throat), great swallows of a hot, greasy liquid, besmearing the lips and beard. The Barbarians know nothing of our delicate mode of eating, where all is silence and decorum whilst in the act. Another most unaccountable thing to a stranger is the robbery allowed by the servants of the High-Caste. If you accept of the hospitality of a great man, you must submit to be plundered by his servants; and, as a stranger cannot know the limits imposed upon this rapacity, it goes far to destroy all the pretence of graciousness in one's reception. When you have eaten at my Lord's table, to think you are to be *fleeced* [pe-ekd] by my Lord's *flunki*!

I was once invited by a High-Caste to come to his house in the country and shoot game. I accepted, and soon went into the copses to hunt for birds for the table. A servant accompanied me by command of his master, to show me the grounds and to wait upon me. He was very civil. The next day, upon my leaving, this man, decked in the livery [bung-shi] of his Lord, closely eyed and stuck to me, till, at length, I perceived he wanted something. Only partially aware of the Barbarian custom, and blushing at the idea of *feeing* [tin-ti] or giving anything in return for hospitality, I awkwardly fumbled in my purse and handed to him a half-crown. He contemptuously looked at the silver piece, then at me; and remarked that the "*gentlemen* of my Lord did not receive gratuities of that colour." Meaning that gold was only fit for such an exalted minion.

CHAPTER XII.
OF THE APPEARANCE OF THE COUNTRY—
AND OTHER THINGS.

THE country is so small, that, riding in the swift steam-chariots, it is traversed in an incredibly short time.

In those parts not disfigured by the smoke vomited out from the huge fire-chimneys of factories, mines, and the like, nor by the nearness of great towns, the country presents a green and cultivated look; nearly as well tilled as our provinces, Quang-tun and Chiang-su. The villages, Temples with lofty towers, great Houses of the High-Castes, here and there; trees, gardens, smooth fields of fine verdure, over which cattle and sheep are feeding; rising hills and sheltered valleys, rich with copses, orchards, and groves—all seen in moving views—give an aspect of peace, comfort, and wealth. You do not see the poverty, nor, too closely, observe the dwellings of the poor.

In winter it is cold, and the whole appearance changes. Far to the North, the sun gives but little light—and, like the climate of our provinces by the great Northern Wall, the cold is severe, and the gloom deeper. Ice is formed upon the streams and canals, and snow frequently covers the ground.

In approaching great towns, you often catch glimpses of the crowded, wretched streets, where misery only thrives. In some places, in the winter cold, smoke and darkness, life becomes intolerable to many. Out of doors you can hardly find your way, and thieves and beggars emerge from covert to ply their trades. In the night, at such times, it is only possible to move by the glare of many torches; and people are often robbed, or bewildered and lost. At this season of darkness many go mad. There is a strong vein of *horror* in the Barbarian imagination, derived from their ferocious ancestors, from their old idolatries, and deepened by the new. In the gloom, the misery, the wretchedness—sometimes in sheer disgust of life—many rush upon self-destruction—throwing themselves under the wheels of the steam-chariots, and from the bridges into the canals and rivers. Many persons are thrown down, maimed or killed in the highways, by horses or by vehicles moving along. Yet, in the grim humour of these barbarians, this is the very time when the High-Castes begin their *revelries*, and the Low-Castes most indulge in drink and riot.

In travelling through the country, you will occasionally notice, seated upon an eminence, some strong Castle, or Place, of hewn stone, belonging to a High-Caste. It will be approached through long avenues of lofty trees, and stand pre-eminent among fine groves, surrounded by broad lands. These wide Parks contain many thousands of acres [met-si], left untilled and unproductive; merely with their green slopes and spaces, interspersed with trees, to give grandeur to the Castle and its Lord. Still, if you look closely, you will discover near by, the squalid huts where *huddle* the *Serfs*, who are starving in the midst of this rich profusion—Serfs, who never have an *inch* [toe] of land of their own, and to whose wornout *carcases* is begrudged a pauper grave!

The inequality between Castes is quite as conspicuous in country as in town. One is born to an abundance, the other to hunger; one to a life of self-indulgence, the other to one of enforced and hard-worked self-sacrifice. The one, at last, is covered by a tomb, emblazoned with Honour; the other is cast into an obscure corner of despised dead, to rot in forgetfulness—though, often, judged upon a true measure of merit, the resting-places should be exchanged—and the idle and vicious *Lord* [chiang-se] descend into ignominious neglect!

You will see deer, pheasants, partridges, hares, and the like, almost tame, in the meadows and copses; but the tillers of the soil must not touch them, though starving—they are carefully *preserved* for the Lord [Tchou]. Not that he needs them, or cares for them for food—*sometimes* he likes to shoot them for idle diversion!

You will notice sturdy *tramps* (beggars) resting, or lazily slouching along by the ways, with heavy staves in their hands; and, if you suddenly come upon these in a secluded place, very likely you will be accosted—"Master, I be'se hungry—will ye give me tuppence?" You do not like the bearing of the man—and would not notice him. But you observe his face and the clutch of his thick stick—and you hurry to hand him a sixpence, and get away! These scamps prowl about, idle, ready for mischief, scornful of honest work—the terror of women and children who meet them, unexpectedly, without protection.

Sometimes the Iron-roads for Steam-chariots are carried over the housetops, in entering towns; sometimes, through long tunnels under the houses, or under hills—and the works in connection with these roads are surprising. The Barbarians of the Low-Castes are forced to incessant labours, to prevent starvation. These must be greatly directed to mines of iron, coal, copper, and tin; and to various things made from these, and from wool and cotton. For the fruits of the land cannot feed the population. The amount of food which must be brought from beyond seas is very great—and to pay for this, the products of industry must be given. Now, other Barbarian tribes make these things also, and; having them, do not require the English; in fact, in more distant parts, undersell them. From this cause, many are unemployed and turned adrift—they have no land to till; they beg, steal, and starve. Should this inability of the English Barbarians increase, there would be no sufficient employment for the Low-Castes—there would not be the means of paying for the food required—and depopulation must ensue! The wealth of the High-Caste must shrink—*the English tribe must decline in strength!*

Many of the High-Caste, already anticipating danger to themselves—fearing not merely loss of revenue, but the savage ferocity of starving multitudes—promote schemes by which large numbers of the poor are shipped off far beyond the great Seas (so that they never shall return)—to starve, or live, as may chance. "England is well rid of them!" they say.

In the neighbouring island, Ireland, an actual starvation of the people in vast numbers happened a short time since. As in England, the poor *serfs*, tilling the soil and owning none; at *the best*, toiling for the High-Castes for such pittance as would buy the cheapest food—*potatoes*; when these failed, could buy nothing—all else too dear. *These failed, the serfs died* by thousands and tens of thousands. Not because Ireland was destitute of food; such was the abundance that ample stores were actually sold for other and distant tribes! but because, in the midst of plenty, the starving were powerless to touch it; it was out of *their* reach—out of the reach of paupers! The potatoes were not—and they must die. The annals of no people record such a depopulation of a fertile land, in the midst of peace and plenty—there is no parallel! A people dying, not from idleness, nor unwillingness to work; not from want of food at hand; not from the ravages of war, nor pestilence; but from sheer poverty! Yet, the English Barbarians boast that no people are so rich, so generous! In our own annals are recorded great sufferings from floods, failures of crops, and natural causes; where our vast populations have been for a time *deficient* in *food*; but we have nothing to compare with this Barbarian horror!

The *Thames* is the only considerable river. This flows through the greatest of all the cities of the West—London. It is an insignificant stream—much less than even the *Quang-tun*, in our chief Southern province.

As it flows through the great city it is, in some places, confined by high hewn-stone terraces [kar-tra]. These are truly great works, and useful, worthy of a strong people. On the river bank is the vast *Hall* of the Grand Council; with its lofty towers, turrets, clocks, and many bells. The architecture is not like anything known to us—it is the *Gothic*, which I have mentioned elsewhere. Why this style, so characteristic and fit in the

Temples, is used in this grand Hall, I know not; but probably because this barbarous form was that of the old Hall, destroyed by fire some time since. And the barbaric stolidity sticks to its habit, however inconvenient and unfit. Not far away, may be seen the Dome and Towers of a fine Roman-Grecian Temple, clear and defined, giving expression to an orderly and trained mind, severe in dignity and beauty. But the *Gothic*, expressing, or trying to express, something very different; and, rising in the Temples of a gloomy, dark Superstition, to a horrible and unformed shape! With *that* the disorderly brain burdened *itself* and the river bank—a pile at once wonderful and abortive!

London is very large, perhaps equal to some of our greatest cities. For the most part very dirty and grim, and badly built. The river shows its great trade—not inland, but from abroad. You can discern, rising above the buildings, the many tall masts of the ships like forests dried up. And you will observe the numerous vessels with high chimneys; these are the vessels moved by *steam*—and the incredible number of small craft. At one point you will remark the tall white towers and the high prison walls of stone, erected by the Barbarian chief from the Main Land who subdued the English tribes in our dynasty *Song*, and made this huge Castle a stronghold and prison.

Lower down rises, close by the shore, one of the best in style of all the Barbarian monuments. It is a fine Palace in carved stone, built, after the Roman forms, to perpetuate the remembrance of *Victories* gained over distant tribes. Within are great Paintings of these Victories. Terrible scenes of devastation and cruelty; bloody fights and dreadful conflagrations, by sea and land; rapine, massacre, unbridled fury! These are the most admired of all things by the Barbarians—by the Low-Castes, who are almost entirely the victims, as much as by the High. The sight of these kindles their passion for bloody force. They *Hoorah!* with an indescribable *yell* [zung] whenever they wish to show their frantic delight at any exhibition of brutal ferocity. This *yell* is greatly gloried in, and vaunted to be far more terrible than that of *any other* tribe—that by it *alone*, when raised upon the air by fierce bands, English Barbarians have routed armed hosts!

When one is in the narrow seas of the English, very many vessels may be seen, and near the coasts fleets of fishing craft. The fishermen live in great poverty, in miserable villages by the seaside. They use lines and snares, sometimes like ours, but are not so ingenious in catching the sea-creatures as are our fishermen. They have never trained birds to the work. Their huts are noisome, and their habits and dress unclean. They wear a curious cover upon the head, like a basin, with a long wide flap behind. This is all besmeared with a thick, black oil—and their clothing is stiff and nasty with the same unctuous stuff. The oil is to exclude the sea-spray and wet. Their speech is nearly unintelligible to the *Literati*, though comprehended by their own *Caste*; they are of the lowest—serfs. Multitudes of these rude and unlettered Barbarians perish amid the waves in the storms of winter—being forced to imperil their lives that they may live *at all*. They are quite a feature in some parts, with their awkward uncouthness. They are addicted to the grossest superstitions of *the* Superstition. They have many legends about the dark *devil-god*, and swear by *him* mostly. They seem to think to cheat him—though they cautiously observe those things which may entrap them, and nothing would tempt them to put to sea on the *devil's day*—Friday. To do so, would be to go to the *devil's Locker* (as they call it) at once! This class is similar to the sailor [mat-le-si] known in our ports, and the character may therefore be fairly judged. The fisherman, in fact, often changes into the ships and goes upon distant voyages.

There are no mountains, only pretty high hills, in the English provinces. The loftiest are in the far Northern parts, where are also some small lakes. In the winter these loftier ridges of land are sometimes white with snow. The inhabitants are savages, having their legs naked and bodies wrapped about in loose robes and skins, secured by a belt, into which a knife is stuck, and to which a long leather pouch is hung. In this pouch they place some dry corn [matze], which, with strong wine in a bottle suspended from the neck, enables them to live for days. Thus equipped, they descend to the valleys, and drive off to their haunts in the rocky hills the cattle of the more civilised people of the plains.

The English Barbarians have never conquered these fierce tribes of the Northern hills, but have contrived gradually to destroy and to remove them. So that, at present, what few remain are quite tamed. A great many, in times past, were cunningly betrayed to the English and put to the sword; but, in latter days, the *head-chiefs* have been bought by the English, and used to entice their ignorant but devoted serfs to enter into the armed bands to be sent beyond seas. By these methods, those distant Northern parts have been, in good degree, depopulated and made quiet.

The Low-Castes furnish the fierce savages so well known in our Celestial Waters as those who live in the great fire-ships.

Now, when the English tribe, being in need of many men for these ships (just about to go away to plunder and to fight), determines to have them, this follows:—Strong, brutal men, are paid to watch for the poor of the Low-Caste, and seize them. These cruel wretches are armed with clubs and swords and small firearms. They are sent into the places where the poor and friendless abound, to seize any man whom they think they can carry off without much *fuss* [pung]. The poor cower and hide away; but these savage bands hunt them out, and bear off from wife and children, it may be, or from any chance of succour, some unfriended man to their dreadful dens. Here they are beaten, or put in irons, or otherwise maltreated; or they may have been brutally knocked down when captured. When gangs [twi-sz] are collected, the victims are forced on board the fire-ships to work in the dark, filthy holes, till, completely cowed, they are made to fire the great cannons, and to learn the art of sailing and fighting!

Many of these slaves of selfish, cruel force, never see their own land again, but are killed in fight, or by accident, or by disease. Multitudes sometimes perish by a single disaster. These are, however, fortunate. They have escaped the brutal whipping, the loathsome diseases, the vile contagions, the inexpressible horrors of a continued captivity!

By these *press-gangs* (so-called) the fire-ships are often supplied with victims snatched from the unprotected Low-Castes; and the Upper enjoy the idle and luxurious security which they rob from the blood and limbs of the friendless and obscure.

This unjust custom, frightful in every aspect, receives the approbation and applause of the Barbarians very generally, who say, "Let the fellows thank their *stars* that they can receive the Queen's money and fight *for* her! Then look at the chance for *prize*!" By *prize*, they mean some pitiful fraction of the plunder taken. The *stars* are referred to, because the Barbarians fancy that everybody is born under the influence of some star!

I once noticed a painting, wherein a young man and maiden were represented as just leaving a Temple, where they had been married. Both were nicely dressed, young and handsome, with roses and *nosegays* [bong-no]. They were walking arm-in-arm, happily engrossed in each other, when, from an alley, out springs a black-whiskered *bully* [kob-bo] with drawn cutlass, followed by a band of half-drunken, armed wretches, wearing the sea-garb of the Queen; he grasps the young man roughly by the collar—the picture attempts to show the indignant surprise of the man, the clinging tenderness, fear, and horror of the maid! But more striking to an observing stranger than even these, is the merely passing curiosity of the people moving about! The scene to them is not so novel. It is merely a *press-gang* doing its lawful work—if, by chance, a wrong sort of man be seized, it is none of the affair of these indifferent passers.

Probably, the picture means to excite some compassionate interest by showing how *very hard* the press-gang system may work!

It would be vain to call the least attention to the matter, if the victim were merely a common labourer; even the accessories of wife and children would not raise the scene into one of compassion. Nor does the representation, for one moment, cause any reflection upon a *system* wherein *bullies* [kob-toe] are employed to waylay and carry off unbefriended and unoffending men, at so much *per head!* For, besides the regular pay, a reward is given for each victim captured!

CHAPTER XIII.
LONDON.

LONDON is the capital city of the British Empire. This is the style assumed by the English when they speak of their whole power. It is a curiously constructed empire—in some respects like that of the old Romans, who, however, obtained their domination more directly by valour and wisdom—whereas the English rather by cunning, accident, and fraud. I say *accident*, because the immense regions possessed by virtue of discovery come under the term; and the vastest of all their distant provinces, that of India, was obtained chiefly by fraud, assisted by force. I say *curiously* constructed, because these Christians are content to wring from Heathen subjects their last bit of revenue utterly indifferent to the idolatries and to the miseries of the people. If the Taxes come in and the wretched Hindoos starve, the main thing is to make the money and support 'our magnificent Empire' (as the English have it). So the wildest excesses may go on, and the native chiefs, who are mere creatures of their distant masters, may oppress the poor inhabitants; still, now and ever, the Master demands money; this secures the yoke upon the neck of the subjugated, and enables the English to make the vast Hindoo world a field where golden harvests are to be reaped. Boasting of liberty at home, there, a tyranny most odious is practised without pity. Then, the distant settlements where the poor English Barbarians go, to cultivate the lands and to trade and plunder, are held in subjection chiefly to give places, with large revenues attached, to members of the Aristocracy, who must be provided for in some way, as they can do nothing for themselves. So this arrangement is very satisfactory, because the stupid Englishman abroad is just as devoted to the Upper-Caste and to the Superstition as at home, and feels honoured to have a "scion of nobility" foisted upon him; and is amply repaid all the cost by the privilege of "cooling his heels" in an ante-room of the great man, when he holds his little Court.

The result is, that back upon London flows all the wealth which the English Barbarians can contrive to get. Having these distant regions, and a greater trade across sea, London has become the greatest mart of all the Western tribes. It is, perhaps, as large and populous as our Pekin. It is the centre of Authority and of business; not only so, but is the Metropolis of all the Christ-worshipping Tribes—or, as the Barbarians phrase it, of *Christendom*.

The population is 3,500,000, or thereabouts. The bulk of this multitude is poor, and a large fraction paupers. Yet the English boast that "it is the richest city in the world!"

Most of the streets, courts, and buildings are very mean. In the winter, nothing can equal the repulsiveness of the place. To the squalor of beggary, the meanness of abject poverty, add the darkness and smoke; and the conditions seem unfit for human life. The rich shut themselves within their houses, drop the heavy draperies over windows, stir up the fires, light the flaring flames of the curious gas-lights, eat, drink, and sleep—shutting out from sight and sound that hideous *outside*. This is the time when the wretched in mind and body find existence too great a burden, and cast it off with a shriek and a rush—plunging into the river or canal, or dashing beneath the wheels of the swift steam-chariots.

At all street-corners one notices the gin and beer shops. These are the homes of the poor, who find in them the warmth and comfort which are wanting in their domestic haunts. These shops are closed at mid-night, when the half or wholly drunken loiterers must straggle off into those holes and corners which *are* their homes. Probably there is no feature in barbaric life so curious and so characteristic as this—this Gin-house of the poor. The Government licenses these places, and derives a great income. The Upper-Castes fatten upon this very thing. What can be said of it—what done with it?

Another remarkable object in the London streets is the *Street Arab*. This is the name given to it by the Barbarians. But the Arab of Asia (if my reading be correct) is nothing like this creature. The London Arab is of the degraded and thieving class—the very sediment—but not yet fully weighted! In years a youth, but in feeling a ravening, sharp, adroit animal, quickened by the exercise of every instinct, and cool and expert from constant habit. He dodges in and out from under the heads of horses and the wheels of vehicles; mounts a lamp-post, or anything by which he may get a sight; seizes the bundle which you may have in hand; touches his uncombed front locks of hair, "Please, Sir, le' me carry it, Sir;" and trots before you, happy if he get twopence. Nobody knows where he sleeps, or eats, nor how he lives, at all. I have suddenly come upon two or more of them, when resting upon an iron grating. Their naked feet and heads, their thin limbs hung about with dirty rags, and their teeth chattering with cold—but never a word of complaint—no seeming thought of anything hard or uncommon. These iron bars cover, sometimes, an area below, into which the warm, moist air of kitchens comes, and rises through the gratings, loaded with the smell of cookery. Upon these bars will huddle together these half-naked and starved outcasts, happy in the partial warmth, and a hope of food—for, if only a bone, or a bit of that steaming soup could by any chance be theirs! Poor girls, of this wretchedness born, shivering upon the wintry swept corners, timidly offer you matches [kin-fue], "Please, Sir, buy"—and will run along by your side, if you give them a half-glance, begging you for pity to buy. Human misery finds no greater examples, nor any form of degradation deeper depths, than the lowest class of London—nor of London only, but of all the great towns.

This degradation takes on every shape of misery and shame. Crime of every kind breeds in it—disease, despair, and death! Is it inseparable from human existence—must excellence in humanity be only for the few?

London has for Misery its Charities—for Crime its vast Stone prisons. The latter are more accessible, and, for the offences of mere poverty, quite as desirable. Pauperism detests the alms-house—it hates subordination; and will, sometimes, starve before it seeks the bread of scornful wealth. Extreme indigence hardens—softness is turned to stone—human instinct feels wronged. "I wish work and pay, not idleness and pauper-bread." The cruel thing with the poor is, that at *first*, there is not debasement. Work is sought—but, continued inability to find work and honest bread, leads in the bad demon—which loves not, cares not, feels not—renders inhuman.

In walking the streets one feels the cold nature of the English Barbarians— one sees its exhibition everywhere. It is intensified by Caste divisions: there is no real sympathy. An Englishman shows in the streets, and in all public places, the indifference of a brute. Nothing moves him, nothing makes him laugh, smile, or give any sign of emotion. In sports, nominally sportive, there is nothing of gaiety—only with the Low-Castes very coarse and rough brutishness; and with the Upper a repulsive cynicism. This mood gives to the life of the streets no pleasing animation—only, at best, mere animal movement, as if each beast was intent upon his own particular hunger. At the Play there is no show of genuine enjoyment—and the dance (somebody said to me once) might be a dance of Death, so far as any lively pleasure appears.

The *Hansom Cab*—of which there are thousands—is a singular and characteristic thing. It is a vehicle of two wheels, drawn by one horse, and carries two passengers. The Barbarians, intent upon gain, allow the driver to urge his horse at speed through the crowded streets, giving no other warning than *hi-hi*! Everybody must look out *at his own peril*; for life and limb are unimportant compared with speed in business. One would not credit this—but as I have been nearly run over by these drivers more than once, not hearing the *hi-hi*! I can vouch for the existence of these privileged vehicles. The use of them is based upon the same rule, which allows of so many other things, to us inhuman or unjust—to say—that 'the convenience of trade' is paramount to trifling risks of life, limb, or soundness of abstract morality.

Another public chariot for passengers is the *Omnibus*. These are very numerous on the great thoroughfares. It is drawn by two horses, and will hold twelve or more inside and fourteen outside, upon the top. These are licensed by the law, and convey people a long distance for a small sum. The name is from the Roman, and means a bus (kiss) for all—a ridiculous term for which I can give no explanation, unless, as women and men ride in them promiscuously, some of the sly and coarse humour of the Barbarians may be meant. I refer, however, to the carriage, to give an illustration of street life, and of the English bearishness [che-liftze]. I have seen women and children waiting at a corner in the mud and rain, for the *'Bus*, and when it has stopped, I have seen men rudely elbow themselves to the front and enter upon the unoccupied seats, leaving the women to the inclemency of winter, or to the rain and sleet. And these not the *Roughs*, but gentlemen. This, too, one would scarcely believe, if one did not see.

The *police* [ki-ti] of London is noted for its stupidity; its members are the perpetual *butt* [la-phe] of farces and plays in the Theatres. Yet the liberty and the good name of the citizens are at their mercy. If a stranger be hustled and mobbed, it will be well for him to get out of the affair without any call for the police, for if one of these should come up, he will be as likely to pounce upon the innocent and injured as upon the wrong-doer. And he likes to make his *arrest* appear guilty before the magistrate—*he* is not mistaken. In selecting policemen, rather strength of body than any moral or mental qualification is looked for. And the theory seems to be that one cannot afford to pay for intelligent men, where merely the liberty and good name of the individual is concerned. Here again, "better that the particular person should suffer than that too much money should be paid;" especially as the Police are not likely to be *hard* upon the upper-Castes. To these they can be conveniently deaf, dumb, and blind.

One wonders, looking along the interminable extent of mean streets, to see the endless shops. It looks as if everybody had something to sell; and where the buyers can be who knows? You may watch some of these places for hours, and you will not see a soul enter or depart. Look in, and very likely some old man or woman is drowsing away, if in summer time, behind a paltry litter of old stuffs, the whole not worth a year's living; or, if in winter, half-perishing with cold, waiting for customers who never come. And these waifs [dri-tze] of a forgotten trade linger on, in old age, eating hungrily the husks of former traffic, which new ways have destroyed. London is an enormous shop with a West End of dwellings; these, however, not by any means shopless. It is a marvel. Thousands and thousands of mean shops, yet supporting the tens of thousands which live by them. One asks how any fair profit can do this. You will see a display of rusty goods, of tawdry ornaments, of dirty books, of mere rubbish; and if you venture inside you will hurry out again. The creatures inside are as unattractive as the wares. Do you believe these are places of honest dealing?

But in what are called respectable tradesmen's houses, profits must be little short of plunder—the business is so small. Yet the English Barbarians, of certain classes, seem to take to this mode of living upon the community with a hawk-like keenness. The difference between the price of an article of food, whether bought first hands, or after it has passed through these intermediaries, is a difference as of one-half to the whole—that is, the price is doubled!

These petty tradesmen glean their livings from the poor, who cannot help themselves; but, in truth, the common feeling is on all hands, "Let us plunder, and be plundered." It is merely a question of securing a good share.

London, therefore, not wanting in a certain air of greatness in some parts, really expresses very clearly the traits of the English Barbarians. It is gloomy, morose, huckstering, repulsive. Huge it is, like the English barbaric power; but incoherent, uninformed, unlovely, without the beauty of refinement.

Still, in the purpose of the Sovereign Lord, one may guess the use of this great centre of barbaric influence—it is to beat down the distant and worse tribes beyond the great seas. As one sort of predatory creature devours another, so these Barbarians destroy worse types of men than themselves, and prepare the way for human advancement. Whether, however, they shall themselves ever emerge into a noble life, is a curious inquiry.

The *West End* is that part where the High-Castes reside when in the Metropolis. It is the seat of Palaces, of Courts, of better built streets, and of the best Parks and ornamental grounds. Here the Theatres and revelries are; the great dinners, the Routs, the Dances, and the stir of High life. Here, in the Parks, the grand dames air themselves, their poodles, and servants. Here, on horseback, they astonish onlookers by the display of figure, and, on foot, by a show of head-dress and draperies, and bright eyes and fashionable forms. Luxury, idleness, show, frivolity, mock the wretchedness which despairs and dies, or robs and cheats in not distant back slums [gna-zti]. Still, along these costly rows of equipages and richly-attired women and men, on whose persons may be single gems which would give bread to thousands, one looks in vain for what would give a human and pleasing touch. If you see a lovely face, it might as well be at a funeral. The whole spectacle is cold and lifeless; the horses only have animation, and they are kept down to the tamest possible step. The world cannot show finer animals, nor wealthier owners, nor more luxurious idlers, nor more unattractive human beings. Joy is unknown, and any touch of natural sentiment, along the long line of devotees of wearisome Time-killers, may be looked for in vain.

When I first walked about the streets, I found myself the victim of Barbarian insolence. My dress attracted rude notice, and I soon adopted the common garb. This, however, only partially removed observation—for my features were different. However, a longer use accustomed me to rudeness, and enabled me to let it pass unnoticed. One part of the town, particularly, appeared to be infested with women, who accosted me and insisted upon walking with me. I could not for some time understand this; but since, I have been informed. The neighbourhood of the Theatres—in fact, many parts of the West End—are the haunts of these poor creatures, many of whom seem to be but little more than children. On one occasion a well-dressed young girl, as I was leaving the Play, smilingly spoke to me, and asked the time! I took out my watch, which was worn in my fob, and holding it up to the gaslight to see the hour, it was snatched from my hand. I merely caught sight of a person vanishing round a corner. The girl exclaimed, "What a pity," and put her hand gently on my arm. I, however, moved away quickly; but all trace of watch and robber was gone, and the young woman too! This would not happen to me now. I did not then know of the state of things in the *centre of Christendom*! Of course I was robbed on several occasions, and in many ways, and shortly found that I must look upon everybody as a rascal, as the English do.

But perhaps there is nothing in London so exasperating as the *Lodging-house keeper*. This is a creature not unknown to other regions, but reserved for its most perfect and exquisite finish for the Metropolis of the World (as the English like to call London).

This being starves you, freezes you, cheats you, waits upon you, steals from you, lies to you, flatters you, and backbites you; reads your private papers, has keys for all your boxes and drawers, and a complete inventory of all your effects. She chooses from your handkerchiefs, smoothes her hair with your brushes, scents it with your perfumes, "makes herself beautiful" at your toilet. She examines your boots, and finds a pair which you "will never miss," for her *James*. She brushes your trowsers, and takes care of any loose change. She waits at your table, counts the oranges, and thinks she will try one.

When you ask for that *pie*, she has given it to the dog—"I thought you were done with it, Sir." She cracks a window pane, and charges it to you in the bill. She eats your bread, drinks your beer, *tastes* your wine; and charges you a shilling for a pinch of salt. She demands pay for coals you have not burned, and for gas you have not used. She gives you sheets that are worn out, and makes you pay the price of new when you stick your toes through them. She demands the *wash* for coverings which you have not soiled, and for *tidys* that were never tidy. She has a lot of cracked cheap glasses and crockery, which she makes you pay "for cracking, Sir"—as she has already made others many times before. In truth, these are invaluable to her—"she get new ones, not she"! (as she says to her drudge of all work).

You pay for clean table-linen and towels weekly (and weakly)—but if you ask for a fresh table-cloth, "I have a friend to dine"—you get it, and a charge for it *extra*. If you intimate that you *could* not have had "so much butter"—you are reminded that you are speaking to a lady, who has been accustomed to have *gentlemen* in her rooms!

You sleep on "hobbles," and are blotched in a curious manner. You hint to the servant that you have seen *something* as well as felt; but "nothing of that sort was ever in my house." At last, when you find it quite impossible to satisfy the ever-increasing rapacity, you "think you will leave." You are very forcibly reminded that you are bound to "a month's notice, Sir." And, happy to get off any way, this you waive and pay for. Nor do you flinch when, on exhibiting the final account, "my lady" has recorded a list of casualties, very startling:—

	(Mental notes:—)
Towel-horse broken	always broken.
Chair-back ditto	ditto.
Door-plate cracked	ditto.
Table-cover stained	old.
Carpet ditto	old, worthless.
Walls injured by boxes	old, knocks.
Candlestick broken	servant.
Postages, and servant for letters	(paid).
Blacking, salt, and pepper (omitted and always charged).	
Wash of coverings, toilets, and counterpanes.	

You glance at the foot, pay it. You think all is done. But "my lady" expects a "slight gratuity, Sir; not for myself, of course, but for Nancy!" I should add that this harpy is a devotee, and is as punctual at prayers as at prey!

One, however, soon finds a change of place is no change of fate. The pickings and stealings may take a little different form, but the result is the same. The only thing is, to get for your money cleanliness and comfort; estimate the whole cost, and consider the plunder a part of it—for you will not escape. The *Lodging House* is only typical. All are preyed upon and prey upon. It is the rule of barbaric life, and *Caste* makes it inevitable. The low think it no robbery to get a share of the plunder enjoyed by the rich. There is, in the general state of things, a rough instinct of justice in it—only innocent people also suffer.

If you live in one of the huge buildings called Hotels, you are no better off. Here, every mouthful is counted; you cannot breathe (so to say) without paying for it. If a waiter look at you, he will expect a *gratuity* [*ti-tin*].

After you have paid everything which an experienced and greedy ingenuity can think of, as you are about to leave, the servants will obsequiously open and stand at doors, hold and brush your hat (already *brushed* bare), catch up some trifle, and generally get in your way, to force gratuities out of your good-nature. If you, at length, reach the vehicle called for you, before you can open the door of it, up will start, as from the ground, a miserable creature, who intercepts your motion, adroitly opening the door for you, and then, when you are seated, stands staring directly into your face, with his hand still on the door-handle, awaiting a gratuity. You have buttoned up your coat, your gloves are on, it is cold; but you cannot refuse the demand.

You are finally off; you arrive at your new quarters. Before you can wink, up starts a first cousin [tw-in-ti] of him who has just stared at you, who, in his turn, seizes hold of the door-handle, and shows in every motion that he has seized you too, at least to the extent of *sixpence*. You step out; he touches his hair (he has no hat); you try not to see him; but impossible—the pennies must come.

But why attempt to delineate these endless methods of prey. The poor wretches who live by these miserable shifts are innumerable and everywhere. One does not begrudge the *pennies*, but detests the nuisance, and the debasement which it demonstrates.

London is an undesirable place of residence, unless for the rich, and to them only for a few months in the year. But it is full of objects of study to him who cares to know anything of barbaric life, or who wishes to investigate the records and literature of the Western tribes.

All great cities are much alike; it is the different aspect of human life which is the noticeable thing. Unless, on the whole, a great city exhibits humanity in a pleasing condition, it is a failure, however rich it may be. London, which was described one hundred and fifty years ago as a "Province of

Houses," certainly contains an immense population bare of attractive features. No doubt much must be put down to climate and fuel. The former is foggy, cold, dark, and disheartening for the larger part of the year; and the latter, by its foul gas [ptrut] and smoke, makes the fog and cloudy air so obscure as to give an unearthly gloom. The poor feel not only the gnawing of hunger but the nipping frost, unrelieved by any smiles in earth or sky. The mud of the streets is like a nasty grease, and one walks or crosses the ways in terror of befoulment. The clothes and the face are exposed not only to this, but also to the defiling smoke which drops a steady drizzle [kri-tze] of black atoms upon everything.

Poor shivering creatures—men, women, and children—are at street crossings and other places, incessantly sweeping away so much of the mud as may enable pedestrians to pass with less weight of nastiness to boots or skirts. These, often very old, or lame, or half-starved and ragged, piteously expect a penny. I have often watched the little girl or boy, or old tottering man, and seen the hurrying passers, on and on, the stream ceaseless, yet have rarely seen a single penny given. I have sometimes put in my outside pocket some copper coins to have at hand; and when I have given to one of these sweepers, the thanking look was well worth the petty trouble; it also showed clearly that the gift was not too common. How these victims of poverty live, where they cover their misery from the wintry cold, I cannot guess. I used to notice one very old and almost imbecile who swept at a place where I crossed frequently. He would stand motionless under a thick, scrubby tree which stood just at the corner of the streets, clinging to its shelter, slight as it was, for protection from wind and rain, and barely touching his head with his finger with a bow when people passed. Occasionally, slowly, and with limbs stiff and back hardly bent to toil, grubbing across the way with his muddy broom, but never giving other sign of vitality. I missed his silent figure one day; another wretch had stepped into his heritage, [qua-ti] and stood beneath the scrubby tree—the old, silent, patient sufferer had found a pauper's grave at last.

Akin to these (indeed cousins-german) are the old creatures who sit at street corners, or by the way-sides, selling trifles, which nobody buys. Through the long, cold days, huddled into a heap, and looking like a pile of rags with a red face a-top, motionless, will one of these sit, bleering and winking with rheumy eyes at the juiceless fruit, or handful of nuts, or ancient cakes, or nasty sweets, displayed upon her little board. If by chance you happen to curiously turn your eyes upon this strange object, some start of vitality appears, but vanishes as you pass on. Who buys, who eats; what can possibly come of this strange traffic? Yet you will see these human things, day after day, sitting, one would think, despairingly, awaiting the buyers who never come. How fine a thing it would be for the idle rich, who like a new sensation, to go about the streets, accompanied by a servant, and buy of these patient crones [ko-tse] a good part of their daily store!

When I first walked about the great places of the city, I was surprised to see very many miserable men punished (as I supposed) by the *Cangue*. They had suspended to their necks two boards, one in front and one behind. Upon these were curious devices. Horses, women, great fires burning, ships blowing up, and the like. Perpetually walking to and fro, just to the measured distance, and never once sitting down, never once speaking, nor being spoken to, these creatures, thus accoutred, walked dismally right in the garbage of the gutters. No one, by any chance, ever noticed them, nor by any chance did they ever do other than, with slow and limping gait, keep up the march of doleful dismalness! For long I puzzled over these ragged apparitions; after many moons I found that they were merely stalking advertisements! [muun-shi].

I might give many other illustrations of life in London, differing from what is known to us. The human dregs are truly dreadful. Their haunts are indescribable. Many settle upon the oozy and slimy river bank, when the tide is out, seeking anything which perchance may have been washed up. Wading in a filth which covers the feet and befouls the whole tattered creature, this being, nicknamed *mud-lark* [pho-ul-sti], becomes an outcast to all decency. Others prowl about the ash-heaps, and sift and pick over any heaps of rubbish, carefully gathering from garbage, bones, rags, anything which can give the merest pittance. It must be certain that human degradation can go no deeper when to debasing and starving poverty is added drunkenness, loathsome brutality, violence, and crime.

Possibly the greatest city of the Barbarians is not worse than the worst of some portions of a great city with us; nor should I refer emphatically to the wretchedness of London were it not for the boastful ignorance manifested by Barbarian writers and literati. These always speak of the preëminence of English civilization—of the grand and humanizing influence of their true religion—of the wealth, the liberty, and the happiness of the people! No other tribe is so humane, so just, so brave, so wise, so free, so prosperous, so contented and happy!

In the face of these declarations, which are to be met with on all sides, London is a marvel! Nor London only, other cities are more marvellous; one wonders what the standard must be, by which is tested this boasted preëminence. If by *other* Western Barbarian life, and compared to that, truly superior, then what must be the condition at large of the Western tribes?

There is a nuisance common enough with us about the streets; and in London it takes every shape. I mean street music. Besides the troops, which infest public places, startling you with a crashing outburst of noise from many brass instruments, there are mendicants, of all ages and both sexes. The halt, the blind, come singing in the most doleful manner, unaccompanied; and others making the night hideous with squeaking wind-pipes, or noisy things of some sort. After annoying you for a long time, one of these will perhaps boldly knock at your door, and demand a gratuity. Some of these creatures blacken themselves, and appear in the courts and squares singing and playing not too decently. Some poor woman, with babes in a kind of basket pushed along on wheels, will try to gain sympathy and pennies by screaming out some woful strain which nobody comprehends, and which grates upon the ear like rasping iron. Sometimes a miserable wretch, shivering with cold, will stand before the bright, warm doors of a drinking place, and sing his feeble note of woe. The most dreadful objects will be those horribly deformed, who, crooked and distorted out of human shape contrive to get along in some strange device of wagon, pushed by their own stumps of hands or feet. Generally these affect to play upon something, no matter what, and drag on an existence too wretched to think of.

But why dwell upon these lowest strata of human existence. It shows out on all hands. Among the gilded idlers of the West End, on the very porticoes of grand Temples. Luxury and pride drive, with mien unconscious of human want and woe; unconscious of "the common lot" awaiting all; almost over the very bodies of these to whom life is so deep a darkness.

London in its sparkling splendours laughs and makes merry. Within its great Parks, in the summer months, musical birds make the air melodious, and flowering shrubs, and fine trees and verdure, give beauty and rest to thousands of the poor—but not to the lowest. These slink away into the fouler haunts, or spread themselves over the green country, seeking new sources of pitiful gain! In the mid-summer the best of London looks almost cheerful; and a sky more pure, and a sun-light which, though not brilliant, *is* soft and warm, render life tolerable to the poor. For the rich and idle, they go out of the City and leave it, as they say, *empty*—for those who remain are *nobodies* [cham-tsi]. Yes, the millions left to toil are nothing. Still, the magnificence of the High-Caste flowers immediately upon that toiling mass—from *it* grows all the spreading splendour which regards it not. The glowing flame cares nothing for the black coal; nor is the money soiled which passes through the hands of despised indigence. London gay and brilliant, glows and glitters upon its dung-heap—as a luminous vapour flashes and flits over a putrescent carcass.

Perhaps one should not be too critical, nor expect other than these inconsistencies in humanity. Misery will be largely its *own* cause. Great populations do not herd together without shocking inequalities of condition; yet, the reflection will arise, Is not the *boast* of refinement and civilization too much for patience—would not humility be better? The boast means self-content—humility would mean a steady work for improvement. One sees not, nor really cares to see; the other sees and feels, and wishes to remove what gives a sense of humiliation and of pain.

Splendid London may disregard the blackness of the East End (as the poorest quarter is called), and think itself a good *Christian* to shun it as a place of horror; but, to my *pagan* wisdom, it seems indispensable to devote that money and energy to the civilization of the English Barbarians, which is now sent to "*the benighted heathen.*" These, no doubt, have the poor and the degraded, the black spots of moral imbecility; nor would one object to any really benevolent enterprise, though not too rational. But the missionary [kan-te] spirit rises so distinctly from an ignorant self-sufficiency and blindness, a merely superstitious notion of a thing to be done as any rite or ceremony is to be done—*for the good of the doer*—that it is impossible to have much respect for it. Then, too, the whole thing shapes into a machine, by the working of which men are to live and get honours and places. If a truly grand benevolence moved the people, it would be impossible to overlook *the Heathen at home.*

CHAPTER XIV.
SOME GENERAL OBSERVATIONS.

IT is the business of a wise man (as our illustrious *Confutzi* and *Menzi* say) to seek the *conditions* of the visible forms of things—whether the things be those which we see, or only those which take form in the mind. The conditions are what the Barbarians call *laws*. We see that the use of a certain earth will enrich some soils, and impoverish others; we examine into the cause; we try to discover the conditions which make this difference. We know that, generally and broadly, the elements are the same, but they are differently combined. The Western Barbarians are of the same race with ourselves—inherently the general nature is the same. What difference of combination of similar elements has produced results so dissimilar?

In the mighty East, where civilization goes back into the most distant and dim antiquity, *the laws* which underlie organized governments and customs, and which give form and life to communities, are very different, and sometimes antagonistic. It is certain, therefore, that man, really the same everywhere, has, in the course of ages, evolved from his own and surrounding nature very different forms of social life in the East and in the West. Man and nature radically the same, have, in different conditions, grown and put forth very dissimilar shapes of growth. The tree and the fruit are rooted in similar soil, have grown in similar air, sun, and rain. Even the trees are not wholly unlike, nor the fruit; yet, most unlike, when duly considered; and, when regarded with a view to usefulness and to perpetuation, *one* may demand the axe, and the *other* only the nice pruning-knife [quin-tse]. But a difference so great implies a different seed-germ— not necessarily; for, from the same germ, one may have a bitter, even a poisonous fruit, which finer culture can make sweet and healthful.

If we assume, then, the same germ, whence so great diversity? In my poor mind, when, among the Barbarians, sad and bewildered by the disorder, confusion, and complexity, this question tediously presented itself—"Is man a creature of chance—is there no perfect rule?" I would say, "Is his *growth* fortuitous like plants, beginning with similar germs and yet dissimilar—so, growing according to the hidden differences and the differing circumstances? Is there no common standard—no fixed measure—no absolute truth?" But, in my poor thought, I also said, "The Sovereign Lord lives in his children, and moral truth (*divine illumination*) must be. *It is simply true*, and can be no other. Human *forms* of social being must be measured by it; and, however complexed and confused, *are so measured*, and will not long exist if radically inconsistent. Yet these forms may be bad without being wholly rootless, and grow *deformed*, strange, and noxious."

In looking upon the disorderly and complex features of Barbarian life, two things prominently strike my poor mind. One is, *a restless activity*, accompanied with love of personal distinction and admiration of strength. The other, is the singular *position of women*. To the former, may be charged the selfish greed, the callous indifference, the delight in forays and plunder.

To the latter, that aspect of dissolute disorder, that curious complexity of ideas and principles, which render the whole Barbarian Society a marvel—I liked to have said *a disgust*—to one unaccustomed to it.

The position of women, as it affects *the family*, no doubt has an all-pervading influence—if that position be wrong, we have, at once, a grand source of evil.

How far the *great Superstition*, super-imposed upon the *olden* Idolatry (dark and cruel) may have deepened the shades of Barbaric nature, and strengthened its old admiration of force and rapine, may be only surmised. Certain it is that the Jewish *Jah* is not unlike the *Odin* of these tribes; and (as I have said) the gentle Christ-god, himself a Jew worshipper of Jah, has been received only as subordinate; in fact, a *Sacrifice* by *Jah* made to himself to appease himself! A character, in fine, not *strong enough* for these fierce tribes.

We have the *government and the family* resting upon a different basis in the West from what they rest upon in the East. In the West, it is difficult to say if there be *any rule* upon which either securely reposes. In the East, the *rule* is as clear, and as clearly recognized, and as undoubtedly *obeyed*, as *any* rule can be. The existence of the Sovereign Lord is not more certainly admitted, and his authority not more implicitly submitted to. This is the rule of OBEDIENCE.

But aside from principles which control comprehensive forms, like the Family and Government, there are secondary growths, usages (perhaps not referable to any marked rule), which have had powerful influence. For instance, the mode of trying persons suspected of Crime, appears to my poor mind to be very fantastic and irrational. The Barbarians, however, boast of the superiority of their way over all other tribes, ancient or modern.

When a crime has been committed, and some one, suspected, has been arrested, he is brought before a Judge, whose duty it is to see if there be good reasons for the arrest. The very first thing, we should think, would be to ask the accused to give any explanation he may wish. Not at all; he is told to say *nothing*, for if he do it will be recorded and may go to *his hurt*. How to his hurt unless he be guilty? How it may be that the accused could, at once, explain everything—but no—the officers who have made the arrest wish to work out a *theory* of their own; and the Judge, listening to these officers, who are uneducated, rude, and often at work for a large prize, commits the accused to prison to be tried over again, really, at a future day, by some other Judge. Meantime everybody who, upon the theory of the officers, is imagined to know anything, is ordered to give security that they will appear at the next trial, and say what they know. And if a witness cannot give this security (frequently the case with the poor), he is also thrust into prison. In this manner persons, who have been so unfortunate as to be fixed upon by these ignorant officers, are treated like the accused, and put to great inconvenience and sometimes suffering, either in themselves, or their families, or affairs. This goes on—the next trial is postponed, delay after delay, whilst the officers are working out *their theory*; and finally the accused is discharged and the witnesses also, the whole disgraceful proceeding being a *blunder*, in which innocent people have been punished as *criminal*, and the *Criminal* has *escaped*! A natural and simple examination of the accused, when first brought before the Judge, would have saved all this loss, suffering, and shame! Such an absurdity can only be to the advantage of the guilty!

A man may be caught under circumstances of guilt so certain that there is no *rational* hypothesis of innocence. Yet, with the very blood and property of the murdered perhaps upon him, surprised, red-handed in the very act, he will be treated as if he were merely *suspect*; *will be cautioned to say nothing*; will have every chance and opportunity to escape by reason of the unaccountable mode of procedure. For he is still innocent. Such is the hypothesis; and disregarding the obvious and simple way of asking for an explanation consistent with innocence (when guilt would be doubly manifest), the other ridiculous hypothesis is maintained, if possible, and the whole community and many innocent people are afflicted and tortured with the most minute and painful investigations (having perhaps no sort of relation to the matter), to see if some doubt may not arise *somehow*, not as to the guilt, but as to some parts of the case as *imagined* to be!

Thus, *theories* of guilt are to be established when the fact is *patent*, if one will simply look at the proofs immediately at hand!

In this case just supposed, too, there is no trial at all of the *man* so clearly seen to be guilty. Twelve men are convened by a sort of inferior Judge, first to see how the dead man came to be dead—it is certain as anything can well be! Yet this kind of Court must go through the long, tedious, and painful inquiry, *how* the man died. Witnesses are dragged from home, from their pursuits, ruined may be; the whole community horrified, and the twelve men kept from home and business, and shocked by the most disgusting examinations of the dead! This whole process seems rather designed to give fees and business to the petty Judge and officers who compose this singular tribunal.

But when this *sham* Court has got through, the accused meantime, and the witnesses, are still awaiting the real inquiry, which may be put off for many weeks.

When, after tedious delays, *twenty-four* petty judges, assisted by an officer, having made up their minds to formally charge the accused with the crime, he is brought before a Judge, who is now for the first time to really try the man, another curious thing occurs. The Judge is not trusted alone to proceed—he must have twelve little Judges, and several Lawyers, to assist him. The little judges are the JURY, not selected for knowledge nor excellency, but any twelve men who can be readily got. Generally they are very poor represervatives of even the average wisdom and morality. They know nothing of law, nor of the Court, nor are they in the least competent to undergo the complex, tedious, and artificial *trial* to which they are about to be put, as well as the accused. However, the business of these twelve is *not* to look directly at the man and at the clear evidence against him—which might be within even their competency—but they are sworn upon the *Sacred Writings and by Jah* (under severe penalties) to try the accused according *to the Law and the evidence.* Now, the Lawyers and the Judge determine as to the law, and the twelve men must obey them as to *that*—the twelve, however, are to determine as to the evidence. This means—they are to see and hear the witnesses, examine the objects of proof (which may take many days); keep all the statements, conflicting, confused, or other; hear all that the Lawyers may say; watch the demeanour of the witnesses, and of the accused—and they must take the *Case* as presented and offered to them, however absurd much of it may be—and, finally, after all, they are not to take *this Evidence* (as it is called) to judge it for *themselves*—no, they must take it *under the direction of the Judge.* They are sworn *to try* according to the Law and the evidence; but *evidence* means *legal* evidence! and the Judge (aided by the Lawyers) directs the twelve men as to what is *evidence.* Under these conditions, one may judge as to the usefulness of this Jury—unless as a contrivance for the torturing of the innocent and the clearing of the guilty!

I was present and examined this matter—for from the common boast of this excellent Jury-mode of *trial,* I wished to see with my own mind.

At length, the twelve men being confined, so that *they* cannot escape, in a sort of box; the Judge and the Lawyers being in their places, attired in the absurd wigs and black gowns [phe-ty-kos] (somebody once whispered in my ear, black-guards) [kon-di-to-ri]; the accused is ordered to stand up. The charge of murder is read;—confused by so much barbarous jargon, that no one but the Judge and the Lawyers understand it—in fact, oftentimes do not understand it—and the criminal often escapes trial because the *proper* jargon has not been used. This *mixed tongue* is the only one allowed in these trials, and must be taken from the fountain of Wisdom (as the Law book is called containing it). The speech is uncertain, only known to the Lawyers; and a mistake spoils the whole charge. Well, after more or less wrangling among the Lawyers, the charge finally stands. I must explain; there are *two sides* of Lawyers—one (hired to do so), by *every means* in its power tries to get the accused discharged, and is helped to do this by all the machinery of the trial—the other merely watches the proceedings, and sees that they are not too absolutely controlled by the other side. The latter, also, open and state the matter, and conduct it; but neither side works simply to obtain the truth. On the side of the accused, if guilty, the truth is *not* wanted; and, on the other side, there is no interest in the matter which greatly moves. But the interest for the accused may be not merely to gratify, in some cases, powerful relatives, but to obtain as large *a sum* of money as the Lawyers can get—which, where life is at stake, may be all the accused has now, or may, if discharged, acquire. In fact, in cases of robbery, the Lawyers for the accused may have received their compensation from the very plunder!

The accused says to the charge either *Guilty* or *Not Guilty*! This is a mere form. Then the names of the twelve men are called over, to see that none have got away—for it is a hateful and disgusting business often, wherein they *instinctively* feel they really have no function—and yet enforced upon them, often to their actual great loss and suffering.

How the scene fairly opens. The twelve little judges in their box; the big one sitting aloft, with pig-tail-ear-flapper wig; the Lawyers in pig-tail wigs and gowns; the officers of the Court; the witnesses, cowering and afraid; the accused in his high, strong cage (or box); and the spectators, friends, relatives, associates of the witnesses and of the accused—women and men—crowding in the dark corners of the Hall of trial.

The Lawyers call and examine the witnesses. These are not permitted to tell the truth in their own way at all. They are sworn upon the *Sacred Writings*, upon pain of penalties of the Law, and the dreadful fear of the awful Jah and Hell, *to speak the truth, the whole truth, and nothing but the truth*! Now, the truth which they are to speak must be that *sort* of truth which the Lawyers and the Judge determine upon to hear—not by any means *that* truth which the witness, in his simplicity, is about to utter! Here, then, an honest and conscientious witness is likely to be at once bewildered; but a callous, self-possessed one, who does not intend to say one word more than he can help, finds himself doing exactly what the Lawyers and the Court understand by the oath—that is, to speak *for* the one side or the other; *not for truth*!

Consider the position of a witness, perhaps a timid woman, or an inexperienced person, never before called upon to take the *awful oath*, never before in such a place! Confronted, made to stand up, *thrust* without respect, sometimes rudely and with positive disrespect; treated, in fact, as if a party to the crime, though perfectly ignorant of anything excepting of some chance *link* required in the *theory* of the charge—thrust forward into the gaze of the Judge, of the whole assembly. Every eye is fastened upon the trembling witness. She is ordered in a rough tone to hold up her hand, to take the *oath*, *to kiss the Sacred Writings*! What with the crowd, the novel and painful position, by this time the poor woman, when asked a question, can scarcely speak. The old, half-deaf Judge, turns his awful be-wigged head to her, raises his ear-flapper and says, "Speak louder, witness; I can't hear you." An officer bawls out, "Silence!" and, not unlikely, the poor witness fairly collapses, faints, and she is allowed to be seated.

The Lawyers examine the witnesses, and if one begins to say something very damaging, if possible, will interrupt him; or, by and by, will insinuate some vile charge against him, to destroy his character with the hearers—not that there be any truth in the insinuation, but merely to effect the purpose of a vile *minion* paid to defend, perhaps, a notorious offender!

Thus the *trial* proceeds; every effort is made on the side of the accused (which is the active side) to mislead, to confuse, to bewilder. The Law, read from big books, is constantly referred to, now to stop a witness in what he is about to say; now to get something *already* said scratched off from the minds of the twelve men; and now to take the opinion of the Judges as to whether this or that should, or should not, be heard by the Jury.

All these things go on day after day, not at all because there is any doubt as to the guilt of the accused, but because by these confused and interminable proceedings, the Lawyers who act for him expect to get him discharged— and discharged, declared by the twelve men to be *not guilty*! This is the great point; for, if this occur, it does not matter at all that the accused himself confess to the crime, *on no account* can he ever be arrested again for the offence! "But how, when the proofs of guilt are present and so certain, can the Lawyers expect to get the twelve men to go against their very senses?" To answer this is to show the nature of the Jury system very plainly.

When all the wranglings and speeches and Law-readings of the Lawyers have at last ended; when the Judge—who has in the course of the trial already loaded the twelve with all sorts of instructions as to what they are to keep in mind as *legal* evidence, and what they are to leave out of mind—has made a long and confused speech (often interrupted by the Lawyers) recapitulating those parts of the conflicting mass of evidence which, and *only* which, *is* evidence, and has told them the manner in which this evidence must be applied to the charge; has finally told them that the crime charged must be the precise *crime* laid down in the Law-books by that *name*, and none other; and that having found beyond all doubt that that crime, upon the *legal* evidence, has been committed, then has *the accused committed the crime* so defined, and so proved? To be certain of this, the accused must not only be found to have done it, but he must have known that he was doing it—that is, he must have been sound in mind. And if in any of these particulars there be any doubt, the accused must be acquitted; and further, every one of the twelve must agree—if any *one* withhold his assent, then the prisoner cannot be declared to be guilty!

With all these clear and simple directions (!) as to how they are to use their minds, an officer leads the twelve into a strong-room, and fastens them in! to consider their *verdict* (as it is called). Not to consider simply and directly upon the plain evidence of their senses, and according to reason ordinarily used, but to consider *their Verdict*—a technical, artificial affair, made by the Lawyers, and only fit for *their* minds—if even *they* could do anything satisfactory to an honest man with it!

The twelve are locked in and guarded by an officer; deprived of food, of rest, of any recreation; perhaps already exhausted from the hair-splitting [di-do-tzi] and intricate directions and proceedings. They are *Sworn* to give their verdict according to the *Law* (first) and the *Evidence* (second). The evidence, however, being *all law*. Then, too, they are to say either *Guilty*, or *not guilty*; and no more.

Now, the Lawyer's expectation may become verified. There is no sort of doubt in any of the twelve that the accused is a horrid wretch, and that he is guilty. But one man has got hold of an idea, based upon something said by the Judge, or perhaps only the suggestion of his own mind; and think of the vanity, the stupidity, the dishonesty, the mere indifference, the obstinacy, the excessive timidity, the weakness, which is likely to be in each of the twelve; one man has got *his* opinion—it is a matter of conscience. The one man is sufficient. Nothing can move him. Hour after hour passes. Night comes on—hunger knocks at the stomach; home is wanted; business is exacting; illness oppresses some, lassitude and sheer exhaustion overpower others—the one persists, only more obstinate by opposition—"The man no doubt is guilty, but I doubt if he be guilty according to law!"

They cannot agree upon a verdict. The Judge and everybody else long since have gone to *their* homes and pleasures. *They* (the twelve) cannot escape unless they agree. To be sure, they may report to the Judge late on the next day that they cannot agree—only, however, to receive new directions (!), and be sent back again and kept till they shall agree!

Human nature gives way. The one, strong and resolute, overpowers the eleven—or, rather, there have been only a part who would not have given over long ago. The fine maxim of English law—"*It is better that a thousand guilty escape than that one innocent suffer*"—turns the scale. There is a *doubt*—or something which looks like it—"let the accused have the benefit of it!"

Now, in this scene, I am taking it for granted that the twelve are really not dishonest—not one of them. But suppose *one* is, in secret, the determined friend of the accused!

Thus, the Verdict of the Jury (not the direct and honest opinion of twelve men in a rational and ordinary use of their minds) is recorded in the Court—*Not guilty*. And a murderer is at once discharged; perhaps escorted with applause from the place by associates of his evil courses. Restored to the community which doubts not his guilt, and which has been horrified, agitated, and oppressed by its frightful details! It will be noticed how admirably everything, in this system, works to procure the escape of the guilty; but it must not be overlooked that it falls with crushing weight upon the *innocent*. Simple and direct inquiry would generally clear him at once. But no—the *theory* in the minds of the officers is, that this *innocency* is a fraud; and the whole machinery works just as irrationally as before; because, the clear evidences of innocency are disregarded—the prisoner's guilt is unreasonably assumed (contrary to the reverse legal maxim) *by the officers*; and the whole crushing blow of this assumed guilt falls upon the innocent. He is thrust into prison; torn from family, friends, human sympathy; his actual trial is put off week after week, aye, month after month, whilst the officers hunt for what does not exist outside of their imaginations; and, finally, from sheer shame, the poor victim is discharged before an *actual trial*—discharged, it may be ruined and for ever tainted with the foul and unjust suspicion. Or, perhaps, finally *tried*, escapes after a long, tedious and confused scene; where the officers, anxious to convict one whom *they* have so long assumed to be guilty, contrive to throw just enough of suspicion upon the victim to render his life ever after insupportable! However, he finally goes at large—ruined by enormous expenses, health shattered by confinement in prison, and *tainted* in character. The victim of an absurd system—for the verdict is, for him, irrational and cruel. If, in the other case, *not guilty* did not mean what the words imply—so, in this, the Jury give a no more meaning *Verdict*. No expression of any actual opinion. No sympathy, no regret; nothing to reinstate the unfortunate victim of official stolidity and conceit. *Nothing* whatever; not so much as any compensation for loss of time and money. Meantime, during this pursuit of the innocent, the real criminal has got safely away.

Now, this strange *Jury system*, boasted of as the *Palladium* of Liberty by the English Barbarians, strikes my poor mind as something very cumbersome, irrational, and hurtful. The criminal class may well esteem it, for it seems exactly contrived to set the criminal at liberty, and to vex, terrify, annoy, and confuse everybody else. Witnesses themselves often fare more hardly than the actual criminal! and Society is shocked by needless and reiterated exposures of every particular of dreadful things to no rational purpose— unless to give fees to Lawyers and a host of busy officials, who live and fatten in these horrors.

One might suspect that the whole machinery was contrived by the Lawyers (called *criminal*) to effect their purpose—that is, to protect their friends and supporters; the numerous men, women, and half-grown youths swarming everywhere, and known as the *criminal class*.

Another unjust custom is when a man offends a Judge, he is not at once brought before him for reproof and proper correction. No; for his disrespect he is compelled to pay a *fine* [tsig] in money which may beggar his innocent family, or prevent his creditors from obtaining their dues; or, *unable* to pay, must lie in prison till it *be paid*, or until released by the angry Judge. Thus making the innocent to suffer! How much better in our *Flowery Land*, where disrespectful conduct is at once reprimanded and, if the disrespect be marked, punished on the spot, in the presence of the magistrate, and under his paternal direction.

These may serve to illustrate usages not readily referable to any principle. They are rooted in old customs, when general ignorance and universal poverty made the mass one, and when simplicity and directness were natural. They are retained now in an artificial and totally different state of society, for no better reason than the English Barbarians have for other abuses and enormities—*they support the fungi which cling to them*! And the upper classes find their interests concerned in maintaining things as they are. The lower classes, too ignorant to see, are made to believe that nothing in human Wisdom and experience excels these very Laws and customs! The Barbarian stolidity, too, in the well-to-do classes, supports these singular views as to the perfection of the Laws and system of administration. These classes constantly mistake this *stolidity* for solidity of character. When an evil is unmistakable, none the less, instead of removing it, they say, "Better bear those ills we have than fly to others we know not of!" (Quoting from their great Shakespeare.) But they do not stop to consider if it must necessarily follow that when one quits one ill he flies to *another*. As if one with a sore finger should refuse to apply any remedy to the *finger* for fear he might thereupon find a sore upon his leg!

Perplexed with these anomalous conditions, and by the stupid conceit and selfish indifference—the callousness and greed of the English Barbarians— I have wondered if, after all, these men were not of a different kind [sty-pho]. Possibly, the Sovereign Lord and Father of men, for wise purposes, may have created different sorts of men. Animals of the same type differ in swiftness, in strength, in intelligence. The Western Barbarians, though of the same type, may be inferior to our Illustrious people in the moral and mental functions. For some purpose in Eternal Wisdom, the Almighty Lord has given them strength of body, energy, and an *intellect* sharp in matters of the *instinct*—which refers to the needs and passions of the body—thus, calculating, ingenious in contrivance, and inordinately selfish; but has not given them a large moral faculty, nor a broad and comprehensive mind. *They are, therefore, incapable of improvement beyond a limited range.*

The Idolatry, and its horrible grotesqueness—the inefficacy of the good in the character of the Christ-god, to influence the least abatement in the passion for Force; the cold-blooded abuses, and the confusion of error and truth, may be thus accounted for.

This, however, suggests a continuance of the evils which have fallen upon *others*. The *All-wise* sees where chastisement is due—and allows the Western Barbarians their time. The offences of the East need chastisement. The quickness, strength, and greed of the Barbarians, unchecked by moral considerations, make them the scourge of other distant peoples not possessing these qualities. The scourge is needed, otherwise it would not be permitted. There is a sufficiency of morality to prevent dissolution; and the Western tribes will no doubt fulfil their appointed task.

Still, in their present forms, rooted in a *lower* type of man, they must disappear; not lost, but absorbed and blended in a better and nobler race. In the East, I suspect this *highest* type has always existed. Here, from immemorial ages and ages [tang-se-yan-se] the simple worship of the Sovereign Lord, and the divine faculty in man, have found their best expression, and taken a fixed and steadfast root in Government and in Society!

I may be mistaken, and it is possible that the Western tribes may be capable of attaining to this settled order—but it must be after very long moons and thousands of moons [lir-re-ty-sin], during which they shall have overturned and reformed existing laws and customs.

I may refer shortly to some of the more striking of these, so curiously and radically different from our notions in the *Central* Kingdom, and so erroneously conceived in respect of the DIVINE ORDER. *First.*—As to the character and worship of the Sovereign Lord of Heaven, and Father of men. Concerning the errors in regard to the true character and proper recognition of the Heavenly Lord, I need scarcely say more. There are wise barbarians who do not differ from my poor thought as to the need of an entire reformation upon this whole matter, which underlies nearly all genuine improvement in morals, in government, and in "Society."

Second.—As to Government. This must be seen to exist in the eternal order and nature of things, and not at all in any *Contract* [Kong-phu], "social" or other. Therefore whatever name be given to its Head, *the Function* is as inviolable as is the Divinity from which it comes. If this Head, however, be incapable of properly representing the divine function, it does not therefore fail, but the nearest *fit*, in the established order acts. The Book of Rites and the great Council of the Illustrious, with us, see to this proper and orderly succession. No one is born to be absolutely Head—the Book of Rites and the Illustrious *Calao*, in our system, may see to it that the Head be fit for the due and divine order. Therefore, no one is born by *right of birth* to govern, nor to make, nor to administer, laws. Wisdom and knowledge only, may entitle their possessors to take rank among those to whom government and administration shall be committed; and these may be changed, degraded, exalted, and removed as they conduct themselves, and not according to any family, nor hereditary distinction. Nor are *Places* created for the aggrandisement of any, continued for the benefit of families, nor, in any case, made hereditary. Places are for the whole, and those who fill them are placed there, in trust, for the good of the whole, and must properly discharge the trust. They are never for the individual—always for the State.

Third.—As to the family. The Family being the *Prototype* [mo-dsi] of Government, should show the Divine order. It must be one; not a divided, unintelligent *accident* [phatsi]. It must have a clear faculty, and understand its true and vital significance—for the community is but an aggregation of families, and as these are so is the State. Then, to have disorder there is to have disorder throughout! There *must*, therefore, be in the Family, obedience to its head, order, and good conduct. If there be insubordination, disorder, immorality, disrespect, and disobedience to the natural head, then that is a disorderly family, and those who are guilty of the disobedience, disrespect, and disorder are *criminals*, to be corrected, restrained, and reformed.

Woman, upon this right conception of the family, finds her proper and her honoured place. She is subordinate, but not in any humiliating sense; she is subordinate, because, in the very nature of her function as woman in the economy of nature, she cannot be otherwise—she *is* timid, defenceless, dependent. She has a right to the tender care and protection of her male relatives; and she, on her part, is bound to be obedient, submissive, orderly; and, upon these, affection follows. Her children are bound to respect and to obey her, and she is bound to have a care for them, and to respect and obey her husband as the unquestioned centre of regard and authority. The father (and husband) *is* the Head of the family; there is no divided nor disputed power. Upon *him* rests the responsibility of due order and proper position.

From her nature and duties, the woman lives retired within her house. If she go abroad, it will be only from necessity, and then in the most quiet, modest, and unobstrusive way. She lives for her relatives, her family; not to attract the admiration of others, nor with the faintest idea that she may shine *abroad*—to be so charged would be to be charged as *shameless*. Only by this degraded *class*, who are barely tolerated without the city, and under the rigid supervision of the officers of order and decorum—could such a purpose be supposed to be thought of? She dresses with neatness, according to the established order, but always with such modesty that nothing is offensive to the chastest eye. She understands the range of her activity and of her affections. It is within the circle of family and relatives. All her accomplishments are to make her home pleasing. Duties and places are settled. She lives for those to whom she belongs, and who also belong to her. Her smiles are for her husband, and for her children, and her relations. She has no thought of going abroad to shine, nor to waste the time and money which belong to her family upon strangers. She never dreams that she has any *mission* which calls her away from her home. She has no *call* to "clothe the ragged," wash other people's dirty children, reform evil-doers, "convert the *heathen*," nor support "Society!" (These are some of the phrases which you will hear among the Barbarian women).

Where women have not husbands, none the less they have relatives, and their home is with them. They have a right to this home, and are bound to do their duty in it, submissively, usefully, and quietly.

If the Western Barbarians would see to it that all women, married or unmarried, were duly cared for in homes of relatives, *as of right*, and that they also made themselves welcome there by their usefulness and obedience, they would find an end of that agitation as *to Women's Rights* existing among them. Rights would be as indisputable as duties—and the first of these would be a quiet, modest, and rational obedience to their natural protectors, who, in turn, would be bound to respect and protect them. And if by any strange chance a woman was absolutely without relatives (a thing nearly impossible in our *Flowery Land*), then the State should see to it that she had a suitable home.

The education of woman, in a well-ordered Society, is also fixed and clear. It has immediate relation to her position and her duties.

She is from the first never disturbed in the natural order. She sees her relatives always quiet, modest, *obedient*. She never thinks this state of things to be wrong. She perceives the manner of female life; its seclusion, its devotion to the family, its purpose, and end. There is no complexity about it, no *outside* glitter, no field for show, no seeking for excitement and display. All her duties are at home—*her* happiness is *there*; *there* she is to be attractive, and there she is to attract—the love and respect of her husband, the regard of her relatives, the affection and obedience of her children!

So, her education needs no straining after effect. It looks directly to her duties, to her natural function and place; and to those accomplishments, of mind and of person, which shall enable her to be happy with books, with music, and the like; and shall add to the pleasures of her home.

All these things are common-place with us—so simple as to appear trivial. Our Illustrious wives and mothers could not *understand* the reasons for their elaboration—they have never seen the women of the Western Barbarians!

The position of women in the *Social* system of the West, on the whole, is the most remarkable thing in it.

I have made sufficiently suggestive remarks in the progress of these *Observations*; and only now have to add a word or two upon the *general* effect.

It gives a wonderful life, restlessness, and colour to the whole aspect of Barbarian life. Think of all the women in our Illustrious Land, at once leaving their homes, the seclusion of their orderly houses and lives, and rushing everywhere with the men, over the Land! And, not only so, dressed in splendid gaiety of colour, and adorned with gems and feathers, crowding into all places of amusement and of travel!

Nor this only, but showing themselves, in public places, with men, where paintings and sculpture, and things here only seen by men alone, are exhibited! And, often, so dressed as to cause even the man to blush!

Why, the face of social life is completely altered. Instead of gravity, dignity, and an undivided attention to the duties of daily life, everything is rendered restless, confused; there seems to be no natural order, nor scarcely natural (cultured) decorum.

But we must not be misled. Nature is too strong to be pushed aside—and with cultivation, even though imperfect, the moral instinct lives and saves. Habit, too, "is a second nature;" (as our divine Confutzi says); and what would be so overwhelming, if at once done, being usual, necessarily *has been* subordinated to some rule—and made, at least, tolerable.

And now, in drawing these *Observations* to an end, perhaps, I may add, in respect of my poor and unworthy thoughts, that if I have said amiss, and which offends, I beg our Illustrious will pardon. To our *Literati*, exalted in wisdom, there is but little to which they may curiously look—but to *our people*, if any there be with whom some discontent may have been caused by too close intimacy with *Missionaries* in our ports; by these let my poor *Observations* be studiously pondered—that they may praise the Sovereign Lord of Heaven, who has given them to live in the *Central and Illustrious Kingdom*; where a true morality and a true worship are known; and where due ORDER AND PEACE, resting upon the unchangeable Heavenly order and peace, are established!

Here, are no brutal worship of Force, and admiration of bloody plunders. Content to the due ordering of affairs, and with peace within, our Illustrious Realm seeks no aggrandisement, dreams of no conquests; and *wishes to do nothing but good.* It has no fears for its own position, nor jealousy of others. It is simply calm, strong, wise, and self-poised. It demands no more from others abroad than that it may peacefully live; and *be treated with that respect which it accords to those who practise moderation and virtue.*

FINIS.

Milton Keynes UK
Ingram Content Group UK Ltd.
UKHW011141220424
441551UK00007B/736